Principles & Practice

of

Pastoral Ministry

By

Dr. Ronald L. Bernier

Copyright © 2009 – Dr. Ronald L. Bernier

All rights reserved. This book is protected under the copyright laws of the United States of America. This book may not be copied or reprinted for commercial gain or profit. The use of short quotations or occasional page copying for personal or group study is permitted and encouraged. Permission will be granted upon request. Unless otherwise identified, Scripture quotations are from the New King James Version of the Bible.

Published by **Vision Publishing**
Ramona, California

ISBN 978-1-61529-000-0

FOR INFORMATION ON ORDERING PLEASE CONTACT:

MASTER BUILDER MINISTRIES, INC.
397 Bay Street
Fall River, MA 02724
508-730-1735

or

Vision Publishing
1-800-9VISION
www.visionpublishingservices.com

PRINTED IN THE UNITED STATES OF AMERICA

Contents

Contents 3
FOREWORD 9
Chapter 1 13
  THE CHALLENGE OF THE PASTORAL MINISTRY 13
    What Is a Pastor to Be and Do? 15
    A Pastor Should Be Humble 16
    A Pastor Has to Shepherd the Flock of God 26
    The Obedient Shepherd 29
Chapter 2 33
  APPROACHING PASTORAL MINISTRY SCRIPTURALLY 33
    A Biblical Philosophy of Ministry 34
    The Purpose of the Church 37
    A Worshiping Community 38
    A Witnessing Community 41
    A Working Community 43
Chapter 3 49
  PRACTICAL APPLICATION OF MINISTRY 49
    #1 - The Ministry of the Word 50
    #2 - The Ministry of Fellowship 51
    #3 - The Ministry of the Lord's Supper 52
    #4 - The Ministry of Prayer 53
    #5 - The Ministry of Outreach 54
    #6 - The Ministry of Missions 55
    #7 - The Ministry of Interchurch Fellowship 55
Chapter 4 57
  ARE WE SETTING UP PASTORS AND CHURCHES FOR
  FAILURE? 57
    Options for Improvement 59
    Team to the Rescue 61
    The Impact of Team Leadership 62
    Challenge Facing Today's Leaders 64
    Six New Leadership Trends in the Church 66
    Pastor's Self-Perception 68

Chapter 5 71
  NEEDING A NEW LEADERSHIP MODEL 71
    Current Ministry Trends Demand Leadership Change 74
    Three Biblical Examples of Team Ministry & Leadership......75
    A Self – Examination – Solo Leadership or Team Leadership 82
    Which Way is Right for You?..84
Chapter 6 87
  RAISING UP LIKE-MINDED LEADERS 87
    Why Do You Need Like-minded Leaders (Amos 3:3)? 87
    The Problem of Wrong Leaders..90
    The Raising Up of Like-minded Leaders..................................91
    Identifying Potential Like-minded Leaders 93
    The Rewards of Raising Up Like-minded Leaders...................94
Chapter 7 95
  CHURCH GOVERNMENT 95
    The Skeletal Structure...95
    God Has Established Government in His Church....................97
    Five Forms of Church Government 98
    Equality and Headship in the Godhead...................................104
    Equality and Headship in the Family......................................105
    Equality and Headship in Israel and the Synagogue..............105
    Equality and Headship in the Local Church 106
    Qualifications for Elders 107
    Summation 108
Chapter 8 111
  THE MEANING OF ELDERSHIP 111
Chapter 9 119
  PASTORAL LEADERSHIP..119
    Shepherd Elders 120
    Protecting the Flock 121
    Spiritually Alert...122
    Courageous..123
    Feeding the Flock..124
    Leading the Flock..125
    Management Skill 126
    Hard Work & Caring for Practical Needs...............................127

Love for the Lord's People	129
Chapter 10	**131**
SHARED LEADERSHIP	131
The Benefits of a Council of Equals	134
First Among a Council of Equals: Leaders Among Leaders	136
Chapter 11	**141**
QUALIFIED LEADERSHIP	141
The Need for Qualified Shepherd Elders	142
The Qualifications for Shepherd Elders	146
Chapter 12	**157**
SERVANT LEADERSHIP	157
Jesus' Teaching on Servant Leadership	157
Three Lessons	164
The Pauline Example of Servant Leadership	166
Elders as Servant Leaders	168
Chapter 13	**173**
DISCIPLINED LEADERSHIP	173
The Foundation for Discipline in the Local Church	174
Why Discipline is Often Neglected	175
Reasons for Church Discipline	180
Important Words Used in Connection with Leadership Ministries	181
Key Biblical Verses Concerning Church Discipline	184
The Purpose of Discipline and Confrontation	189
The Kinds of Sins that are to be Disciplined by the Church	192
The Levels of Discipline (Matthew 18:15-20)	192
Prerequisites for Effective Church Discipline	194
Excommunication	196
The Attitude of a Restorer	199
Practical Steps of Church Discipline	200
Public Announcement	201
Conclusions about Discipline	202
Chapter 14	**203**
HOW AN ELDERSHIP FUNCTIONS	203
Elder's Governance Process Policies	204
Chapter 15	**225**

APPOINTMENT OF ELDERS 225
   Elements in the Appointment Process: Desire, Qualification,
   Selection, Examination, Installation, and Prayer 226
Chapter 16..235
   RELEASING GIFTS AND MINISTRIES 235
     The Initiation of the Body of Christ..236
     Releasing the Body to Function 238
     A Nation of Priests 239
     Entering into the Doctrine..240
     Hindrances to the Function of the Body of Christ 241
     Preaching is not the Highest Calling..241
     Full-Time Ministry is for Everyone 242
     Ministry Occurs Outside the Church Service..........................244
     Leaders Must Decrease 245
Chapter 17..247
   HOUSE-TO-HOUSE MINISTRY...247
     The Great Commission 247
     A Strategy for Success 248
     The Present-Day Challenge..249
     The Need for a Strategy 250
     Toward a Solution – Exodus 18:13-26 252
     The Jethro Principle 253
     In Jesus' Ministry...254
     In the Early Church..255
     Today's Challenge 255
     The Two-Pronged Attack...256
     Multiple Facets of Small Groups 257
     Models that have Proven Effective 259
     A Net for the Harvest...267
Chapter 18..269
   WORKING WITH MINISTRY TEAMS 269
     Ministry Task Teams 269
     Ministry Leadership Teams..270
     Shaping a Team Vision 278
Chapter 19..285
   ORGANIZATION FOR PASTORS 285

Introduction to Organization 287
Tips on Personal Organization 289

Chapter 20 293
SETTING AND ACHIEVING GOALS 293
  Goal-Orientation and Problem Solving.............................295
  How can a Problem-Oriented Organization Become Goal-Oriented? 296
  How Can We Apply MBO Principles to Ministry? 298
  Four Stages in the Process of Goal-Setting........................300

Chapter 21 303
SHORT-AND LONG-RANGE PLANNING 303
  What is Strategic Planning? 304
  What are the Common Pitfalls of Planning?......................305
  Where Do We Commonly Go Wrong?................................306
  Foundations for Effective Planning 307
  Common Questions about Effective Planning 309
  Concluding Thoughts on Planning.....................................312

Chapter 22 315
ASSESSING NEEDS, GIFTS, AND CALL 315
  Effective Leadership Centers in Spiritual Gifts 322
  Effective Leadership Requires Clarity of Call 325

Chapter 23 329
RECRUITING EFFECTIVE VOLUNTEERS 329
  Determine High Standards 330
  Design an Atmosphere of Service......................................333
  Develop Effective Servants..336

Chapter 24 343
BUILDING THE LEADERSHIP AND RESOLVING CONFLICT 343

Chapter 25 351
TRANSITIONING TO LEADING WITH TEAMS 351
  Common Mistakes Pastors Make......................................355

Chapter 26 361
BIG PASTORS OF SMALL CHURCHES 361

Appendix 1 365

Expanding on the Qualifications for Spiritual Leadership
Delineated in the Constitution of Master Builder Ministries.....365
    "Qualifications for Spiritual Leadership" 365
    Practical Questions a Potential Leader Can Ask to Evaluate His
    Own Character Development. 388
Appendix 2 391
    Marriage, Divorce and Remarriage in the Bible: 391
        Marriage 391
        Divorce..393
        Remarriage 402
        "Dealing With Divorce and Remarriage" 404
        Divorce, Remarriage and Church Leadership.......................405

FOREWORD

It's been my privilege to know the author for about five years. I am a missionary with Ministry to Educate and Equip, and Ron is on the board of directors for my mission. I also direct the Institute for the Development of Christian Leadership, headquartered in Kiev, Ukraine, and Ron was among the first to volunteer to teach in our masters program when it began.

It's been a pleasure to watch the evolution of this book as its various parts have been formed and refined for use in our masters program and elsewhere. What you have in your hands is the product not only of a great deal of effort and energy, but also experience. The book is a thorough treatment of the basis for pastoral ministry and in fact all ministry accomplished by the Church. These are not untested theories, but rather tried and true structures and methods that have been embraced by church leaders in different countries, including those of the former Soviet Union where our Institute operates.

The response we have received from the Pastors and leaders who have received Ron's ministry have been greatly encouraging. Recently I received a letter from one such pastor who wrote:

> Greetings to the Institute for the Development of Christian Leadership and Master Builder Christian Church!
>
> I want to present my deep appreciation to the Institute for having invited and to Master Builder Christian Church for having delegated Doctor Ron.
>
> A good testimony of his skillful teaching for the past years was confirmed during our classes. This person really corresponds to his high title. And it was seen not only in perfect theoretical and practical combination but first and foremost in his character and relationship. This is a godly person – it can be seen without any titles! The audience was not only under the influence of a healthy teaching, but also

under the influence of the Holy Spirit, Who was present in the lecturer.

I admire those accents (priorities) that Brother Ron postulated during the course of "Pastoral Theology and Administration". The Lord blessed him to show us in this teaching a true standard of a leader-servant, reflecting the nature and heart of Christ and His methods of administrating and building relations. The Holy Spirit spoke so deeply to my heart through the simple and humble manner of teaching, that by the end of the course I felt a great responsibility in the position of a leader and a blessing at His commandment "to shepherd God's flock".

Dear church, I want to say thank you for your "sacrifice of communication" in your pastor's person and for the maturity in Christ to let and bless him for the edifying of the body of Christ in the other part of the world, realizing, how much you lack pastor Ron during this period. May God bless you abundantly! And may your heart be always big enough to "cast thy bread upon the waters; for thou shalt find it after many days".

With love and thankfulness in Christ,

Oleg Nerodin
Pastoral leader of a Messianic Church (Zhitomyr, Ukraine)

Pastor Peter Kovalenko, who is part of Pastor Larry Stockstill's global team of church planters and presently pastoring a local church in Kharkov, Ukraine which had grown to over 3,000 believers and is impacting the entire nation along with hosting a national television program that ministers in a practical way, recently invited and hosted Pastor Ron at his church. Pastor Peter has been involved with IDLC by serving as a member of our board of directors. Peter met Ron last year while attending Ron's class on the Principles and Practice of Pastoral Ministry. After Pastor Ron ministered in Kharkov, Peter wrote:

On behalf of many people in our church I would like to thank the saints of Master Builder Ministries for blessing us with letting Pastor Ronald Bernier minister to our congregation. His deep understanding of sound doctrine of the Word of God and the ability to present an overall picture are the key factors that made a huge impact on our church. Pastor Ronald's solid message impelled many church members to redefine their walk as believers and get back to the core of what it means to be God's servant and representative in this world. A lady doctor texted me after the church service that she needed to hear that message and previous circumstances in her life had prepared her heart for it.

Additionally, I would like to thank Pastor Ronald for the Pastoral Theology course last year. It is important for me as a pastor to get a fresh view of that subject in order to move forward and not to become spiritually stiff. Pastor Ronald's teaching on that subject helped me in a practical way and provided answers to a number of questions on pastoring that I had.

Since our church is heavily involved in church planting in Russia and Belarus we see a tremendous need of quality training for young pastors. I strongly believe that a solid training course by Pastor Ronald will be a great tool to influence lives of many people in Russia through ministry of well trained pastors.

We have received testimonies from many leaders who have communicated how Ron's training and ministry has impacted their lives and churches. One pastor from Budapest, Hungry recently expressed how discouraged she was in her ministry, but upon completing the Pastoral Ministry training her heart for her congregation had changed. Now she is encouraged and ready to give herself fully to the call of pastoring in her city.

Many pastors and leaders have continued to build a relationship with Ron, and he has been invited to minister in many churches throughout Ukraine as well as many other countries where Ron has ministered including Belarus, Kenya, Ghana and Zimbabwe.

We are very grateful for Ron's commitment to raise up and equip pastoral leadership worldwide, and we look forward to many more years of fruitful collaboration with him and with Master Builder Ministries.

Paul Shotsberger, PhD
Kiev, Ukraine

Chapter 1

THE CHALLENGE OF THE PASTORAL MINISTRY

In many churches today, it seems that the pastor just cannot do anything right. It does not matter how sincere he may be, or how hard he tries, there are always some who stand ready to find fault and to criticize. Someone has expressed the situation in this way:

- If the pastor is young, they say he lacks experience; if his hair is gray, then he's too old for the young people.

- If he has 5 or 6 children, he has too many; if he has no children, he's setting a bad example.

- If he preaches from his notes, he has canned sermons and is dry; if his messages are extemporaneous, he is not deep.

- If he is attentive to the poor people in the church, they claim he is playing to the grandstand; if he pays attention to the wealthy, he is trying to be an aristocrat.

- If he uses too many illustrations, he neglects the Bible; if he doesn't use enough stories, he isn't clear.

- If he condemns wrong, he's cranky; if he doesn't preach against sin, they say he's a compromiser.

- If he preaches the truth, he's offensive; if he doesn't preach the truth, then he's a hypocrite.

- If he fails to please everybody, he's hurting the church and ought to leave; if he does please everybody, he has no convictions.

- If he drives an old car, he shames his congregation; if he drives a new car, then he is setting his affection upon earthly things.

- If he preaches all the time, the people get tired of hearing one man; if he invites guest preachers; he's shirking his responsibility.

- If he receives a large salary, he is a mercenary; if he receives a small salary, well, then they say it proves he isn't worth much anyway.

As a result, when a pastor is called to a church today, he is expected to have almost superhuman qualifications. He must be a good speaker, a deep Bible student, a spirited evangelist and a compassionate pastor. He must be a man with the wisdom of Solomon. One who has a pleasing personality, is good looking and has a wife who is compatible with all the members of the church. He must be a good businessman, an effective and efficient administrator, creative and original and must have the gift of dreaming up startling sermon topics to draw a large Sunday morning crowd.

A good pastor must have:

- The strength of an ox,
- The tenacity of a bulldog,
- The daring of a lion,
- The wisdom of an owl,
- The harmlessness of a dove,
- The industry of a beaver,
- The gentleness of a sheep,
- The versatility of a chameleon,
- The vision of an eagle,

- The hide of a rhinoceros,
- The perspective of a giraffe,
- The disposition of an angel,
- The endurance of a camel,
- The bounce of a kangaroo,
- The stomach of a horse,
- The loyalty of an apostle,
- The faithfulness of a prophet,
- The tenderness of a shepherd,
- The fervency of an evangelist,
- The devotion of a mother,
- And then, he would not please everybody!

What Is a Pastor to Be and Do?

A vast amount of material is available to advise pastors on how to conduct their ministries. Books, tapes, journals, and seminars abound. In fact, so much material is available that a pastor could easily spend all his time absorbing it – and have no time left for actual ministry! How can a pastor sift through this mountain of information to discern what is really important in ministry? Can what a pastor is to be and do be boiled down to a few basic principles?

The apostle Peter read no books or journal articles on pastoral leadership. He attended no seminars and heard no tapes. However, with the wisdom of long years of experience, Peter distilled the essence of pastoral leadership into two simple admonitions: be humble, and do the work of shepherding the flock. He expressed these foundational principles in 1 Peter. 5:1-3:

> Therefore, I exhort the elders among you, as your fellow elder and witness of the sufferings of Christ, and a partaker also of the glory that is to be revealed, shepherd the flock of God among you, exercising oversight not under compulsion,

but voluntarily, according to the will of God; and not for sordid gain, but with eagerness; nor yet as lording it over those allotted to your charge, but proving to be examples to the flock.

Peter modeled the humility he enjoined for pastors. Although the acknowledged leader of the twelve apostles, he humbly described himself as "your fellow elder." He refused to lord his exalted position over the other elders. And in verse 2 he gave the pastor's calling, to "shepherd the flock of God" entrusted to his care. Humble shepherds are what God requires to lead His flock.

A Pastor Should Be Humble

We live in a world that neither values nor desires humility. Whether in politics, business, the arts, or sports, people work hard to achieve prominence, popularity, and fame. Sadly, that mind-set has spilled over into the church. Personality cults exist because pastors and Christian leaders strive for celebrity status. The true man of God, however, seeks the approval of His Lord rather than the adulation of the crowd. Humility is thus the bench-mark of any useful servant of God. Spurgeon reminds us that "if we magnify ourselves, we shall become contemptible; and we shall neither magnify our office nor our Lord. We are the servants of Christ, not lords over His heritage. Ministers are for churches, and not churches for ministers . . . Take heed that you be not exalted above measure, lest you come to nothing."[1]

Examples of Humility

Until his time, John the Baptist was the greatest man who had lived (Matt. 11:11; Luke 7:28). He was the last of the Old

---

[1] C. H. Spurgeon, *An All-round Ministry* (reprint, Pasadena, Tex.: Pilgrim, 1973), 256-57.

Testament prophets, privileged to be no less than the immediate forerunner of the Messiah. Yet he was a humble man and expressed that humility when he said of Christ, "He must increase, but I must decrease" (John 3:30). Except for Jesus Christ, the apostle Paul is the greatest spiritual leader the world has known, but he described himself as "the least of the apostles" (1 Cor. 15:9), "the very least of all saints" (Eph. 3:8), and the foremost of sinners (1 Tim. 1:15-16).

Five marks of Paul's humility are identified in 1 Corinthians 4. First, he was content to be a servant: "Let a man regard us in this manner, as servants of Christ, and stewards of the mysteries of God" (v. 1). The word he used for "servants" is *huperetes*, which refers literally to an under rower, one who rowed in the lower tier of a war galley. Such rowers were unknown, unheralded, and unhonored. "When all is said and done," Paul says, "let it be said of me that I pulled my oar."

A second mark of Paul's humility was his willingness to be judged by God. In 1 Cor. 4:4 he wrote, "The one who examines me is the Lord." Paul did not seek the accolades of men, nor did he care what they thought of him. God was the audience before whom he executed his ministry; God was the one he sought to please, whatever the cost. Any human evaluation of his ministry, whether by others or himself, was meaningless.

Third, Paul was content to be equal with other servants of God. In 1 Cor. 4-6 he cautioned the Corinthians not to compare him with Apollos. He did not want his readers to presume to elevate one over the other. Paul and Apollos were not in competition with each other, nor did Paul consider himself better than Apollos. The puritan Walter Cradock's description of a humble man fits Paul perfectly:

1. When he looks upon another that is a sinner, he considereth that he has been worse than he.
2. A humble heart thinks himself to be worse still.
3. It is God that hath made it and not anything in himself.

4. He considereth that the vilest sinner may be, in God's good time, better than he.[2]

Fourth, Paul was willing to suffer (1 Cor. 4:12-13). He suffered for the cause of Christ as few men in history have suffered, thus fulfilling the Lord's prediction at his conversion (Acts 9:16). Paul details some of that suffering in his letters to the Corinthians (1 Cor. 4:9-13; 2 Cor. 11:23-33). His exhortation to Timothy to "suffer hardship with me, as a good soldier of Christ Jesus" (2 Tim. 2:3) is his challenge to every pastor, for all will face suffering. As Sanders notes, "No one needs aspire to leadership in the work of God who is not prepared to pay a price greater than his contemporaries and colleagues are willing to pay. True leadership always exacts a heavy toll on the whole man, and the more effective the leadership is, the higher the price to be paid."[3] Spurgeon gives a reason pastors may expect suffering: "It is ofneed be that we are sometimes in heaviness. Good men are promised tribulation in this world, and ministers may expect a larger share than others, that they may learn sympathy with the Lord's suffering people, and so may be fitting shepherds of an ailing flock."[4]

Finally, Paul was content to sacrifice his reputation. A pastor's goal is not to be popular with the world. Those who preach boldly against sin and live godly lives will sacrifice their public reputation and prestige. They will suffer rejection, face opposition, and endure slander. Paul described his own loss of reputation when he wrote, "For, I think, God has exhibited us apostles last of all, as men condemned to death; because we have become a spectacle to the world, both to angels and to men. We have become as the scum of the world, the dregs of all things, even until now" (1 Cor. 4:19, 13).

---

[2] Cited by I. D. E. Thomas, *A Puritan Golden Treasury* (Edinburgh: Banner of Truth, 1977), 148-49.
[3] J. Oswald Sanders, *Spiritual Leadership*, rev. ed. (Chicago: Moody, 1980), 169.
[4] C. H. Spurgeon, *Lectures to My Students: First Series* (reprint, Grand Rapids: Baker, 1972), 168.

Keys to Humility

True humility flows from a correct view of God. How a pastor lives his life and functions in the ministry relates directly to his view of God. A humble man, with a proper view of God, will be confident in God's power, committed to God's truth, commissioned by God's will, compelled by God's knowledge, and consumed with God's glory.

A humble pastor will be confident in God's power. In 1 Thess. 2:2, Paul reminded the Thessalonians that "after we had already suffered and been mistreated in Philippi (see Acts 16:19-24), as you know, we had the boldness in our God to speak to you the gospel of God amid much opposition." Paul's humble confidence in God's power translated into boldness and courage in his ministry. He was confident that God was more powerful than any opposition he would face. That gave his ministry strength and tenacity. It enabled him to speak out no matter what the response and consequences were.

In the ministry, pressure to compromise, to mitigate the message, and to avoid offending sinners will always exist. However, the preacher's job is to expose sin, to confront the lost with the hopelessness of their condition, and to offer the cure for their wretchedness in the saving gospel of Jesus Christ. Doing those things will lead to confrontation and opposition. The courage to stand firm derives from a humble dependence on God's power. It comes from being "strong in the Lord, and in the strength of His might" (Eph. 6:10).

A humble pastor will be committed to God's truth. We live in a day when most are ignoring Paul's exhortation to Timothy to "preach the word" of God. Instead of the Word of God, all too often from the pulpit come the uncertain sounds of political rhetoric, social commentary, and pop psychology. Such "persuasive words of [human] wisdom" (1 Cor. 2:4) are a prostitution of the preacher's true calling. The pulpit is not a place for the pastor to express his opinion, demonstrate his erudition, or browbeat those who oppose him. Such prideful exaltation of self is the antithesis of humility. John Stott believes that:

> The less the preacher comes between the Word and its hearers, the better. What really feeds the household is the food which the house-holder supplies, not the steward who dispenses it. The Christian preacher is best satisfied when his person is eclipsed by the light which shines from the Scripture and when his voice is drowned by the Voice of God.[5]

A man committed to God's truth is a man dedicated to "handling accurately the word of truth" (2 Tim. 2:15). His greatest fear in preaching is that he might present the Word inaccurately to his flock and so mislead them. Paul stressed the importance in his own ministry of handling the Word accurately in 1 Thess. 2:3. In that passage, he gave a threefold response to the charge of teaching false doctrine.

First, he declared that "our exhortation does not come from error." *Plane* (error) comes from a verb meaning "to wander or roam." From it the English word *planet* is derived, since the planets appear to wander through space. To be in error is to wander from the truth, to roam from the divine standard and be out of control. Paul's teaching was not in error. He was neither deceived nor a deceiver. He guarded the truth of the Word of God, even as he twice exhorted Timothy to do (1 Tim. 6:20; 2 Tim. 1:14). That concept of guarding the truth has largely been lost today. Yet pastors *are* guardians of the truth, responsible for keeping it pure and handing it on to the next generation. The measure of a pastor, then, is not how clever or interesting he is, but how well he guards the truth. Anyone who fails to do so "advocates a different doctrine, and does not agree with sound words, those of our Lord Jesus Christ, and with the doctrine conforming to godliness" (1 Tim. 6:3).

---

[5] John R. W. Stott, *The Preachers Portrait* (Grand Rapids: Eerdmans, 1979), 30.

Such a man "is conceited and understands nothing" (v. 4). He has failed in the most important aspect of his ministry.

One of the most provocative verses in all the Pauline literature is 2 Cor. 2:17, where the apostle declares, "We are not like many, peddling the word of God, but as from sincerity, but as from God, we speak in Christ in the sight of God." *Peddling* is from *kapeleuo*. It describes the activity of those spiritual hucksters and con men who peddle the Word of God, insincerely for their own enrichment. Unfortunately, they are as common today as they were when Paul wrote. False prophets, spiritual phonies, and associated cultists, crackpots, and swindlers abound, unceasingly laboring "to make crooked the straight ways of the Lord" (Acts 13:10). To combat this onslaught, the church needs pastors humbly committed to proclaiming the truth of God's Word.

Merely proclaiming the Word is not enough, however; the pastor must live out its truths in his life. Paul declares that his teaching was free of impurity (1 Thess. 2:3). While that word can refer to uncleanness in general, it often refers to sexual uncleanness. That sexual uncleanness and false doctrine go hand and hand is evident from the many scandals that have rocked the church in recent years.

In his classic work *The Reformed Pastor*, Richard Baxter addressed pastors with some of the most pointed words ever penned regarding living the truths they preach:

> Take heed to yourselves, lest your example contradict your doctrine, and lest you lay such stumbling-blocks before the blind, as may be the occasion of their ruin; lest you unsay with your lives, what you say with your tongues; and be the greatest hinderers of the success of your own labours. It much hindereth our work, when other men are all the week long contradicting to poor people in private, that which we have been speaking to them from the Word of God in public, because we cannot be at hand to expose their folly; but it will much more hinder your work, if you contradict yourselves, and if your actions give your tongue the lie, and if you build

up an hour or two with your mouths, and all the week after pull down with your hands! This is the way to make men think that the Word of God is but an idle tale, and to make preaching seem no better than prating. *He that means as he speaks, will surely do as he speaks.* One proud, surly, lordly word, one needless contention, one covetous action, may cut the throat of many a sermon, and blast the fruit of all that you have been doing . . .

It is a palpable error of some ministers, who make such a disproportion between their preaching and their living; who study hard to preach exactly, and study little or not at all to live exactly. All the week long is little enough, to study how to speak two hours, and yet one hour seems too much to study how to live all the week . . . Oh how curiously have I heard some men preach; and how carelessly have I seen them live! . . .

Certainly, brethren, we have very great cause to take heed what we do, as well as what we say: if we will be the servants of Christ indeed, we must not be tongue servants only, but must serve him with our deeds, and be "doers of the word, that we may be blessed in our deed." As our people must be "doers of the word, and not hearers only"; so we must be doers and not speakers only, lest we "deceive our own selves." . . .

Maintain your innocency, and walk without offence. Let your lives condemn sin, and persuade men to duty. Would you have your people more careful of their souls, than you are of yours? . . .

Take heed to yourselves, lest you live in those sins which you preach against in others, and lest you be guilty of that which daily you condemn. Will you make it your work to magnify God, and, when you have done, dishonor Him as much as others? Will you proclaim Christ's governing power, and yet contemn it, and rebel yourselves? Will you preach His laws, and willfully break them? *If sin be evil, why do you live in it? If it be not, why do you dissuade men from it?* If it is dangerous, how dare you venture on it? If it be not, why do you tell men so? If God's threatenings be true, why do you not fear them? If they are false, why do you needlessly trouble men with them, and put them into such frights without a cause? Do you "know the judgment of God, that they who commit such things are worthy of death"; and yet will you do them? "Thou that teachest another, teachest thou not thyself? Thou that sayest a man should not commit adultery," or be drunk, or covetous, art thou such thyself? "Thou that makest thy boast of the law, through breaking the law dishonourest thou God?" What! Shall the same tongue speak evil that speakest against evil? Shall those lips censure, and slander, and backbite your neighbour, that cry down these and the like things in others? Take heed to yourselves, lest you cry down sin, and yet do not overcome it; lest, while you seek to bring it down in others, you bow down to it, and become slaves yourselves: "For of whom a man is overcome, of the same is he brought into bondage." "To whom you yield you yield yourselves servants to obey, his servants ye are to whom ye obey, whether of sin unto death, or of obedience unto righteousness." *O brethren! It is easier to chide at sin, than to overcome it.*[6]

The preacher who wants his words taken to heart by his congregation must first take them to heart himself.

Finally, in 1 Thess. 2:3, Paul's preaching was free of deceit. He moves from preaching to living to motive, and now asserts that his motives were not deceitful. Paul had no hidden agendas and did not seek to trick or ensnare anyone. He was not like the false teachers, who had lust or profit as their motive (2 Pet. 2:15-18; Jude 2). He was like David, who "shepherded [Israel] according to the

---

[6] Richard Baxter, *The Reformed Pastor* (Edinburgh: Banner of Truth, 1979), 63, 64, 65, 67-68 (emphasis added).

integrity of his heart" (Ps. 78:72). It is humble men, men of integrity, whom God desires to shepherd His flock.

A humble pastor is commissioned by God's will. All believers have the right and the duty to share the gospel wherever and whenever they can. However, no one should hold the office of pastor who has not received a call to that ministry from God. Those who pridefully exalt themselves to that position will not have God's blessing. God will say of them what He said of the false prophets of Jeremiah's day: "I did not send those prophets, but they ran. I did not speak to them, but they prophesied" (Jer. 23:21).

Paul certainly did not exalt himself to the ministry. Indeed, becoming a minister of the gospel was the last thing he expected to do with his life. But on the Damascus Road, God redeemed him and called him to the ministry. No doubt that incident was in his mind when he wrote to the Corinthians, "If I preach the gospel, I have nothing to boast of, for I am under compulsion: for woe is me if I do not preach the gospel. For if I do this voluntarily, I have a reward; but if against my will, I have a stewardship entrusted to me" (1 Cor. 9:16-17). Unlike the false teachers who dogged his steps and unlike their present-day counterparts, he did not appoint himself to the ministry. Instead, Paul was "approved by God to be entrusted with the gospel" (1 Thess. 2:4).

The knowledge that we did not earn the right to preach through our own efforts or abilities should humble us. God called us to the ministry, God trusted us to proclaim His Word, and God chose us to lead His flock. To forget that is to take the first step toward disqualification from the ministry.

A humble pastor is compelled by God's knowledge. God's omniscience is a further key to and motive for humility. While it is possible to fool others by an outward façade of piety, God knows the secrets of the heart. "What [a] minister is on his knees in secret before God Almighty," wrote John Owen, "that he is and no more."[7] God's omniscience means accountability in the ministry. It keeps a man focused on pleasing God, not men. God

---

[7] Cited by Thomas, *Golden Treasury*, 192

scrutinizes the desires, motives, and intentions of the heart, and He knows what is done to please others and what is done to please Him.

Paul was quite aware of the implications of God's knowledge about his life. To the Thessalonians he wrote, "Just as we have been approved by God to be entrusted with the gospel, so we speak, not as pleasing men but God, who examines our hearts. For we never came with flattering speech, as you know, nor with a pretext for greed – God is witness" (1 Thess. 2:4-5). He knew he was commissioned by God to preach the gospel of God, not by men to preach a man-pleasing gospel. In Gal. 1:10 he added, "For am I now seeking the favor of men, or of God? Or am I striving to please men? If I were still trying to please men, I would not be a bond-servant of Christ." Remember God's omniscience kept Paul from seeking to be a man-pleaser.

A humble pastor is consumed with God's glory. This key achieves the epitome of humility, for it is impossible to seek self-glory and God's glory at the same time. It is the New Covenant that is glorious (2 Cor. 3:7-11), not its ministers (2 Cor. 4:7). If all the rank-and-file believers do is to be for God's glory (1 Cor. 10:31), how much more the work of the ministry?

In 1 Thess. 2:6 Paul wrote, "nor did we seek glory from men, either from you or from others, even though as apostles of Christ we might have asserted our authority." Paul was no Diotrephes (3 John 9), seeking preeminence; he did not seek esteem, honor, or praise. His preoccupation was the glory of God (2 Cor. 4:5).

What marks a man effective in the ministry?

- Tenacity – he trusts totally in God's power
- Integrity – his life is consistent with his doctrine
- Authority – he receives his commission from God, not himself
- Accountability – he is constantly aware of the implications of God's omniscience
- Humility – he is consumed not with himself, but with the glory of God.

Only such a man is humble enough to shepherd God's flock

A Pastor Has to Shepherd the Flock of God

Of all the titles and metaphors used to describe spiritual leadership, the most fitting is that of shepherd. As shepherds, pastors are to guard their flocks from going astray, lead them to the green pastures of God's Word, and defend them against savage wolves (Acts 20:29) that would ravage them. The shepherd metaphor is the one chosen by Peter in 1 Pet. 5:1-3. There he discusses the primary objective of shepherding and gives wise counsel on how to shepherd and how not to shepherd.

The Primary Objective of Shepherding

A shepherd who fails to feed his flock will not have a flock for long. His sheep will wander off to other fields or die of starvation. Above all, God requires of His spiritual shepherds that they feed their flocks. In fact, the one ability that distinguishes an elder from a deacon is that an elder must be "able to teach" (1 Tim. 3:2; Titus 1:9). Charles Jefferson writes,

> That the feeding of the sheep is an essential duty of the shepherd-calling is known even to those who are least familiar with shepherds and their work. Sheep cannot feed themselves, nor water themselves. They must be conducted to the water and the pasture . . . Everything depends on the proper feeding of the sheep. Unless wisely fed they become emaciated and sick, and the wealth invested in them is squandered . . . When the minister goes into the pulpit, he is the shepherd in the act of feeding, and if every minister had borne this in mind, many a sermon would have been other than it has been. The curse of the pulpit is the superstition

that a sermon is a work of art and not a piece of bread or meat.[8]

Jesus forcefully drove home the importance of feeding the sheep to Peter in His encounter with him described in John 21. Twice in His command to Peter, Jesus used the term *bosko*, which means "I feed" (vv. 15, 17). The shepherd's goal is not to please the sheep, but to feed them – not to tickle their ears, but to nourish their souls. He is not to offer light snacks of milk, but substantial meals of solid biblical truth. Those who fail to feed the flock are unfit to be shepherds (cf. Jer. 23:1-4; Ezek. 34:2-10).

How to Shepherd

Besides feeding them, the shepherd has two primary duties to his flock. He must exercise oversight of them and must lead them by the example of his life. Peter challenged his fellow elders to "shepherd the flock of God among you" by exercising oversight" (1 Pet. 5:2). God entrusted them with the authority and responsibility of leading the flock. Shepherds are accountable for how they lead, and the flock for how they follow (Heb. 13:17).

However, being a shepherd does not mean merely getting the over-all picture from a distance; it requires getting right in among the flock and leading by example. It is not leadership from on high so much as leadership from within. An effective shepherd does not herd his sheep from the rear but leads them from the front. They see him before them and imitate his actions. The most important asset of spiritual leadership is the power of an exemplary life.

How Not to Shepherd

In his exhortation to his fellow shepherds, Peter warns them of two pitfalls. First, they must avoid doing what they do

---

[8] Charles Jefferson, *The Minister as Shepherd* (Hong Kong: Living Books For All, 1980), 59, 61.

unwillingly. A good shepherd does his work "not under compulsion, but voluntarily" (1 Pet. 5:2). Sheep can be disagreeable, dirty, stubborn, exasperating animals. Former sheep rancher W. Philip Keller observes that "No other class of livestock requires more careful handling, more detailed direction, than do sheep."[9] A lazy shepherd is an ineffective shepherd. The temptation that Peter cautions against is merely going through the motions – i.e., merely doing the work of the ministry only when under compulsion. Shepherding God's flock must be done spontaneously, voluntarily, with eagerness, and with a knowledge of its vital importance.

Another more sinister pitfall to avoid is doing the work of the ministry for sordid gain. "I have coveted no one's silver or gold or cloths," Paul said to the Ephesian elders (Acts 20:33). "No one can serve two masters," Jesus declared, "for either he will hate the one and love the other, or he will hold to one and despite the other. You cannot serve God and mammon" (Matt. 6:24). That is doubly true of pastors, whom God requires to be "free from the love of money" (1 Tim. 3:3). It is the false prophets who engage in the furious pursuit of monetary gain (see Isa. 56:11; Jer. 6:13; 8:10; Mic. 3:11; 2 Pet. 2:3).

It is not wrong for a pastor to be paid; in fact Scripture commands it. "Let the elders who rule well be considered worthy of double honor," Paul wrote to Timothy, "especially those who work hard at preaching and teaching" (1 Tim. 5:17).[10] What is wrong is allowing financial gain to be one's motivation in the ministry. That not only produces insincere, ineffective leaders but also degrades the ministry in the eyes of the world.

A humble man, dedicated to shepherding the souls God has entrusted to his care, "will receive the unfading crown of glory" in that day "when the Chief Shepherd appears" (1 Pet. 5:4).

---

[9] W. Phillip Keller, *A Shepherd Looks at Psalm 23* (Grand Rapids: Zondervan, 1979), 71

[10] For Paul's defense of his own right to be paid for his ministry, see 1 Cor. 9:6-14.

The Obedient Shepherd

If Peter were still alive, I would like to ask him, "Could you be more specific as to what the humble shepherd should do?" Though we do not have Peter's specific response, we do have God's thorough answer to the question through the pen of Paul in the two epistles to Timothy in the New Testament. Paul had personally mentored the young pastor, but Timothy encountered severe trials when assigned the task of leading the church at Ephesus out of sin and error. He struggled with fear and human weakness. He apparently experienced the temptation to soften his preaching in the face of persecution. At times he seemed ashamed of the gospel.

Paul had to remind him to stand up for the faith with boldness, even if it meant suffering: "Do not be ashamed of the testimony of our Lord, or of me His prisoner; but join with me in suffering for the gospel" (2 Tim. 1:8). The two rich epistles from Paul to Timothy outline a ministry philosophy of being and doing that challenges the prevailing practice of today. Paul instructed Timothy in the first letter that he must:

- Correct those teaching false doctrine and call them to a pure heart, a good conscience, and a sincere faith (1 Tim. 1:3-5).
- Fight for divine truth and for God's purposes, keeping his own faith and a good conscience (1:18-19)
- Pray for the lost and lead the men of the church to do the same (2:1-8).
- Call women in the church to fulfill their God-given role of submission and to raise up godly children, setting an example of faith, love, and sanctity with self-restraint (2:9-15).
- Carefully select spiritual leaders for the church on the basis of their giftedness, godliness, and virtue (3:1-13).
- Recognize the source of error and those who teach it, and point these things out to the rest of the church (4:1-6).
- Constantly be nourished on the words of Scripture and its sound teaching, avoiding all myths and false doctrines (4:6).

- Disciple himself for the purpose of godliness (4:7-11).
- Boldly command and teach the truth of God's Word (4:12).
- Be a model of spiritual virtue that all can follow (4:12).
- Faithfully read, explain, and apply the Scriptures publicly (4:13-14).
- Be progressing toward Christ-likeness in his own life (4:15-16).
- Be gracious and gentle in confronting the sin of his people (5:1-2).
- Give special consideration and care to those who are widows (5:3-16).
- Honor faithful church leaders who work hard (5:17-21).
- Choose church leaders with great care, seeing to it that they are both mature and proven (5:22).
- Take care of his physical condition so he is strong to serve (5:23).
- Teach and preach principles of true godliness, helping his people discern between true godliness and mere hypocrisy (5:24-6:6).
- Flee the love of money (6:7-11).
- Pursue righteousness, godliness, faith, love, perseverance, and gentleness (6:11).
- Fight for the faith against all enemies and all attacks (6:12).
- Instruct the rich to do good, to be rich in good works, and to be generous (6:17-19).
- Guard the Word of God as a sacred trust and a treasure (6:20-21).

In his second epistle, Paul reminded Timothy to:

- Keep the gift of God in him fresh and useful (2 Tim. 1:6).
- Not be timid but powerful (1:7).
- Never be ashamed of Christ or anyone who serves Christ (1:8-11).
- Hold tightly to the truth and guard it (1:12-14).

- Be strong in character (2:1).
- Be a teacher of apostolic truth so that he may reproduce himself in faithful men (2:2).
- Suffer difficulty and persecution willingly while making the maximum effort for Christ (2:3-7).
- Keep his eyes on Christ at all times (2:8-13).
- Lead with authority (2:14).
- Interpret and apply Scripture accurately (2:15).
- Avoid useless conversation that leads only to ungodliness (2:16).
- Be an instrument of honor, set apart from sin and useful to the Lord (2:20-21).
- Flee youthful lusts, and pursue righteousness, faith, and love (2:22).
- Refuse to be drawn into philosophical and theological wrangling (2:23).
- Not argue, but be kind, teachable, gentle, and patient even when he is wronged (2:24-26).
- Face dangerous times with a deep knowledge of the Word of God (3:1-15).
- Understand that Scripture is the basis and content of all legitimate ministry (3:16-17).
- Preach the Word – in season and out of season – reproving, rebuking, and exhorting with great patience and instruction (4:1-2).
- Be sober in all things (4:5).
- Endure hardship (4:5).
- Do the work of an evangelist (4:5).

To sum it all up in five categories, Paul commanded Timothy (1) to be faithful in his preaching of biblical truth, (2) to be bold in exposing and refuting error, (3) to be an example of godliness to the flock, (4) to be diligent and work hard in the ministry, and (5) to be willing to suffer hardship and persecution in his service for the Lord. This is how every pastor should exhort and encourage his leaders.

Discussion Questions:

1. Name the five marks mentioned in the reading of Paul's humility and identify the correlating scriptures.
2. Define humility and how it affects a pastor's ministry.
3. What scripture is an exhortation to suffering and why must a pastor be willing to suffer?
4. How does a pastor shepherd his flock by "exercising oversight"?
5. What two pitfalls do we find in the pastoral ministry that Peter warns his fellow shepherds?

Chapter 2

APPROACHING PASTORAL MINISTRY SCRIPTURALLY

Pastoral ministry is a unique divine calling bestowed upon God's elect ministers of His Word and servants of His church. Men called to such a work feel both unworthy (1 Tim. 1:12-17) and unqualified (2 Cor. 3:4-6) for such a precious task. Yet to those set aside for this ministry, the claim of the apostle Paul applies: "We have this treasure in earthen vessels, that the surpassing greatness of the power may be of God and not from ourselves" (2 Cor. 4:7).

The sinfulness of man and the schemes of the evil one complicate the task of pastoral ministry, but our own ignorance of the basic purposes of the ministry add to the confusion. All too often no awareness can lead him to embark on erroneous and dangerous courses.

An understanding of the biblical philosophy of pastoral ministry can serve as a means of helping the minister enter into his vocation properly and in addition can facilitate the proper execution of that vocation. This chapter will deal with two basic tenets: first, the definition and benefits of a basic biblical philosophy of ministry, and second, biblical discussions on the purposes of the church, in the execution of which it is the pastor's function to lead. Some may wonder why we have a discussion of the purposes of the church in connection with a pastor's philosophy of ministry. The answer is in the question, how can a pastor minister effectively if he cannot identify, clarify, simplify, and execute the purposes of the church he leads? He will be serving in a fog unless he fully understands the importance of biblical purposes.

A Biblical Philosophy of Ministry

Every profession needs a mission statement that answers the questions: "Why am I in this role?" "What am I supposed to be doing?" and, "How am I to accomplish this task?" Like one on a journey, a pastor needs to know where he is going. The formulation of a statement of purpose is another way of referring to a philosophy of ministry. For the pastor, a philosophy of ministry must come from the mandates addressed to Christ's church.

We need to stress here the importance that every pastor knows and owns the biblical philosophy of pastoral ministry. No variety in philosophies of ministry exists. There is only one! It comes from the Scriptures and applies to all pastors.

Some today endeavor to have churches adopt a particular purpose, such as "a church for the families," "a church for the poor," etc. These may be proper, but they must be part of a larger context of the overall purpose of the church. As we shall see, the church has a purpose, and every minister is called into service to help accomplish this purpose. We dare not enter His service with our preconceived ideas on our personal agenda or a new theory on church ministry. As God said to Moses, so He says to us: "See...that you make all things according to the pattern which was shown you in the mountain" (Heb. 8:5).

Definition

What then is a philosophy of ministry? As already noted, it is a statement of purpose. It spells out exactly what we are to accomplish in ministry. It identifies the reason for the existence of the church and, thus, the reason for the existence of Christian ministry. The ministry does not exist independent of the church but rather as the means for fulfilling the purpose of the church. Paul reminds Timothy of this when he writes, "I am writing these things to you, hoping to come to you before long; but in case I am delayed, I write so that you may know how one ought to conduct himself in the household of God, which is the church of the living God, the pillar and support of the truth" (1 Tim. 3:14-15). He tells Timothy his role in the purpose of the church.

For this reason, a pastor's philosophy of ministry becomes a guide for his personal ministry. Once established and understood, it will guide the pastor's ministry accordingly. It becomes the map to keep him on track, a guide for his course of action – to correct him when blown astray by the hazards of ministry – and an encouragement to his life when the weight of the task burdens and almost overcomes him.

Benefits

Many benefits accrue from having a biblical philosophy of ministry. Five are worthy of emphasis. First, *it forces us to be biblical.* When we look to the Scriptures themselves for our reasons for ministering, it keeps us on a biblical track. The church drifts from its biblical foundation when its leaders abandon the biblical course. Ministers can apostatize by degrees, hardly noticing the slippage. They need constant reminders of the grave responsibility to keep the church firmly rooted and grounded upon the Word. The biblical writers and founding apostles have made clear the divine instructions as to the church's pattern, purpose, and practices. Even its power is to be from God. Hence we read of traditions (1 Cor. 11:2; 2 Thess. 2:15; 3:6) and practice(s) (1 Cor. 11:16). The earliest churches of God held the same philosophy of ministry (1 Cor. 14:33, 40). Any attempt to abandon that philosophy was a sign of apostasy, either in doctrine or in practice (2 Thess. 3:6; 3 John 9).

A biblical philosophy of ministry includes the means as well as the goals. A shallow and flippant understanding of the divine purposes for the church will lead to pragmatic, carnal, and even sinful approaches to the accomplishment of these ends. The winds of social change, the currents of liberal theology, and the influence of carnal stowaways will surely take the ship off course unless its captain stays faithful to the divine course.

A second advantage to a philosophy of ministry is that *it makes practical sense*. We must have a definite goal; there must be an aim to what we do. Paul said it best: "Therefore I run in such a way, as not without aim" (1 Cor. 9:26). He would not spend his life shadow-boxing. Ministerial burn-out usually lies at the feet of a lack of direction.

Efficiency is a third reason for a philosophy of ministry. Knowing his course of action will allow the pastor to concentrate his resources on accomplishing those aspects of ministry that are most essential. Too often, issues, programs, and efforts that have little or nothing to do with the church's overall purpose consume the pastor's resources as well as the church's. The temptation to waste its apostolic energies on social issues came to the early church but was averted through the wisdom of church leaders (Acts 6:1-7).

Fourth, the most obvious result of efficiency is *effectiveness*. He who aims at nothing hits it every time. A clear delineated battle plan, architectural blueprint, or work detail ensures success. Ministers laboring under the hit-and-miss philosophy will have little to show after a lifetime of faithful service. Even those with meager personal resources and on difficult ground will have something to show for their labors if they toil under the guidance of a divine blueprint. This undoubtedly was the secret to the church's success in the first century. The church knew what it had to do and went about doing it. In a short while the church had gained a reputation of upsetting the world (Acts 17:6).

The fifth benefit of holding to a biblical philosophy of ministry applies to a minister's *personal call to be faithful* (1 Cor. 4:2). We must one day give an account to the Lord for the ministry entrusted to us. How can we stand before Him and plead ignorance and ask for pardon for a blundering ministry? How can we claim a reward when we have not followed the charted course? Faithfulness includes the wise execution of our work. Men do not reward failure, no matter how much effort goes into it. Neither does God. Only those like Paul achieve the prize (Acts 20:24, 27; 1 Cor. 9:24; 2 Tim. 4:7).

Using another framework, Johnson summarized eight advantages for having a philosophy of ministry.[11] He said that a church that can articulate its philosophical foundations:

1. Can determine the scope of its ministry.
2. Can continuously re-evaluate its corporate experience in the light of its message.
3. Can evaluate its ministry in the light of thoughtful criteria rather than on the basis of a program's popularity.
4. Is more likely to keep its ministry balanced and focused on essentials.
5. Can mobilize a greater proportion of its congregation as ministers.
6. Can determine the relative merits of a prospective ministry.
7. Can be a clear, attractive alternative community to people seeking relief from systematic failure.
8. Can choose to cooperate or not cooperate with other churches and parachurch ministries.

The Purpose of the Church

The biblical purpose of the ministry must be rooted in biblical ecclesiology. To understand one's role as a minister, one needs to understand the role of the church. Getz puts it this way:

> Anyone who attempts to formulate a biblical philosophy of ministry and develop a contemporary strategy, a methodology that stands foursquare on the scriptural foundations, must ask and answer a very fundamental question. Why does the church exists? Put in another way,

---

[11] Rex Johnson, "Philosophical Foundations of Ministry," in *Foundations of Ministry*, ed. Michael J. Anthony (Wheaton: Victor, 1992), 55-59.

what is its ultimate purpose? Why has God left it in the world in the first place?[12]

Upon discovering the answers to these questions, the minister can then answer the question, "What is *my* purpose in the overall purpose of the church?"

Prior to His death, our Lord predicted the establishment of His church, which would be victorious over all foes (Matt. 16:18) and would consist of all believers becoming His body (Eph. 1:22-23). The church replaces Israel as God's people in the present administration and becomes a community of believers, redeemed by Christ's precious blood, with a three-fold function. The church is a *worshiping* community, a *working* community, and a *witnessing* community. In other words, the church is to *exalt* the Lord, it is to *edify* its members, and it is to *evangelize* the world. Everything the New Testament commands the church to do falls under these headings. Only an understanding of these functions can enable an individual believer to fill his or her role in the body of Christ. Only as the minister comprehends the mission of Christ's church can he properly serve his Lord and execute the pastoral ministry. We shall examine these three purposes in further detail.

A Worshiping Community

The ultimate purpose of mankind is to worship God and to enjoy His creation. The greatest commandment is to love God with your total being and then to love your neighbor as you love yourself (Matt. 22:36-40). The church's foremost calling is to exalt the Lord, to magnify His character, and to glorify Him before all creation. Saucy states, "Worship is central in the existence of the church. The words of the apostle Paul that God has chosen and predestined sons unto Himself in Christ 'to the praise of the glory of His grace' (Eph.

---

[12] Gene Getz, *Sharpening the Focus of the Church* (Chicago: Moody, 1974), 21.

1:4-6) suggests that the ultimate purpose of the church is the worship of the one who called it into being."[13]

Hence we understand the words of Peter as identifying the express purpose of Christ's church to be the exaltation of God through word and deed:

> You also, as living stones, are built up as a spiritual house for a holy priesthood, to offer up spiritual sacrifices acceptable to God through Jesus Christ. But you are a chosen race, a royal priesthood, a holy nation, a people for God's own possession; that you may proclaim the excellencies of Him who has called you out of darkness into His marvelous light (1 Pet. 2:4, 9).

The church is a redeemed community of sinners set apart to worship God in Christ. The minister is himself a worshiper of God. He must worship and then assist the community in the worship.

What is worship? "Worship is the honor and adoration directed to God," says MacArthur.[14] Martin says, "Worship is the dramatic celebration of God in His supreme worth in such a manner that His 'worthiness' becomes the norm and inspiration of human living."[15] Hence, "to worship God is thus to ascribe Him the supreme worth to which He alone is worthy." We are worshiping God when we give ourselves "completely to God in the actions and attitudes of life."[16]

The New Testament minister must see the clear distinction between worship patterns of Israel and those of the church. A dramatic change transpires between the delineated pattern of worship in Israel and that in the new order in which God is worshiped "in spirit and in truth (John 4:24). The church has no prescribed format, no temple or holy place, no sacrificial system, and no priesthood. Any attempt to institute any of these old features

---

[13] Robert L. Saucy, *The Church in God's Program* (Chicago: Moody, 1983), 14.
[14] John MacArthur, Jr., *The Ultimate Priority* (Chicago: Moody, 1983), 14.
[15] Ralph R. Martin, *The Worship of God* (Chicago:Moody, 1982), 4.
[16] Saucy, *The Church*, 166.

into the church faces the danger of trying to turn the church back into Israel.

The church is spiritually a temple in that it is the habitation of God and is called a "spiritual house" (1 Cor. 3:16; 1 Pet. 2:5). The church does not contain a priesthood but rather is a priesthood, which in turn offers up spiritual sacrifices to God (Rom. 12:1-2; 1 Pet. 2:5; Rev. 1:6). The New Testament writers, through employing similar terminology in describing the worshiping function of the church, were careful not to impose upon the church the "old wine" that was intended for the "old wine skins."

The absence of a prescribed order introduces some unique and particular ways in which the church offers worship to God. These spiritual sacrifices become the Christian's ministry to the Lord. The New Testament speaks of these sacrifices, often employing sacrificial terminology, but with an obvious distinction from the Old Testament system implied. The Christian is to be involved in the ministry of the gospel (Acts 6:5; Rom. 15:16; 2 Tim. 4:6), the ministry of holy living (Rom. 12:1-2; 1 Pet. 1:12-16), the ministry of prayer (Acts 6:6; 13:2-3; 1 Tim. 5:5; Rev. 4:8, 10-11), the ministry of serving others (Rom. 12:1-8; Phil. 2:17, 30; Heb. 13:16), the ministry of gratitude (Eph. 5:19-20; Col. 3:16-17; Heb. 12:28; 13:15), and the ministry of giving (Rom. 15:27; 2 Cor. 9:12; Phil. 2:4; 4:18; Heb. 13:16).

A casual glance at these aspects of New Testament worship reinforces what has been true since the beginning of time – that all of life is to be an act of worship. Moule offers this distinct summary: "All Christian life is worship, 'liturgy' means service, all believers share Christ's priesthood, and the whole Christian church is the house of God (1 Cor. 3:16; Eph. 2:22)."[17]

The New Testament presents but a sketchy picture of any particular type of the actual corporate worship experience in the early church. Here and there, we have a brief glimpse at the meetings of New Testament believers. We know they were

---

[17] C. F. D. Moule, *Worship in the New Testament* (London: Lutherworth, 1961), 85.

"continually devoting themselves to the apostles' teaching and to fellowship, to the breaking of bread and to prayer" (Acts 2:42). They came together for seasons of prayer (Acts 4:31; 12:5). The best glimpse of church service is in Paul's correction of the Corinthian catastrophe over the use of tongues (1 Cor. 12-14). Believers obviously met to exalt God both in prayers and prophecies, as well as in singing (see 1 Cor. 14:26). The intent of all was the worship of God (14:16, 25) and with the purpose that all be edified (14:26).

The function of the pastor is to lead the church in the attainment of this grand design, the worship of God. Obviously, the minister himself must be a true worshipper of God. He must practice in a personal and authentic way the worship of God. Then he must assist the congregation in the worship of God by helping them to understand the New Testament aspects of worship for the believer and to lead in the corporate worship of God during the various gatherings of the Christian community. He must teach the church to worship, lead them in worship, and join them in worship.

A Witnessing Community

It is not unusual to view the second and third grand purposes of the church as extensions of the first. Witnessing and ministering to one another are, in a sense, individual acts of worship. Hence two more ways to worship God are to win lost people and to help God's people. At times "only a few things are necessary, really only one" (Luke 10:42), the simple worship of God! Yet we have chosen for the sake of simplicity and development to keep the next two purposes distinct from the first.

The second grand purpose of the church is to evangelize a lost world. The church is to be a community witnessing to the saving grace of Christ. The Gospels are unanimous regarding the Great Commission given to the church by Christ (Matt. 28:18-20; Mark 16:15-16; Luke 24:46-47; John 17:18). The book of Acts not only concurs with this commission (1:8) but records the church's obedience to the Great Commission, from Jerusalem to the remotest part of the earth.

Evangelism is not an option to be accepted or rejected by the church. Outreach is a command. Evangelism is not limited to the gifted or to the church leadership. It is the mission of the entire church. To the truly faithful, evangelism is not merely a command but a compulsion (Acts 5:42; Rom. 1:14-17; 1 Cor. 9:16-18). Evangelism is the heart and soul of the New Testament church. The mandate is clear "that repentance for forgiveness of sins should be proclaimed in His name to all the nations, beginning from Jerusalem" (Luke 24:47-48).

Carrying out this purpose follows two approaches in Acts. The first is contact with the lost in the immediate surroundings, whether it be the person next to us (Acts 2), the house next door (Acts 5:42), the next town (Acts 8:5), or people of a different ethnic makeup (Acts 10). The early church did not understand the Great Commission as a mandate to do specialty evangelism. There was but one church composed of all peoples (see Rev. 7:9).

The second approach was to reach out to those in the regions beyond (cf. Rom. 15:18-29), which involved commissioning special men with the mission of taking the gospel to the remotest parts of the earth (Acts 13:1-3). The church was not negligent in obeying the Lord's command, either in soul winning or in planting churches in other communities.

The purpose of the church has not changed today. The Great Commission still stands. Modern technology has not annulled it. Pressing social needs have not abrogated it. Spiritual problems in the church have not surpassed its importance. Neither Christ nor Paul would stay longer than necessary in one particular place. They moved on so that others might hear the gospel.

In our biblical approach to pastoral ministry, the pastor must see his role in leading the congregation in fulfilling the Great Commission. The minister is by Christ's design himself a missionary. His church is to be a missionary church to those across the street or around the world. He is to be a world-class leader. He must have a vision beyond the pews in his facility. He should lead the way in praying for new fields, praying for God to thrust out laborers (Matt. 9:37-38), praying over the selection of missionaries (Acts 13:1-3), and supporting missionaries and the evangelistic enterprise. If he is a faithful minister, he can do no less and he dare not do otherwise.

A Working Community

The third purpose of the church is to build itself up through the interworking of various members of the Body of Christ. The function of the Christian is to edify or spiritually build up fellow members in the Body of Christ. Gertz states, "The church is to become a mature organization through the process of edification so that it will honor and glorify God."[18]

The New Testament contains a number of references to this vital but neglected purpose of the church (Matt. 28:18-20; Acts 20:17-35; Rom. 12:1-8; 1 Cor. 12-14; Eph. 4:7-16; Col. 1:24-29; 1 Pet. 4:10-11). A summary of these texts is that God expects the church, which is a living organism, to grow spiritually in Christlikeness and that God has given every believer a unique spiritual gift that is intended not for self-growth but to enhance the spiritual development of fellow Christians. The role of the pastor, himself gifted for his task, is to help believers discover and utilize their gifts for the growth of the Body of Christ. A mature church can thus remain united, firm in its devotion to Christ, functioning according to the purposes of God, and able to stand against the attacks of Satan.

Paul understood his pastoral ministry well, as he states: "And we proclaim Him, admonishing every man and teaching every man with all wisdom, that we may present every man complete in Christ. And for this purpose also I labor, striving according to His power, which mightily works with me" (Col. 1:28-29). This passage serves

---

[18] Getz, *Sharpening the Focus*, 53

well in pointing out the express purpose of a Christian minister. Consider these observations from this text:

1. *The purpose* – "That we may present every man complete in Christ." Paul makes clear that the purpose of every pastor is not to fill the auditorium with people, nor is it to preach wonderful sermons or entertain a congregation or collect a salary. The minister's task is to help every believer become Christlike, to prepare every child of God for meeting the Lord and Savior on that great day (see 1:22). "A glorious aim," states Eadie, ". . . the noblest that can stimulate enthusiasm, or sustain perseverance in suffering or toil."[19]

2. *The plan* – "We proclaim Him, admonishing every man, …teaching …with all wisdom" (1:28). Paul's plan was simple, direct, complete, and effective. Paul preached Christ and Christ alone! (See 1 Cor. 1:23; 2:2) His goal was to present Christ to every man, exhorting men to repent from their sins and to understand the totality of what a believer has in Christ. Paul felt "the necessity of employing the highest skill and precedence in discharging the duties of his office."[20] By warning and teaching Paul sought to bring about this maturity.

3. *The pain* – "For this purpose also I labor, striving…" (Col. 1:29). Paul's purpose was all-consuming, taxing. As an athlete does, Paul strove for a perfect mission. It was no light work, no pastime; it made a demand upon every faculty and every moment. The work of winning and discipling believers is not easy, nor is it for the fainthearted. The motivation must be the all-consuming goal of presenting mature believers to Christ (see. Eph. 5:26-27).

---

[19] John Eadie, *Commentary on the Epistle of Paul to the Colossians* (reprint, Minneapolis: James and Klock, 1977), 104.
[20] Ibid., 103. Eadie also gives an earnest admonition here.

4. *The power* – "According to His power, which mightily works…" (Col. 1:29). No minister is adequate for such a task. There must be absolute dependence upon the strength that only Christ can and will supply to those whom He calls and who humbly depend upon His strength, grace, and effective power. Paul elsewhere states that "our adequacy is from God" (2 Cor. 3:5).

Thus we see that Paul saw his role as a minister of the Word to bring about the maturity of every person. His was not an exclusive gospel, but an all-encompassing message.

Another text to consider in discussing the purpose of the church as a working community is Eph. 4:11-16. This passage is important not only in understanding the purpose of the church, but also because it is one of the few places that explicitly tells the role of the pastor in relation to that purpose.

Paul's epistle to the Ephesians is the epistle on ecclesiology. Chapter 4 treats the relationship believers should have with one another, namely harmonious loving unity. A means of promoting unity in the church is the gracious giving and exercise of these gifts. Paul proceeds in verses 7-16 to expound on this truth. Four observations are apropos.

1. *The distribution of gifts* (vv. 7-11). Paul first speaks of the divine distribution of gifts whereby each member of Christ's church receives a spiritual gift. The gifts vary in nature and effect but have one goal: the benefit or the common good, that is, the building up of one another (see 1 Cor. 12:1-11; Rom. 12:3-8). The distribution of these gifts to the church in general (v. 7) also includes gifts to a particular group of people who fill the offices of apostles, prophets, evangelists, and pastors and teachers. The intent of the apostle Paul is to highlight the specific nature of these gifts so as to indicate the part they play among the rest of the gifted brethren.

2. *The destination of the gifts.* Paul states that the purpose of the gifted men is "the equipping of the saints for the work of service, to the building up of the body of Christ" (v. 12). The plain order of the phrases and the arrangements of the prepositions yield the simple sense "for the perfecting of the saints unto all that variety of service which is essential unto the edification of the church. The role of the pastor-teacher is to mature the saints, to mend them, to instruct them in the Word of God. These mature saints are then duly qualified and fit to perform the work of ministry, to exercise their spiritual gifts to serve one another. The purpose of the work of the minister to the saints is that the body of Christ is built up.

God did not design the pastor to be the church's errand boy. Nor is the pastor the only one gifted to do the ministry. In fact, he does not possess all the gifts necessary for the proper and complete building up of the body. His gifts are equipping gifts, whereas the other members of the body have the useful gifts for a well-rounded ministry to the whole body. It is foolish for a church to expect its pastor to do all the ministry, as it is equally foolish for a minister to see himself as the only one capable of serving saints. His job is to equip. Theirs is to minister to one another. The end result is an edified church.

3. *The description of edification.* Paul goes on to explain what building up the body means by giving three parallel descriptions (v. 13). The goal of the church is to be united in the faith and in the full knowledge of the Lord Jesus. A partial comprehension of Christ obviously breeds disunity as history so well testifies. The church is to grow in stature, to move from infancy to manhood, from childhood to maturity. Finally, it is to fill up the measure of Christ's fullness, to be all that Christ is and that Christ expects the church to be.

4. *The design of edification.* Paul shows what will be the ultimate result of a mature church (vv. 14-16). It will no longer be a church resembling an easily deceived child with an unstable personality. The church will not be carried about by different doctrines and glaring error. Nor will it be susceptible to the tricks of Satan, but because of its full knowledge of Christ, it will detect, deter, and defend itself against the wiles of the devil. While upholding the truth in love, the church will grow into all the aspects of Christ. It will become like Christ (conformed to Him). Christ is really the ultimate source of all power and energy for the accomplishment of the growth of the body (Eph. 4:16). The ultimate goal is a loving community united by the strongest bond of all – God's divine love.

The pastor, then, has the special duty of equipping the members of his congregation so that they will discover and utilize their respective gifts for the spiritual maturity of one another. Some use the analogy of a coach and his team. The coach teaches the team the fundamentals of the game, and the team plays the game. The church is designed to be a working community where each individual member is faithfully serving the Lord by ministering to the rest.

The apostle Peter concurs with Paul and exhorts the pilgrims in his Epistle:

> As each one has received a special gift, employ it in serving one another, as good stewards of the manifold grace of God. Whoever speaks, let him speak, as it were, the utterances of God; whoever serves, let him do so as by the strength which God supplies; so that in all things God may be glorified through Jesus Christ, to whom belongs the glory and dominion forever and ever. Amen (1 Pet. 4:10-11).

The New Testament picture of a shepherd and his sheep provides an excellent model for the church and its leadership. Just as the shepherd leads, feeds, equips, encourages, protects, and multiplies the flock, so the pastor is to view his role with his flock. The parallels are marvelous and illustrative. In modern terms, the church's leaders must provide direction to Christians by pointing them toward the truth. The leader is to teach the congregation the whole counsel of God as it is revealed in Scripture by the faithful exposition of the whole Bible (see Acts 20:27; 2 Tim. 4:1-5). The pastor must see to it that every member of his flock moves through a harsh environment. Because of many dangers from the world, the flesh, and the devil, the minister must protect the flock (Acts 20:28). His watchfulness for wolves and snares ensures a safe and maturing flock. The obvious goal of the pastor is that the church grows both in numbers and in Christlikeness. He will not be content with a few sheep or with a flock so decimated by sin and Satan that they resemble "sheep without a shepherd" (Matt. 9:36).

The pastor plays a vital role in the establishment of a working community. Although the church is an organism, God sees to it that the church has direction and protection by providing a godly leadership for Christ's body. The minister's task is obviously never done, but he can see his flock progressing in maturity as it functions together, ministering to the needs of one another.

Discussion Questions:

1. Name five benefits that come from having a Biblical philosophy of ministry.
2. What are the three major aspects of the purpose of the church?
3. Define worship as it is discussed in the reading.
4. What distinction must be made about Old Testament worship that a New Testament minister must adopt?
5. How does the pastor develop spiritual maturity in the members of his church besides preaching the word?

Chapter 3

PRACTICAL APPLICATION OF MINISTRY

Having proposed a definition and suggested some benefits for a biblical philosophy of pastoral ministry, and having summarized the basic purpose of the church, we can now offer a general statement of the biblical purpose of Christian leadership. The role of the pastoral leadership, composed of a select group of men from the church of redeemed believers, is to provide guidance, care, and oversight for the church so that it fulfills its Christ-ordained mandate of evangelizing the entire world, growing into the likeness of Christ, and existing for the exaltation and worship of God.

The question remains as to how this biblical philosophy fleshes out in the practical ministry of the local church. What programs or practices should the pastor implement in his church to bring about the fulfillment of the church's purpose? Again, the New Testament is silent on rigidly specifying regulations, rituals, and practices that are to be the pattern for every congregation. The early churches were not clones of one another. Rather than precise patterns, the Lord gave the purpose of the church and the basic means by which the purpose was to be accomplished. We should look for principles rather than patterns. In some instances the apostles are specific (see 1 Cor. 14); in most cases, they present the ministry of the church in generalities, thus leaving room for each church to adapt its ministry in its own culture and context.

Though the New Testament does not furnish specific programs to implement, it is not lacking in illustrations of how the early church functioned so as to accomplish its goal. Some concepts and practices are quite adaptable and furnish a bare minimum by way of New Testament examples of what should be taking place in every local assembly. The Scriptures indicate seven ministries for accomplishing the three basic purposes of the church: exaltation, evangelism, and edification.

#1 - The Ministry of the Word

Acts 2:41-42 provides the first hint of the practice of the early disciples: "So then, those who had received his word were baptized; and there were added that day about three thousand souls. And they were continually devoting themselves to the apostles' teaching and to fellowship, to the breaking of bread and to prayer."

Entrance into the church came through repentance and baptism accompanied by the gift of the Holy Spirit (Acts 2:38). The newly formed church then devoted itself to a number of activities that resulted in numerical and spiritual growth (see 2:47; 4:32-35). First on the list of practices was continuance in the apostles' teaching. The Christians learned the Word of God or doctrine of the apostles, and they not only heard it but put the Word into practice. The preaching and teaching of the Word was central to the ministry of the apostles. The Word is the primary means of bringing a Christian to maturity (2 Tim. 3:16-17; cf. Ps. 19:7-11) and must not be neglected (Acts 6:2).

The pastor, then, is responsible for the teaching of the Word of God to the local church. Whether this is done through a preaching service, a Sunday school class, a discipleship group, cell groups, or home Bible studies does not matter ultimately. What is important, however, is that the Word of God be taught. If the Word of God is taught, the church will grow in faith and love (Rom. 10:17). Yet to introduce innovative programs for the sake of change and excitement without actually concentrating on teaching the Word of God is to change dinner plates without concern for the actual food that is served on those plates. The church leader must see to it that God's people continually devote themselves to the study and practice of the Word of God.

#2 - The Ministry of Fellowship

Luke mentions a second practice of the church. They devoted themselves to the fellowship – to the oneness and the commonality of the body of Christ. Rackham states,

> This fellowship was begun by our Lord, when He called the apostles to leave all and follow Him. So they formed a fellowship, living a common life and sharing a common purpose. When the Lord was taken up, the common life continued: and the most characteristic words in the early chapters of the Acts are *all, with one accord, together*.[21]

The job of the leadership is to incorporate new believers into the local body of Christ by visible acceptance into the membership of the church, to develop the use of their spiritual gifts, to place them in a useful spiritual function in the church, and to care for their spiritual welfare (see Acts 2:44-45; 4:32-37; 6:1). The focus of the Christian community is a continual devotion to caring for one another. "Christians," adds Getz, "cannot grow effectively in isolation! They need to experience each other."[22]

Leaders need to get Christians involved with one another. They should create meetings, occasions, ministry opportunities, and structures and funnel social patterns so that Christians are involved with one another. The church is not to be a theater, a lecture hall, or a spectator event. Rather, it is to be a community, a body, a mutual sharing of lives (see 1 Cor. 12:14-27). MacArthur gives these insights into fellowship:

> Fellowship involves being together, loving each other, and communing together. Fellowship includes listening to

---

[21] R. B. Rackham, *The Acts of the Apostles* (reprint, London: Methuen and Co., 1957), 35.
[22] Getz, *Sharpening the Focus*, 117.

someone who has a concern, praying with someone who has a need, visiting someone in the hospital, sitting in a class or a Bible study, even singing a hymn with someone you've never met. Fellowship also involves sharing prayer requests."[23]

There are no gimmicks to fellowship, nor can it be artificially maintained. Either Christians care for one another or they do not. They have a sense of belonging or they do not. True maturity in Christ-likeness does not develop adequately in assemblies filled with anonymous, non-committed spectators. Pastors must strive for the opposite and look for ways to make it happen.

#3 - The Ministry of the Lord's Supper

The early church participated regularly in "the breaking of bread," which may be taken in the general sense of eating meals together or in the specific sense of partaking of the Lord's Supper. We take it as the latter, although there is evidence that the Lord's Supper as practiced by the early church was accompanied by a common meal (see 1 Cor. 11:17-34).[24]

The Lord's Supper, like the ordinance of baptism, is not trivial practice, but is one that lies at the heart of the Christian message (1 Cor. 11:23-26). The symbolism, solemnity with celebration, and the sanctity required by all participants makes it one of the most inspirational and worshipful services of the Christian community. Lindsay, speaking of the early church and its practice of observing the Lord's Supper, recalls its importance as an act of worship: "And the Holy Supper, the very apex and crown of all

---

[23] John MacArthur, Jr., *Shepherdology: A Master Plan for Church Leadership* (Panorama City, Calif.: The Master's Fellowship, 1989), 54; rev. ed., *The Master's Plan for the Church* (Chicago: Moody, 1991).
[24] Thomas M. Lindsay, *The Church and the Ministry in the Early Centuries* (reprint, Minneapolis: James Family, 1977), 50-52).

Christian public worship, where Christ gives Himself to His people, and where His people dedicate themselves to Him in body, soul and spirit, was always a sacrifice as prayers, praising and alms-giving were."[25]

If the church's worship service never or seldom includes the Lord's Supper, it falls short of the intentions of the Lord (1 Cor. 11:23) and the practices of the early church (Acts 2:42). Great spiritual benefit comes to the church when the Lord's Supper is properly observed and is not trivialized as an appendix to a sermon or musical celebration. Pastors must teach and encourage the congregation to celebrate the Lord's Supper in a way that will be meaningful, uplifting, and edifying to the soul.

#4 - The Ministry of Prayer

We observe in Acts 2:42 that the church was devoted not just to prayer, but to *"the* prayers." The expression probably refers "to their own appointed seasons for united prayer within the new community."[26] Rackham says that "the expression *the Prayers* almost implies that there were regular hours of prayer, corresponding to the Jewish Synagogue prayers, but we have no information on the subject."[27] Prayer was an important part of the church's life (Acts 1:14; 3:1; 4:23-31; 6:4; 10:9; 12:5, etc.). The church prayed for its leaders (6:6), its missionaries (13:3), its sick (James 5:14-18), governing authorities (1 Tim. 2:1-2), and just about anything one could think of (Phil. 4:5-7).

Prayer moves God; prayer changes things. Effective prayer accomplishes much. A praying church will be a victorious, growing, maturing community. The wonder of today's church is that so much goes on with so little praying. The answer to many of the church's problems is not more seminars, programs, and

---

[25] Ibid., 37.
[26] F. F. Bruce, *Commentary on the Book of the Acts* (Grand Rapids: Eerdmans, 1970), 80.
[27] Rackham, *Acts of the Apostles*, 41.

promotional gimmicks but more intercession on the part of God's people, both as a group and in the closet.

#5 - The Ministry of Outreach

Another aspect of the ministry that needs incorporation into the life of the church is educating, involving, and motivating the church to reach out to the lost community around them. Early believers were concerned for the unsaved and made it a lifestyle to testify about the gospel of Jesus Christ. Luke makes this observation about the church's leadership: "And every day, in the temple and from house to house, they kept right on teaching and preaching Jesus as the Christ" (Acts 5:42). The record of the Acts of the Apostles is a description of the spread of the gospel as Christ had commanded.

Evangelism is expected of the believer, and especially of the local church. The church today commits two grave errors when it comes to evangelism. The first is the notion that the pastor's role is to teach the people and then the church will naturally go about the business of evangelism. The other fallacy is that evangelism is the task of the pastor or church leadership. They are the "hired ones," paid to do evangelism. More recently, some have suggested that evangelism is a gift held by some who in turn are to do the work of evangelism for the church.

We contend that evangelism is both caught and taught. Pastors must practice personal soul winning as well as teach evangelism to their congregations. A church that does not know how to reproduce and does not reproduce is in reality an immature congregation, regardless of its intellectual comprehension of Scripture or the sophistication of its corporate programs.

#6 - The Ministry of Missions

The obvious results of attempting to fulfill the Great Commission will be the incorporation of a missions program into the local church. Faithfulness to the Lord's command to disciple all the nations will include a directed effort, regardless of the magnitude, at reaching the regions beyond the local church's immediate locality. The local church will have a missions program where they participate in selecting, sending, supporting, and interceding for special Christians who are sent out from them to reach the lost in other places.

The pastor will lead the way in establishing and maintaining the missions program. It is not a task to leave to the women's missionary society or the missions committee. Missions is world-class work and needs top-level guidance and support. The early church considered missions a matter of extreme importance (Acts 13:1-3; 14:27; 15:36-40). It was not a secondary or minor program. Every church, large or small, should have its own involvement in the great missionary enterprise of the body of Christ.

#7 - The Ministry of Interchurch Fellowship

New Testament churches were autonomous congregations under the supervision of their own eldership or leadership. They share in similar traditions and practices, while being distinct congregations. Yet there was a great amount of interdependence. They shared in discipleship efforts (Acts 11:26), in common relief efforts (Acts 11:27-30), and in active relationship with one another so that each church saw itself as a part of the whole.

The same needs to be true today; churches should belong to a larger group of churches for mutual support and cooperative efforts. This may be done by belonging to a denomination, an association of churches, or a fellowship of like-minded ministries. The result will be the same.

The pastor should be careful not to become the proverbial lone ranger, isolating himself and his congregation from the rest of the body of Christ. This will result in his own loss and the diminished ministry of his congregation. The minister must lead the church in these cooperative efforts and implement the programs that will sustain and invigorate these fellowships.

As one can see, there is no end to specific ways that the pastor can flesh out the purpose of the biblical church in his particular congregation. Yet he must make sure that he begins with the Scriptures. The Holy Spirit in His sovereign wisdom gave biblical principles that can be applied during all ages to all cultures. The rest is up to Christian ministers.

Discussion Questions:

1. What are the seven ministries noted in scripture that fulfill the purposes of the church?
2. What results can be found from the ministry of the Word?
3. Describe the job of leadership towards new believers.
4. What two common errors do we find in the church today concerning evangelism?
5. How does a pastor motivate his congregation for missions? List several practical ways the ministry of outreach can be incorporated in the church.

Chapter 4

ARE WE SETTING UP PASTORS AND CHURCHES FOR FAILURE?

Most of us have bought into an unhealthy understanding of leadership. We have been taught that leadership is about one individual's performing all of an organization's critical tasks – motivating, mobilizing, directing, and resourcing people to fulfill a vision – at a level of excellence and influence that separates him or her from the bulk of humanity. The combination of skills and abilities required to be a great leader has caused many people to lament the absence of leaders in our society.

Let me share why I believe we have unrealistic expectations for our leaders. In a nationwide survey conducted by Barna Research among 1,005 adults, people identified those things they feel are "very important" for a leader to do.

Here is the profile:

- 87% expect leaders to motivate people to get involved in meaningful causes and activity.

- 78% believe leaders should negotiate compromises and resolve conflicts when they arise.

- 77% look to leaders to determine and convey the course of action that people should take in order to produce desirable conditions and outcomes.

- 76% rely on leaders to identify and implement courses of action that are in the best interest of society, even if some of those choices are unpopular.

- 75% expect leaders to invest their time and energy in training more leaders who will help bring the vision to reality.

- 63% want leaders to communicate vision so that they know where things are headed and what it will take to get there.

- 61% say leaders are responsible for the direction and production of employees associated with the leader's organization or cause.

- 61% think leaders should analyze situations and create the strategies and plans that direct the resources of those who follow them.

- 56% hold leaders responsible for managing the day-to-day details of the operations.

The list goes on, but it clearly shows that we have developed an unreasonable notion of what a leader should do. Look at the breadth of tasks and abilities demanded by the expectations reflected in that survey – and realize, of course, that many people hold additional expectations beyond those listed. We expect the central leader not only to provide the corporate vision, but also to:

- direct activity
- encourage participants
- supply resources
- evaluate plans and progress
- motivate participants
- negotiate agreements
- strategize
- manage people
- reinforce commitments
- recruit necessary colleagues

- communicate conditions, plans, and assignments
- train new leaders
- resolve conflicts, and so on

Who could possibly meet such a wide range of disparate expectations? Would you agree that a person would have to be superhuman to accomplish all of these tasks? Yet that's what we expect a leader to do. No wonder we are consistently disappointed by leaders who seemed to hold such promise before assumed positions of significant authority and responsibility. Barnas' surveys have shown that during the past two decades there has been a continual decline in satisfaction in churches, governments, nonprofit organizations, schools, businesses, and families.

When you reach a point of frustration or incapacity, one useful strategy is to go back and question your assumptions to determine if they were errant and therefore contributed to the blockage. If we take that approach to our consternation regarding leadership, we will most likely conclude that the real problem is not our leaders but the unhealthy expectations we have of them. Few men or women have the individual capacity to deliver all that we have come to expect of those in positions of authority. We set leaders up for failure by holding them to absurd performance standards. We set organizations up for failure by intimately tying the success and well-being of the institution to the quality of leadership it receives. We set people up for frustration, disappointment, and failure by basing their present and future well-being upon the capacity of the individual leader whom they most closely follow in any given dimension of their lives.

Options for Improvement

Once we understand the problem, there are several options we might consider for improving the situation – some good, some not so good.

First, we could accept the situation as a reality that is certainly imperfect but cannot and will not change. From that perspective, our responsibility is simply to make the best of it. No matter how many superior scenarios we dream up, we might assume that they are not likely to become reality, so we feel we might as well not tantalize ourselves with unrealistic potentials. While such an analysis may have some appeal, it is undoubtedly a defeatist, lazy-minded perspective. It is hard to imagine any scenario in life in which improvements are impossible.

Second, we could argue that the real problem is our failure to identify the most qualified leaders. *If we could get those people in place, things would improve.* This is a common complaint heard within the political arena: The system and the election process scare away the most capable and qualified candidates, leaving only those so desperate for the job that they will do whatever it takes to win elected office. Once again, this view is not very realistic. True leaders rarely shrink from a reasonable challenge, especially if one of their potential accomplishments is changing the system to facilitate better outcomes and to make the task more attractive to other leaders.

Third, we might take the position that past and present leaders have failed to meet our expectations because they have not been adequately trained. This notion is undermined by ample evidence that suggests our leaders often receive the best training available, whether in school, in the field, or through mentoring. Effective leaders have many traits – among them a strong desire to succeed – that often drives them to gain the training, information, experience, and skills needed to accomplish their goals. While there are many examples we could cite of leaders not having enough training, this explanation appears insufficient to describe dearth of effective leaders, especially in our churches.

Finally, a wiser alternative, in my view, would be to accept the fact that the current system does not work because it has an inherent flaw in its foundation that must be addressed. Such broad thinking opens up a world of possibilities and conjecture. What hypotheses are worth testing? If we were to build the "ideal model" of leadership, regardless of what models now prevail, what would that model look like? Working backward from a clear-cut notion of "effective leadership," what would we strive to facilitate? In other words, rather than try to enable existing leaders to live up to the extremely high levels of performance we demand of them, how could we reconceptualize and innovatively redefine the leadership process?

Team to the Rescue

Let me confess that it took me a long time to realize that the first three options described above – that is, accepting things as they are, recruiting better-quality leaders, and providing leaders with better training – will not necessarily produce the results we are seeking. As a product of the institutions and methods that produced the problem in the first place, I had been completely blinded to alternatives to the leader-as-superstar approach.

Over the past several years I have had the privilege of discovering what many other people already knew and practiced: Leadership works best when it is provided by teams of gifted leaders serving together in pursuit of a clear and compelling vision.

In the past decade, more than four thousand new books on leadership have been published. Most discuss the indispensable skills needed to become king of the hill; few downplay personal superiority or emphasize serving within a team context. Almost every leadership book or training course discusses what the central leader can do to satisfy people's demands and outperform everyone else; rarely do leadership books or courses dare to suggest that leadership is best accomplished without a high-profile, multitalented, popular icon in the center-stage spotlight. But we have found that the "superstar" model of leadership, while appealing and not without some experiential validity can do more to decimate the health of an organization than to facilitate its well-being.

The greatest challenges in our society stem from the absence of quality leadership. We live in an increasingly complex and sophisticated society. People are constantly bombarded by opportunities, challenges, and choices. No one can deny that we do, indeed live in a land and age of opportunity.

But as human beings we are prone to chase outcomes that may not be realistic or even in our own best interest. Often we ignore the common good for the personal good. As often as not we make choices that we later regret or that reflect poor judgment. Making good choices, discerning appropriate priorities, and staying focused and on track is exceedingly difficult. What will enable us to make progress toward outcomes that honor God, improve people's quality of life, and facilitate joy and meaning? Quality leadership.

But the answer does not lie in unearthing more superhero leaders who satisfy the grandiose, ever-expanding demands of the people. The answer lies in combining the talents of gifted leaders to create synergistic outcomes. Team leadership is the only approach that carries the promise of satisfying the needs of our society. Solo leaders will always have an important place in our present and future reality. But I believe that teams hold the key to the future.

The Impact of Team Leadership

We are not aware of just how much our lives have been impacted by leadership teams. Consider just a few examples that you may have overlooked.

- **Major political decisions are made at both the federal and state levels by executives whom we have elected – specifically, by the president of the United States and by the governor of your state.** But do you realize that those two individuals, while elected to lead, each rely heavily upon a cabinet – a small group of advisors who are leaders in their own right and who provide substantial input into the key strategic decisions made by the chief executive? It is the rare – and usually unsuccessful – government leader who makes important, life-impacting decisions without careful study and discussion among a handful of selected counselors whose experience, skills, and abilities complement those of the chief executive.

- **Your physical safety had been sustained by the military.** You may be aware that key military decisions are rarely the choice of one individual, such as a general, but they are the outcome of a small group of experienced, trained professionals who work together to make important decisions. At the policy-making level, we might identify the Joint Chiefs of Staff as such a leadership team. Within a given branch of the military there are other teams at work, enabling the chief leader of the branch to make significant decisions.

- **Sports teams use multiple leaders to devise effective strategy, representing a team behind the scenes as well as the team that you enjoy watching on the field.** In football, the head coach works with a team of assistant coaches including a defensive coach, an offensive coach, a special teams' coach, and a tactician who has studied the opponents to understand their strengths and weaknesses. In basketball you may have the head coach working in tandem with a coach of the guards, one who focuses on the forwards and centers, and another who tracks what the opponents have been doing. Baseball teams have coaches who help the manager by focusing on various functions such as hitting, pitching, scouting, and conditioning.

- **The board of directors of many large corporations uses an "executive committee" that shapes policy and other core decisions for the corporation.** That committee is usually a handful of people – from three to seven individuals – who assist the board chairperson in developing key outcomes. The team often includes individuals of divergent, complementary backgrounds covering areas such as finance, human resources, management, marketing, and technology.

Clearly, teams of leaders affect every day. In many cases we may not realize the depth and range of leadership competence provided simply because a team works so smoothly – almost as if it were one indivisible entity rather than a collection of individuals. In these situations the team embraces one unified position, speaks with one voice, gains a single image in the public eye, and operates with such unity that we remain unaware of the multiple parts that work cooperatively behind the scenes. When those parts are working in lockstep, all we see – or care about – are the results.

A major advantage of being led by a team is that the results almost always transcend what any individual from the team could have produced without the assistance of the other leaders involved in that team.

Challenge Facing Today's Leaders

To sense the full impact of the importance of shifting from solo leadership to team leadership, take a moment to consider some of the challenges that face our culture today.

- **Population growth.** Already the third most-populated nation in the world, the United States will add another thirty million people to its population this decade. That growth will result in a wide variety of new pressures, needs, and expectations.

- **Morality.** One of the growing concerns of Americans is the moral and ethical decline of our nation. This is a decade which as Americans we have been overtaken by moral anarchy – an environment in which people do whatever they feel is in their personal interest regardless of the law, the common good, or the needs of the groups with which they are associated. While a remnant is deeply concerned about moral decay, most people have come to accept it and strive to cope with it – primarily by honing and excusing their own decadent practices.

- **Expectations.** People expect to have the best of everything at a low cost and delivered immediately. Having abandoned God as the center of our lives, we seek fulfillment from other sources, especially our material possessions and entertainment experiences. We resent anything that gets in the way of our being able to achieve maximum pleasure.

- **Families.** Soaring levels of divorce, "gay marriages," legal abortions, latchkey children, family poverty, in-home violence, and out-of-wedlock births among both adults and teenagers, combined with fewer mothers staying home to nurture young children and the declining quality of communication within families have made a pipe dream of the notion that the family is the primary delivery agent of appropriate values and behavior. Families themselves no longer turn inward for direction and resources they need for maturation and quality of life; instead, they turn outward to get what they need, which leads to further weakening and disintegration of the family unit.

- **Values.** Traditional values such as absolute moral truth, personal integrity, and respect for authority have been twisted beyond recognition. The new values in place have shaped our relationships with people and institutions.

The list of challenges facing leaders could go on for pages. The severity of the cultural shifts we have witnessed in recent years emphasizes that one person is not likely to provide the breadth and acuity of leadership demanded by such an environment. Expecting any one individual to meet such extraordinary demands is not only naïve, but borders on being cruel to the leader and unjust to the enterprise he or she leads.

Six New Leadership Trends in the Church

We continue examining the context in which leadership occurs by studying some of the shifts happening in churches. Consider the following six trends that are reshaping leadership in ministry:

1. **Increasing numbers of senior pastors are shifting from the role of preacher-counselor to that of leader-trainer.** Without diminishing the importance of preaching and counseling, there is a heightened realization that the congregation relies upon the senior pastor for vision, motivation, and mobilization. The result is a redefining of how pastors use their resources to have impact.

2. **Four forces are converging to change the role of laity in leadership.** First, people are demanding participation in the development of their current experience and future conditions. Second, Christians are becoming more aware of their spiritual gifts – and more eager to use those gifts in personal ministry and for the benefit of their church. Third, most of our seminaries are still oriented more toward producing preacher-counselors than toward training effective leader-trainers. As a result, many churches must look elsewhere for individuals who have been called by God to lead, have been trained to do so, and have solid leadership experience. Fourth, pastors are increasingly open to sharing the leadership of the church's ministry with competent and committed laity. The outgrowth of these new realities is that churches are identifying, training, and deploying congregants as key leaders within the ministry. Ministry leaders are

increasingly being raised up from within the congregation instead of being chosen from resumes presented by outsiders.

3. **More churches are striving to accurately determine the health of their ministry.** To facilitate that transition, attention is being shifted from the church growth – primarily qualitative in nature – to church health, which addresses ministry quality. This change in emphasis will necessarily demand a different leadership focus and new skills.

4. **In the past decade, the Holy Spirit has received greater attention and devotion than at any time in the past half-century.** One implication of this "comeback" by the third Person of the Trinity is that church leaders must now consider the appropriate blending of business-oriented skills with sensitivity to the prompting of the Holy Spirit. This produces a better balance of head and heart in leading the ministry.

5. **Extensive research over more than three decades has confirmed the view that although leadership skills can be taught, leadership will always be an art, not a definable science.** As such, while methodology is important and techniques can be taught to bring about superior outcomes, the acceptance of leadership as a "soft science" frees churches to concentrate on leadership as a ministry rather than as a discipline that facilitates ministry. The bottom line is that leaders minister by serving others.

6. **Congregants demand excellence and relevance from their church.** This perspective has changed the way in which people want to be treated when they invest themselves in ministry. Rather than being described as volunteers, unpaid laypeople want to be regarded as "ministry professionals." Churches are changing the terms they use to describe volunteers and the quality of resources made available to

them, and they are providing different forms of supervision to these ministry partners. This alters how full-time church leaders perceive and carry out their work within the congregational context.

Each of these trends points to a meaningful shift in how people think, interact, work, and perceive ministry. When the context changes, leadership must adapt. The changes described above demand that leaders perform the same fundamental functions – giving people a sense of where to go and how to get there – but deliver the related resources in ways that fit the new cultural context.

Pastor's Self-Perception

Recent research has shown that most pastors neither see themselves as leaders nor aspire to be leaders. A recent national survey of Protestant senior pastors asked them to identify their spiritual gifts. Only 12 percent said that they had a gift of leadership. In contrast, two-thirds of pastors surveyed said they had the gift of teaching or preaching. They have accurately recognized that teaching and leading are two very distinct responsibilities and activities that require different skills that produce different results.

Despite the trends highlighted above, the continuing, prevailing mind-set among pastors is that their primary job is to preach from the Bible and to take advantage of other opportunities to teach. Studies show that there is a very high level of frustration among pastors, they went to seminary to learn how to preach and pastor, not how to lead – yet their people expect strong visionary leadership in addition to practical, challenging, and life-changing teaching.

Another relevant finding from research is that less than one of every ten senior pastors can articulate the vision for the ministry he or she is trying to lead. Combine pastors' personal convictions that they have not been called to lead with the inability to articulate

God's vision for their ministry, and you can clearly see that we will be in trouble if we rely upon senior pastors to provide all or most of the leadership in our churches. A church can compensate for the absence of many skills and resources, but it cannot overcome the absence of effective leadership. If that leadership is not going to come from pastors, then it must come from somewhere else.

And that is where team leadership enters the picture.

Discussion Questions:

1. How can the unhealthy expectations of the role of leadership be reversed?
2. Give one example of how team leadership produces results.
3. What is the major advantage of being led by a team?
4. Name three social demands facing our leaders today and explain how the latest trends can help meet those challenges.
5. What are the four forces that are changing the role of the laity in leadership positions?

Chapter 5

NEEDING A NEW LEADERSHIP MODEL

There are two common traditional leadership models.

1. **The Solo Leadership Model.** This model allows the leader/pastor to say, "I know where we are supposed to go next; follow me." This model focuses on one leader having all the vision, decision-making, and control over the ministry.

2. **The Majority Rule Leadership Model.** This model allows the group/congregation to say, "We know where we are supposed to go next, and we've hired professional ministers to take us there." This model allows 51% of the overall group or congregation to determine the direction. Usually a smaller subset of the majority in the group influences and controls the majority to get their way.

Both models have inherent weaknesses. The weaknesses in the Solo Leadership Model is that it sets up the senior leader to eventually fail and hinders the group (team) from active, involved participation.

When the solo leader's creativity proves inadequate, or his decisions prove flawed, he loses credibility in the eyes of his followers. Even if mistakes are not made, burnout from carrying that heavy burden is inevitable. While the group must trust their solo leader, if they are not included in the decision making process, they usually find it much more difficult to be committed to the decision. What often results is compliance rather than commitment.

Compliance is what you have when your followers agree to follow but don't necessarily agree with the direction. Commitment is what you have when common agreement has been reached and everyone works together toward a common goal. No one lives in compliance forever. They will either move to commitment by coming into agreement with the direction of the ministry, or they will move away from the ministry.

Solo leadership does not prepare leaders for the future. Those solo leaders who survive often establish a "hero" mentality in which the ministry does not survive after the leader is gone. It remains only a one generational ministry.

A few extremely gifted leaders manage to minimize mistakes and maintain energy over the long haul. The ministry members learn to be dependent on their solo leader. They do not learn to lead. The result has a deep leadership void when the solo leader leaves. This violated the principle of generational transfer.

> **2 Timothy 2:2** *And the things that you have heard from me among many witnesses, commit these to faithful men who will be able to teach others also.*

Point to Ponder: George Mueller built a ministry based on his individual leadership. General Booth built the Salvation Army based on a team model. George Mueller's ministry no longer exists. The Salvation Army is the largest charity in the world.

There are also weaknesses of the Majority Rule Leadership Model.

Majority Rule Leadership (Congregational rule) is ineffective. It does not encourage the pursuit of excellence in leadership. Often the weakest members of the group wind up setting the standard for the whole. It actually facilitates the ability of a few forceful people to dominate the decisions of the group and control the agenda.

Majority Rule Leadership is usually inefficient. A growing ministry must be able to make decisions and plans, and remain flexible in the accomplishment of goals. Majority Rule does not naturally facilitate those needs. When unexpected issues arise it takes considerable time (which you sometimes don't have) to call a meeting of the membership and inform them of the issue.

Majority Rule Leadership is not based in Scripture. In Scripture, the recurring pattern shows God speaking to His chosen vessel who takes the message to the people.

- God told Moses to flee Egypt and lead the Israelites out. Joshua received instruction from God and Joshua conveyed them to his leaders and the people before entering Canaan.

  Joshua 1:2-3 *"Moses My servant is dead. Now therefore, arise, go over this Jordan, you and all this people, to the land which I am giving to them--the children of Israel Every place that the sole of your foot will tread upon I have given you, as I said to Moses."*

  Joshua 1:10-11 *Then Joshua commanded the officers of the people, saying, "Pass through the camp and command the people, saying, 'Prepare provisions for yourselves, for within three days you will cross over this Jordan, to go in to possess the land which the Lord your God is giving you to possess.'"*

- Paul was led by the Holy Spirit on his various missionary endeavors.

  Acts 13:2-4 *As they ministered to the Lord and fasted, the Holy Spirit said, "Now separate to Me Barnabas and Saul for the work to which I have called them." Then, having fasted and prayed, and laid hands on them, they sent them away. So, being sent out by the Holy Spirit, they went down to Seleucia, and from there they sailed to Cyprus.*

- The only example of majority rule in Scripture is found in Acts 27:9 and it failed. Paul told the captain about God's instructions to wait to sail or the ship would be lost. The captain chose to take a vote among the sailors. The majority wanted to set sail. They lost the ship.

Point to Ponder: The concept of democracy did not originate in Scripture. The people to counter the misuse of power and mistrust of leaders framed it in the Greek world. There is a difference between a democracy and a republic (representative government).

Social trends are challenging what have become the traditional models in the contemporary church.

- Population growth is increasing while church attendance is shrinking. We are not reaching our current culture.

- Even in cultures previously thought of as "Christian," absolute values and morals have been replaced by relativism.

- The modern family functions very differently from the families of the previous century. There are fewer two-parent families. In the United States, many families have both parents working full-time, allowing less time for the family as a central unit.

Point to Ponder: The challenge of every leader is to remain biblically sound and yet culturally relevant.

Certainly there are no shortages of challenging opportunities today. In these extraordinary times, the challenges seem to be increasing – and through our responses, we have the potential to profoundly change the world in which we live and work.

Current Ministry Trends Demand Leadership Change

- **Increase role of the Holy Spirit.** There is an increased role of the Holy Spirit in ministry life and leadership among effective ministries. Leaders are required to embrace a balance between business skills and sensitivity to Holy Spirit promptings (Acts 13). Leaders must have a better balance of the heart and head in leading the ministry.

- **Increased ministry role of volunteers.** The relationship between laity and clergy is changing. There is an increase of volunteers serving in key ministry roles. In a world of increased education, ministry members bring expertise with them to the ministry and an expectation that they will be able to use those skills. Ministry members are seeking to discover their gifts and to be empowered and released to use them. Effective ministry leaders are becoming leader-trainers. Ministries and congregations depend on them to provide vision, motivation, and mobilization through skill training.

- **Increased expectations by members.** There are increased expectations by ministry members for excellence and relevance to everyday life. Ministries that prioritize excellence and relevance thrive, while those that don't are stagnant or losing numbers.

Point to Ponder: The bottleneck to the harvest of souls is leadership. The bottleneck to leadership is old wineskins.

Three Biblical Examples of Team Ministry & Leadership

Moses learned the value of team ministry.

Moses was a fascinating leader. Reluctant to lead from the start, he learned many leadership lessons the hard way. Two insights stand out about Moses and his involvement with teams.

First, he clearly recognized that while God called him to lead, he was hampered by severe limitations and was reticent to take on such responsibility. His reaction was to ask God to provide him with colleagues who would compensate for his overt weakness – that is, to let him lead as part of a team in which he would (by God's design) serve as the directing leader and captain of the team. In response, God provided other leaders, such as Joshua and Caleb, to share the burden.

The second insight relates to the potential inefficiencies of solo leadership. Even though Moses had capable teammates, he retained much of the responsibility of directing the people, making public policy, and supervising the operations of their venture. In Exodus 18, Moses' father-in-law Jethro, pays Moses and his family a visit. He observed Moses' typical workday and is appalled by the bottleneck Moses has created by striving to be all things to all people. Jethro offers some advice: Divide the leadership duties into manageable portions and delegate some of the responsibility to a leadership team of other gifted servants. That advice changed Moses' life, freeing him to focus on aspects of directing the nation that only he could perform. Solo leadership can take you only as far as your individual capacity; increasing the leadership capacity through teamwork enhances the quality of life for the people as well as for you, their leader.

Moses learned several valuable lessons about teamwork and leadership when Jethro challenged him to stop trying to meet everyone's needs by himself (Ex. 18:13-26).

- **Recognize the no one can do it all alone (Ex 18:13-18).** Moses realized that his previous leadership approach was flawed and that he needed help.

- **Be willing to receive advice (Ex 19:19a).** Moses humbly received correction from his father-in-law, Jethro. He was teachable and was willing to be a continual learner and make needed changes. This applies to all leaders.

- **Maintain a spiritual perspective of your duties (Ex 19:19b).** As Moses stepped back from doing everything himself, he was able to focus more on spiritual matters. We have to be reflective in ministry, not just reactionary.

- **Focus on teaching and training others (Ex 18:20a).** Moses was challenged to teach the people life principles so they could learn to make good decisions on their own, rather than merely telling them what to do. Here Moses became intentional. Sometimes we think it is easier to do it ourselves; but not in the long run.

- **Model and be an example of what you teach (Ex 18:20b).** Moses needed to practically demonstrate how to apply the principles he was teaching.

- **Communicate expectations clearly (Ex. 18:20c).** Moses was challenged to clearly communicate the expected duties the people were to perform. When expectations are clear, people are not as dependent on the leader to do their part.

- **Select and develop high character leaders (Ex 18:21a).** Moses was shifting (making a transition) from doing it all himself to being committed to raising up qualified leaders who would manage the work. A leader must focus on developing leaders. Leaders don't just show up. (I Tim. 3:2-7; Titus 1:5-9; Acts 6:2-3; II Tim. 2:2)

- **Empower the emerging leaders to do their job (Ex 18:21b).** Once the leaders were picked and trained, Moses released them into action. The temptation is to hold them back, or micromanage. A leader must empower others to serve. Give the proper authority to match responsibility.

- **Delegate the easy things; retain the hard tasks (Ex. 18:22).** Moses learned to give away as much responsibility as possible, spreading out the workload. He retained the tasks and problems the others could not handle.

Jethro instructed Moses that there would be two key benefits from team leadership (Ex 18:23):

1. **Leaders last longer when they work in a team.** When the load is shared, leaders can focus on the overall vision and keep a long-term view.

2. **The needs of the people get satisfied.** This model is best for the leader and the people. More needs get met when there are more people involved in the ministry process.

Nehemiah models team leadership principles.

Through his campaign to restore the city walls, Nehemiah relied heavily upon teams of gifted individuals with complementary skills to facilitate the fulfillment of the vision God had given to him. At different times throughout the campaign he organized different teams for divergent purposes. The walls would never have been built if he had relied upon a more traditional style of one-man leadership.

Nehemiah knew the importance of teams. He undertook the difficult challenge of rebuilding the city wall around Jerusalem (Neh. 1-6).

We can identify several key principles related to leadership and teams.

- **Recognize the need (Nehemiah 1:1-3).** When Nehemiah heard of the plight of his brothers in Jerusalem, he didn't just talk about the problems, he mourned and fasted and prayed for the need to be met.

- **Accept responsibility – repent and respond (Nehemiah 1:4-11).** Nehemiah's response to the need was to repent for his own failures and those of his nation. He then responded to God's call to do his part.

- **Risk failure and step out in faith (Nehemiah 2:1-6).** Every great leader comes to the place in which he steps out in faith in response to the call of God.

- **Request help and be supplied with resources (Nehemiah 2:7-9).** There is no leader who has all the resources he needs to accomplish God's mission. God intended it that way so we would not attempt to go alone.

- **Include the leadership team in the decision process (Nehemiah 2:11-20).** From the very beginning of surveying the damaged wall to the decision to build, Nehemiah had a select group of leaders with him. Together they reached common agreement to accomplish the rebuilding of the wall.

- **Establish teams to perform the task (Nehemiah 3).** There are multiple task teams that each had their own leader. The leaders must have been a part of Nehemiah's leadership team. (If every task team built their section uniquely, then all the various parts of the wall would not have matched up!)

- **Work together to overcome opposition (Nehemiah 4).** Half of the people watched for enemies while the other half worked on the wall.

- **Experience the powerful results of effective teams (Nehemiah 6:15).** The building of the wall was completed in 52 days.

Jesus developed, empowered, and released teams.

Doesn't it seem sensible that to accomplish a spiritual end, Jesus would have turned to the people most interested in spirituality – the religious leaders of the day? And wouldn't you expect Him, given barely three years in public ministry, to pursue alliances with high-profile individuals whose resumes proved that they knew how to lead effectively?

But, as usual, Jesus broke all the rules. He called upon a group of uneducated, low-key, ill trained individuals whose character seemed pretty solid and who were willing to sacrifice whatever they had to in order to be apprentices to the master leader.

Clearly, Jesus' intent was not to raise up eleven future hotshots whose stellar performances would wow the world, but rather to prepare a humble group whose limitations would force them to work together to complete the assignment He had given them while remaining focused on Him. Jesus was training teams of leaders, not potential members of the Future CEO Club.

Jesus modeled the use of ministry teams in His own ministry and then gave the gift of leadership teams to the body of Christ.

- **Ministry teams.** Jesus invested His life in team building and consistently developed, empowered, and released teams.

    o Inner circle of three: Peter, James, John (Mark 9:2)

    o Team of 12 disciples (Mk 3:13-19, Matt. 10:1-4)

    o Ministry team of 70 (Luke 19:1, 17)

    o Wider circle of 120 followers (Acts 1:15)

    o Multitudes into groups of 50 (Mk. 6:40; Luke 9:14)

- **Leadership teams.** Jesus gave the "church" leadership teams in the form of five fold ministry gifts (Eph. 4:11-13)

- o The Apostle governs, the Prophet guides, the Evangelist gathers, the Pastor guards and the Teacher grounds.

Point to Ponder: It is a human tendency to overestimate what we can do by ourselves and to underestimate what we can do as a group. As the body of Christ we can accomplish more together than we could dream possible working by ourselves. How important it is then that the leadership team models this?

Paul

On his missionary journeys the most prolific of the apostles always traveled and ministered with a team. Whether it was in the company of Barnabas, John, Simeon, Lucius, or Manaen (Acts 13), serving with Timothy, Judas, or Silas (Acts 15-16), or ministering alongside various combinations of other leaders, Paul was the quintessential team player.

His advice in Ephesians 4:12, *"to prepare God's people for works of service, so that the body of Christ may be built up,"* remains one of the central challenges to the church to train laity to do the entire work of the ministry.

His entries regarding spiritual gifts (1 Corinthians 12 and Romans 12) not only identify leadership as a core gift, but further suggest that rather than focus on one individual who can do it all, God's intent was to prepare each of us to be a role player, not a superhero.

Only One Ministry Superstar

There are other Bible passages in both the Old and New Testaments that address the importance of leadership provided through teams of gifted individuals. The point is not to diminish the value of individual leaders but simply to recognize that the Bible does acknowledge teams as a viable leadership strategy.

The longer we deny the benefits of team leadership, the less likely it is that we will experience the power of God in the church, in society, or in our personal efforts. There is only one ministry superstar: Jesus Christ.

If we persist in seeking to lead churches through the display of talents and abilities resident within only a few unusually capable individuals, rather than allowing the community of believers to use their significant-but-less-inclusive leadership skills in an orchestrated unison to accomplish synergistic outcomes, the church and society will pay the price for such defiance.

A Self – Examination – Solo Leadership or Team Leadership

Occasionally life's choices are either-or propositions: Either you choose one option, or you are left with the other. Americans dislike having such limited choices. We prefer the sense of control and power, as well as the pleasure, of having truly disparate alternatives from a broad range of possibilities.

In choosing your leadership approach – solo leadership or team leadership – it appears that you have an either-or challenge. Which option is best for you? As you consider your answer, keep the following observations in mind:

- Churches can grow only as much as their leaders will facilitate. The degree of growth made possible by teams of gifted leaders working together will generally exceed the growth feasible under a group of solo leaders.

- The more a church allows leaders to use their gifts and skills for ministry, the more leaders the church will attract and retain. The more leaders the church attracts and retains, the more likely the church is to develop a full orbed, healthy ministry.

- It seems most likely that God's design for leadership is for individuals to work together in teams – and thus minimize personal glory – than for a single, solo leader to strive to make everything happen and receive the brunt of the church's attention. Team leadership helps keep the focus on God, while solo leadership may deflect the spotlight from Him.

- When personnel changes happen, a church is less likely to be crippled by the departure of one team member than by the departure of the solo leader. The church will struggle in both situations, but the struggle will be less profound in the case of losing one team-based leader.

- Quality in leadership is enhanced by constant and objective performance. Solo leaders have a relatively poor track record of self-evaluation when compared to the self-assessment of leadership teams.

- In a solo leadership model, the qualification standards may be high but the production standards are often unmet. In a team leadership model, the qualification standards are not as lofty but the productivity level is typically met or exceeded. The question for a church is whether it is more interested in impressing people with the quality of a single or small number of leaders or in the quality and ministry impact of what a larger number of team-based leaders produce.

Team-based leadership – utilizing the wealth of talents and abilities that God has invested in laypeople – is not the answer to every challenge and dilemma facing the church. The continued refusal to exploit those talents and abilities, however, leaves churches at a disadvantage. The team approach may not solve every problem, but it often increases the potential for eliminating many of the vexing issues that perplex churches large and small.

Which Way is Right for You?

To arrive at the best choice for your church, you might take an inventory of how your leadership process and output is presently faring. I encourage you to prayerfully answer the following questions and reflect on whether team leadership or solo leadership is likely to facilitate improvements in the ministry impact of your church.

1. **What is the vision for your church's ministry?** How widely known and owned is that vision among your congregants?

2. **What goals have you set in the past year in relation to your vision?** How satisfactorily did your church meet all of those goals?

3. **Is the senior pastor of your church a true leader?** How well does he or she work with and develop other leaders? Would the pastor's productivity and personal well-being improve if your leadership model shifted?

4. **What is your church's philosophy of leadership and leadership development?** How confident are you that your philosophy is an ideal match with your congregation's needs?

5. **How does your church identify potential lay leaders?** How viable is that approach?

6. **Once lay leaders are identified, what happens with them?** What types of preparation and development do

your lay leaders receive? How many of them voluntarily stay heavily involved as leaders for an extended period of service?

7. **How do you ascertain the leadership aptitudes of your leaders?** If you identify those distinctions, how do you apply that knowledge to the assignments given to your leaders?

8. **Does your church culture foster team leadership or solo leadership?** Is that intentional?

9. **How many lay leaders have left your church because they felt that their gifts would never be adequately or appropriately used?** How many lay leaders have left your church because they were burned out by your ministry?

10. **How difficult is it to keep your lay leaders motivated to stay sharp and involved?**

11. **How does your church evaluate the effectiveness of its leaders?** How effective is that evaluation process? How could it be improved?

12. **Which approach would be of greatest benefits to your church: solo leadership or team leadership?** If your church were to transition from one to the other, what price would be paid for that change? In what ways would the results be worth the price?

Whether you determine that lay-leadership teams or solo-based leadership is the best path for your church to pursue, my prayer is that you will empower every leader God has brought to your church to live up to his or her ministry and leadership potential. And all things being equal, I pray that your church will strongly consider the merits and benefits of employing lay-leadership teams as your strategy for unleashing God's greatest blessings upon your ministry and those whom it will influence.

Discussion Questions:

1. What detriments come from using the 'Majority Rule' model of leadership?
2. How can a church implement the team concept effectively?
3. What social trends are challenging the traditional models of leadership in the contemporary church?
4. Name two samples of how Jesus used the team model of leadership.
5. What are two major benefits found in team leadership? What biblical example demonstrates these benefits?

Chapter 6

RAISING UP LIKE-MINDED LEADERS

"But I trust in the Lord Jesus to send Timothy to you shortly, that I also may be encouraged when I know your state. For I have no one like-minded, who will sincerely care for your state. For all seek their own, not the things which are of Christ Jesus. But you know his proven character, that as a son with his father he served with me in the gospel. Therefore I hope to send him at once, as soon as I see how it goes with me. But I trust in the Lord that I myself shall also come shortly" (Philippians 2:19-24).

When you think of this verse that Paul penned, who comes to mind in your ministry that is like-minded? Who will judge as you do, or care for others as you would? For the Apostle Paul, Timothy was like-minded. He was Paul's son in the Gospel. Timothy had proven character. Paul had confidence that Timothy would judge as he would.

Why Do You Need Like-minded Leaders (Amos 3:3)?

- Like-minded leaders give you personal strength and encouragement.

  Ecclesiastes 4:9-12 *Two are better than one, because they have a good reward for their labor. For if they fall, one will lift up his companion. But woe to him who is alone when he falls, for he has no one to help him up. Again, if two lie down together, they will keep warm; but how can one be warm alone? Though one may be overpowered by another, two can withstand him. And a threefold cord is not quickly broken.*

- Like-minded leaders add unity of counsel and direction.

    1 Corinthians 1:10 *Now I plead with you, brethren, by the name of our Lord Jesus Christ, that you all speak the same thing, and that there be no divisions among you, but that you be perfectly joined together in the same mind and in the same judgment.*

- Like-minded leaders bring greater power and accomplishment.

    Matthew 18:19 *Again I say to you that if two of you agree on earth concerning anything that they ask, it will be done for them by My Father in heaven.*

    Genesis 14:14 *Now when Abram heard that his brother was taken captive, he armed his three hundred and eighteen trained servants who were born in his own house, and went in pursuit as far as Dan.*

- Like-minded leaders enhance your ability to minister to more people.

    Deuteronomy 32:30 *How could one chase a thousand, and two put ten thousand to flight, unless their Rock had sold them, and the Lord had surrendered them?*

- Like-minded leaders give you a personal release into your primary ministry.

    Acts 6:4 *but we will give ourselves continually to prayer and to the ministry of the word."*

- Like-minded leaders multiply your ministry.

> **2 Timothy 2:2** And the things that you have heard from me among many witnesses, commit these to faithful men who will be able to teach others also.

- Like-minded leaders give you additional personal relationships and friendships.

> **1 Timothy 1:2** *To Timothy, a true son in the faith: Grace, mercy, and peace from God our Father and Jesus Christ our Lord.*

- Like-minded leaders give you personal accountability.

> **2 Timothy 3:10** *But you have carefully followed my doctrine, manner of life, purpose, faith, longsuffering, love, perseverance,*

- Like-minded leaders are necessary for the sake of future generations.

> **Psalm 78:6** *That the generation to come might know them, the children who would be born, that they may arise and declare them to their children,*

> **Genesis 18:19** *For I have known him, in order that he may command his children and his household after him, that they keep the way of the Lord, to do righteousness and justice, that the Lord may bring to Abraham what He has spoken to him."*

Leaders who follow biblical patterns invest their time and energy in others. Jesus invested and reproduced His life in His chosen disciples. In similar ways, church leaders give their strength to others to see Christ's self-sharing life and spirit reproduced. Reproduction of the life of Christ in His followers brings Him glory on earth. Christ's leadership is more than a historical curiosity. It is an ongoing reality. The same choosing, investing and reproducing goes on now and should continue throughout the twenty-first century.

Developing like-minded leaders who can assist you in your ministry work is part of God's plan for succession and success in ministry. Now that you are excited about what can be accomplished by having like-minded leaders working as a team, let me give you a word of caution: You must be careful to raise up the right kind of leaders. So far we have focused on like-minded leaders. Let's look at what I would consider the wrong kind of leaders.

The Problem of Wrong Leaders

Proverbs 25:19 *Confidence in an unfaithful man in time of trouble is like a bad tooth and a foot out of joint.*

There are at least four characteristics of leaders that should caution you in the selection of those who would serve on a team in some way. This is not to say that each person is perfect. However, if their character is bent toward these characteristics they will create more harm than good.

- *Double-minded leaders* create a wavering and unstable church that does not move forward in a constant way (James 1:8).

- *High-minded leaders* seek their own advancement and recognition (Phil. 2:21; II Tim. 3:1-7).

- *Carnally- minded leaders* exploit the body for their own purposes (Rom. 8:6).

- *Earthly- minded leaders* may not care for your people as they would their own or as you would (Phil. 2:19; 3:19).

The Raising Up of Like-minded Leaders

Like-minded leaders are made, not born. All men are born in sin and prone to self-will. Pastors must take the responsibility to raise up like-minded leaders.

You cannot expect leaders to come to you fully trained. Nor can you expect someone else to train them. Like-minded leaders must be discipled (Matt. 18:19-20). Discipling involves several things:

- Discipling involves <u>spending time with them</u>

    Mark 3:14 *Then He appointed twelve, that they might be with Him and that He might send them out to preach,*

- Discipling involves <u>praying for them</u>

    Luke 22:32 *"But I have prayed for you, that your faith should not fail; and when you have returned to Me, strengthen your brethren."*

- Discipling involves <u>systematic instruction</u>

    Matthew 28:19-20 *Go therefore and make disciples of all the nations, baptizing them in the name of the Father and of the Son and of the Holy Spirit, teaching them to observe all things that I have commanded you; and lo, I am with you always, even to the end of the age." Amen.*

    - Bible (II Timothy 3:15); doctrine (I Timothy 4:6); philosophy of ministry; traditions; character qualifications and manner of life (2 Thessalonians 3:6-9)

- Discipling involves <u>training experience</u>

> **Luke 10:1** *After these things the Lord appointed seventy others also, and sent them two by two before His face into every city and place where He Himself was about to go.*

- Discipling involves <u>accountability</u>

   > **Luke 10:17** *Then the seventy returned with joy, saying, "Lord, even the demons are subject to us in Your name."*

- Discipling involves <u>pastoring them</u>

   > **1 John 3:16** *By this we know love, because He laid down His life for us. And we also ought to lay down our lives for the brethren.*

- Discipling involves <u>sharing of one's life</u>

   > **1 Thessalonians 2:8** *So, affectionately longing for you, we were well pleased to impart to you not only the gospel of God, but also our own lives, because you had become dear to us.*

- Discipling involves <u>encouragement & exhortation</u>

   > ***1 Thessalonians 2:10-12*** *You are witnesses, and God also, how devoutly and justly and blamelessly we behaved ourselves among you who believe; as you know how we exhorted, and comforted, and charged every one of you, as a father does his own children, that you would walk worthy of God who calls you into His own kingdom and glory.*

Identifying Potential Like-minded Leaders

In identifying potential like-minded leaders there are factors that should serve as "green lights" to you. There are several questions that you could ask yourself to form an evaluation. As you have observed the potential leaders does he or she demonstrate:

- Faithfulness in all areas.

- Humility when corrected or adjusted.

- Willingness to serve in menial areas.

- A high level of personal integrity.

- Responsiveness to your preaching and teaching.

- Genuine love for people.

- Sensitivity to the needs of others.

- Continued personal growth.

- Successful relationships on the personal, family and work level and a strong hunger for the Lord and the Word of God.

Factors that should serve as "red lights", of course, would be the opposite of all the above. In addition to these we could add:

- An inability to keep confidences

- Hasty in decision making

- Constantly making poor judgments (even after instruction)

- Aggressive and domineering in relationships
- Emotional instability
- Pushing for promotion and recognition
- Constantly on the wrong side of decisions
- Continual conflicts with those under their charge
- Continual justifying and blame shifting

The Rewards of Raising Up Like-minded Leaders

There are many rewards of raising up like-minded leaders. You can have great peace of mind when you are away. You will know that the work that you left behind will be cared for well. You will experience endurance and multiplication of your vision. One can put a thousand to flight but two can put ten thousand to flight. You will build a lifetime of good relationships and companions in the Gospel. And ultimately you will have a sense of accomplishment at the end of your course.

Discussion Questions:

1. Name five of the nine qualities like-minded leaders possess.
2. What are the characteristics of a leader that would be potentially troublesome?
3. What does discipling a leader involve?
4. How can one identify a potentially good like-minded leader?
5. In your own estimation what are the rewards of raising up like-minded leaders?

Chapter 7

CHURCH GOVERNMENT

The New Testament does give us a structure for government in the church. The church is not a one-man operation or dictatorship. It is not a democracy where every member gets an equal vote. It is not to be ruled by committees composed of those willing to serve.

God has a form of government outlined in the New Testament that could best be described as team ministry. The church is not to be led by one person but it is to be led by a team of called individuals, under Christ, who meet the biblical qualifications for leadership. This team is led by a set-man or chief elder who gives vision and momentum to the group.

Church structure is certainly not to be our daily focus, but if the church is going to have the ability to be led by the Head of the church, the Lord Jesus Christ, its government must be of such a nature that the will of the Lord may indeed be done.

The Skeletal Structure

Church structure can be compared to the skeletal structure of the human body. Every person has one. Every person's skeleton is very much alike. Every person's skeleton is vital to the body's ability to fulfill function. However, in day-to-day life we don't really focus on a person's bone structure. What we tend to focus on is the way the flesh is arranged on the structure and the personality that is expressed by the individual. The skeleton is quietly going about its job, and it is only noticed when there is a problem. It is rarely noticed when everything is functioning according to design.

Church government is much the same. If you would ask the average church member what form of government their local church practices, they most likely would not be able to tell you. If you asked the average church member if they had ever read the constitution and by-laws of the church, most of them would probably say, "No!" As a rule, people are not interested in all of that "dry stuff." They are interested in the life and personality of the church. What interests them is the preaching, the pastor, the friendliness of the people, the children's ministry, or some other program of the church. They don't want to think about church government.

Yet in the overall scheme of things, church government may be the most important part of the church. The government of the church will either hinder or enable the church to do what God has called it to do.

The issue of church government is an issue that historically has distinguished one church from another. To some it has been important enough of an issue over which to either establish or break fellowship.

When one studies the names of various churches or church groups, it becomes clear that their names are based on several things. Their names can be based on the person who founded the church or group of churches (e.g. Lutheran, Mennonite, etc.). It may be based on a particular belief or distinct doctrine that they uphold (e.g. Baptist, Pentecostal, etc.). It may be based on what they believe about themselves (e.g. Assembly of God, Church of God, etc.). Or it may reflect their form of church government (Presbyterian, Episcopal, Congregational, or Independent).

In any case, the fact that churches are named after government styles show the importance of this area in people's minds and the fact that people have been willing to establish or break fellowship over governmental issues.

The government of the church can be the most important aspect of a church's life. Your government will affect many things. It will affect the local church's ability to fulfill the will of God. It will affect a church's ability to reach the vision that God has given to its leaders. It will affect a church's ability to be led and directed by the Holy Spirit.

If the leaders of the local church (i.e. those who are responsible to make decisions) are not personally under the authority of the Holy Spirit in their lives, listening to the voice of the Lord, and submitted to His Word, the church will not be able to be led and directed by the Lord of the church. Christ exerts His leadership through God-ordained and God-appointed leaders

God Has Established Government in His Church

Most people will acknowledge the fact that there is government in the family realm (Eph. 6:1). They understand that children are to obey their parents and respond to their authority. Most people will also acknowledge authority that exists in the realm of government (Rom. 13:1). They understand that they are to be subject to the governing powers because they are established by God. But many of those same people do not see the local church and its leaders as an authority in their lives. They see the authority in the local church as advisory in nature at best.

The Bible indicates that there is authority in the local church that is to be an important aspect of every believer's life. It indicates that believers are to respect and respond to those who have the rule over them (Heb. 13:17).

The concept of ruling includes directing, managing, exercising control over, regulating behavior, and influencing the affairs of something. It includes setting and promoting goals, establishing and enforcing boundaries, and producing and maintaining order, all for the sake of accomplishing vision and purpose.

The local church has been called to achieve a great purpose. For this to be accomplished, God has given leaders to the local church. He has established government. These are those who rule in the house of God (Heb. 13:17, 7, 24; Rom. 12:8); with no such government there will be a lack of order (1 Cor. 14:40; Col. 2:5).

Not only has God established the local church as a place where order is present, He has prescribed the order for it. God has a plan. He did not find it necessary to consult with His creation regarding that plan. He simply lays it out for us. The local church is God's idea. He is the architect. He is the one who will live in it. He is the Lord of the church, and He has a workable plan.

God identifies the rulers in His house (1 Tim. 3:5; 5:17). All throughout the Bible, both Old and New Testament, God's leaders are referred to as elders. In the local churches that Paul established, he set in elders who would function as the pastors, teachers, and leaders. The elders were always plural in number and seem to have worked as a team with a senior or chief elder.

There are many forms of government that God could have chosen. God was not short on ideas. He was not limited in His understanding or limited by history to a few options.

Five Forms of Church Government

Dictatorship or One-Man Rule

There are five main types of government or variations of them seen in various churches in the world today. *The first one could be called dictatorship or one-man rule.* No one would ever say their government was a dictatorship, and certainly on paper they would not use the word "dictator." But in actuality that is how many churches operate.

The leadership of such a local church would consist of a board made up of the senior pastor, his or her spouse, brother, uncle, and best friend. While business is conducted as needed (usually just a couple of times a year), it is clear that one person really makes all of the decisions, and the board is really nothing more than a rubber stamp for those decisions.

Dictatorship is a very simple form of government. Decisions can be made very quickly. No one has to get "bogged down" in lengthy discussions and frequent meetings.

Often the leader of such a church would refer to the church government as a "theocracy" or a church ruled by God.

Unfortunately, it is not always God who is making the decisions but "Theo" (the senior pastor). In these cases, decisions are not usually up for discussion because "the Lord told me." No one wants to argue with "the Lord." The authority in this system is usually supported by heavy teaching on "the anointed of the Lord" and warnings about touching "the Lord's anointed." Well-meaning people line up behind such a leader to hear the voice of God to them.

The problem is, however, that no leader is perfect. Even in the best of cases no one has perfect wisdom at all times. Since the dictatorship is built on one person, the local church is only as strong as that person. If the leader falls, the church falls with him. Dictators have few (if any) checks and balances to ensure that they and their churches will stay on track.

Too much power in one person has the tendency to corrupt even the best of leaders. In addition it does not prepare adequately for the future. Often when such a leader steps out of that role because of age, health issues, or death, the church is left in a very difficult situation. The church was really built on a singular personality.

Democracy

Another form of government today is democracy or "rule by the people." Sometimes, because we see democracy as a viable or superior form of government in the world order, we want to bring that same government into the church. God was not ignorant of such a form of government when the local church was established. He simply did not want to subject His plan and purpose to popular opinion. Simply stated, the majority is not always right.

The local church was built for growth. In a growing church the new people (those who have been saved or have come to the church) will always outnumber those who have been Christians for a long time. As a result, democracy ends up being a "rule of the immature" since they will always have the swing vote.

New converts do not always have the ability to hear from God clearly. Sometimes they do not have the ability to do the difficult thing. One experiment in democracy, the Laodicean Church (Laodicea means "people's rights" and was a city that became an experiment in democracy) was characterized by lukewarmness.

Democracy would never work in the natural family, and it will not work in the local church. I can't imagine submitting all of the decisions of my household to a vote of the family members.

Central Control or "External Control"

A third form of local-church government that is widely practiced in the church world today is what I call central control or external control. This is government that comes from outside of the local church. While the local church congregation may have some latitude on decision making and the development of vision, the primary or critical decisions in these churches are in the hands of those who are not a part of the local scene.

Many denominational churches are structured in this way where control is exercised by a headquarters or central agency. This external board maintains its ultimate control by several means. They maintain control by owning the physical building, ordaining, licensing, and placing the ministers, maintaining a central board for all missions and mission funds, and educating leaders through a central seminary or Bible school.

Often churches under this system operate fairly independently of the central board when it comes to the day-to-day affairs. Where control is seen most clearly is in the case where a local church bucks up against the headquarters' policy, strays from a central doctrinal position, or has a serious problem particularly as it relates to removing or replacing leaders. In such cases local assemblies must submit to the outside authority or face the possibility of losing their building or license to minister.

While the outside support of such organizations can appear to be a great benefit, this form of government can hinder the local church in tailoring its programs to the unique nature of its city or community. It can also inhibit leaders from following the voice of the Holy Spirit in the growth and development of that local assembly. It assumes that one size fits all in church programming, that we have complete understanding of all that God has for us in biblical revelation and understanding, and that God has nothing more to say to us concerning His plan.

Local churches should be as unique as people are. Yes, there are many things that every person has in common that makes them part of the human race. But every person also has a uniqueness about them that makes them particularly suited to the individual ministry that God has given them.

True biblical local churches will have much in common. These common things are those structures and elements clearly revealed to us in the Bible. But beyond this, local churches must be free to respond to the individual leading of the Holy Spirit as they attempt to fulfill the Great Commission in the city where God has placed them. God may have a unique strategy for them that is not part of anyone's instruction manual.

Local churches in the New Testament were not controlled by other local churches or outside boards. Some would attempt to use the meeting in Acts 15 as an instance where the Jerusalem church was acting as a central authority and issued decrees to the rest of Christendom.

When you study what was actually happening here, you realize that people from the Jerusalem church were preaching without commission in churches that Paul had established, causing a great deal of doctrinal confusion. The only way to solve the problem was to take the problem to the source of the problem, Jerusalem, and let the leaders of that church discuss it and see if they could help to undo some of the damage caused by these teachers who claimed to be ministering in the name of the Twelve. The result was that the Jerusalem church sent some of their key leaders to many of the churches to help clarify their position and rectify any damage.

Church Council or Deacon Board

The fourth type of church government that is commonly practiced is what could be called rule by a church council or deacon board. The board may be referred to in several ways including board of trustees, financial board, the deacons, or simply, the board.

This form is often seen in churches that have some form of external control as well. It is characterized by a church board that is elected by the members of the congregation. Usually members of such a board are selected from among the congregation by a nominating process. They may or may not have any specific qualifications apart from the fact that they are members of the church and have a desire to serve in this way.

Members of such a board are often seen as faithful members who have natural talents in the financial and business areas. They usually serve a term of office of one to three years with limitations on how many successive terms they may serve. This board often serves alongside a pastoral team or even what are called elders, but this group has the financial power in the church. Whoever controls the finances of the church controls the vision of the church.

In these situations there may or may not be biblical or spiritual qualifications for those who serve. Whether or not these individuals can hear the voice of God is not usually necessary to nominate them to the office. Whether or not the senior pastor of the church feels good about the nomination is not often considered.

In most cases it is this board that has the power to hire and fire the pastor. As a result, the board often sees their main responsibility as keeping the pastor in check or protecting the people from abusive leadership. Usually decision making is a fairly long process, and the spiritual leadership of the church must come "hat in hand" to the board to have their vision approved.

With board members rotating and pastors coming and going, the local church has a difficult time sustaining growth and vision over a long period of time. People are often coming and going as well, and usually the church has a difficult time stretching for growth.

Some would use the servants who were appointed in Acts 6 as an indication that deacons were appointed in the church to control the natural affairs of the church. The truth is, the word *deacon* is never used to apply to the seven in Acts 6. In addition, the job description to these individuals who were appointed was to distribute food to the needy.

There is no evidence in the New Testament that a group of deacons met as a board with any corporate function. There is especially no evidence that elders (spiritual leadership) had to submit their vision to a second board that controlled the finances of the church. When Paul wanted to talk to those in authority in any local church, he called for its elders (Acts 20:17). When Peter addressed the leaders of the local churches, he addressed the elders of the church (1 Peter. 5:1-4).

Eldership Management or Team Ministry

God could have chosen any form of government for His church that He so desired. God did not choose any forms that we have discussed to this point. God chose what I would call eldership management or team ministry.

When the New Testament talks about authority in relation to the local churches of that era, it talks about it in terms of a group of individuals called "elders" (1 Tim. 5:17).

Elders were the pastors and teachers of the local assembly much like elders who were established in the Old Testament community and in the Jewish synagogues of Jesus' day. Elders of the local churches were its bishops or, literally, overseers who were responsible for giving guidance and direction to the affairs of the church, pastoring the members of the congregation, protecting the church from corrupting influences, and teaching the congregation the good word of God (Acts 20:28-31).

It is clear that once local churches had been established by apostolic ministry, the goal was to set in elders to give ongoing guidance and leadership to the assembly (Acts 14:23; Titus 1:5).

When setting in such elders, the early church leaders never set in just one elder. Elders of the church are always referred to as plural in number (Acts 20:17; 1 Tim. 5:17; James 5:14). Actually, in order to have some checks and balances, there needs to be at least three elders established in a church to function effectively.

New Testament local churches had many elders, but at the same time they had one senior or chief elder (Acts 12:17; 15:4-7, 12, 13, 22; Phil. 4:1-3). There are some today who are trying to establish an eldership form of government where there is no such head elder or senior pastor. These efforts usually end in failure. They usually end up with three or more visions, with the congregation choosing their personal favorite (1 Cor. 1:12).

In situations where this form of government is attempted, the eldership is of necessity limited to a small number of individuals, because to have a coequal plurality would be difficult with five, ten, or twenty individuals. With this type of government it is easy to get to a stalemate or to find some measure of power struggle within the group. Eventually if this system works at all, it is because one of these individuals is recognized officially or unofficially as the principal voice.

God's plan for the church is plurality of elders with a chief or senior elder. This has always been God's form of government. God has always used plural leadership with one of those leaders placed as head. There is a sense of equality among the leadership team with a recognized head to be the official leader or spokesperson for the team.

Equality and Headship in the Godhead

God demonstrated this principle for us first in His own person and nature. God has revealed Himself to us in a divine mystery. He is three yet one. There are three distinct persons of the Godhead who are distinguishable but indivisible.

There is the Father, the Son, and the Holy Spirit (1 John 5:7). The Bible clearly teaches that the Father is God, the Son is God, and the Holy Spirit is God. There exists within these persons an equality of person (Phil. 2:6). And yet there is at the same time an order of headship (1 Cor. 11:3). The Father sent the Son, the Son sent the Spirit. The Spirit bears witness to the Son and the Son bears witness to the Father. The Father becomes the ultimate figure in the Godhead (1 Cor. 15:27-28). For the sake of mission fulfillment each person of the Godhead recognizes His particular function and role responsibility.

Equality and Headship in the Family

When God established the natural family, He followed the same governing principle (Gen. 2:24). Each natural family has plurality of ministry or team ministry. Each natural family is led and directed by two mature ones (elders) who are established as the parental authorities in that home. The man and the woman are equal before God. And yet for the sake of mission fulfillment, God has differing role responsibilities to each one.

Within this equality is an order of headship. The husband is the head of the wife as Christ is the head of the church (Eph. 5:23; 1 Cor. 11:3). This does not mean that the husband is more important than the wife or that he leads as a dictator independently of the wife. It does mean that for the sake of order and the ability to function, one of the members of this team has been placed in a position of headship as the chief elder.

Equality and Headship in Israel and the Synagogue

This is the same form of government under which Israel walked during the wilderness wanderings. In Israel, God established His chosen senior leader or "set man," Moses. Along with Moses a team of elders served to give leadership to and care for the needs of that nation (Num. 11:16-17; 27:16-17).

This is the same pattern that the Jews used in the synagogue (Acts 13:15; 18:8, 17). Each synagogue had its group of elders who presided over the affairs of the community. Within that structure there was a chief elder who served as the set leader or team captain among the elders.

Equality and Headship in the Local Church

As has already been stated, a team of elders (Titus 1:5; Acts 21:18) led each New Testament local church. Even though the Bible seems to imply that various elders had different functions or anointing, they all seemed to function as a group. But as with the other patterns mentioned above, they too had a senior elder or general overseer.

The clearest pattern for this seems to be the Jerusalem church, the one about which historically we know the most. The twelve apostles seemed to have served as the initial eldership for the first church. After some time, however, other elders joined their ranks and served with them to form the leadership team (Acts 11:30; 15:2). Among their ranks one person emerged as the leader of that team. It is interesting that the leader was not one of the original twelve apostles but James, the brother of the Lord. As you read through the pages of the book of Acts, it is clear that James functioned as the senior elder or senior pastor of the church at Jerusalem.

In Acts 12 when Peter escaped from prison by divine intervention, it was James to whom he felt personally accountable (Acts 12:17). In Acts 15 when the church leaders met to discuss how to handle Gentile converts, it was James who made the final judgment and brought a conclusion to the discussion (15:13-19). In Acts 21 when Paul was bringing a relief offering to the church in Jerusalem, he presented it to James in the presence of the other elders (21:18).

The Jerusalem elders worked as a team, but James acted as the first among equals who assisted in bringing resolution and impetus to their efforts. This seems to have been true of other churches as well. When the Lord addressed the local churches in the book of Revelation, He addressed His letter to the set-man or the *"angelos"* (messenger) of each of the churches (Rev. 2:1).

Qualifications for Elders

God determines the kind of individuals that are to be rulers in His house (1 Tim. 3:1-7; Titus 1:5-9). Through the apostle Paul, He gave us very specific guidelines for identifying those who would serve in this capacity. Strict adherence to the guidelines given in the New Testament is the only thing that will ensure this form of government being any better than any of the other forms of government that we have discussed.

In fact if these guidelines are not strictly adhered to, eldership can be an even worse form of government than some of the others that we have discussed, because with an eldership you could have the wrong people in office and have no ability to remove them.

These qualifications that Paul gives are to ensure that the leaders of the church have demonstrated through their personal lives that they are personally submitted to Christ, are an example for others to follow, and have a track record of hearing from God.

It is these qualities that make them candidates for leadership. Christ is to be the head of the church. He exercises His headship through His leaders. Christ can rule through these kinds of leaders.

We can summarize the qualifications listed by Paul into four categories:

- **Potential elders must be people with proven character.** That is, they have allowed the work of sanctification to take place in their lives and they manifest the fruit of the Spirit.

- **Potential elders must be people of spiritual vision.** That is, they have a vision to see God's purposes established, and they have the maturity to make sacrifices in the present to see those purposes come to pass.

- **Potential elders must be people with their homes in order.** That is, they have demonstrated their ability to rule and provide pastoral covering for the church by virtue of the fact that they have established the Kingdom of God in their own homes.

- **Potential elders must be people with the spiritual gifting for this ministry.** That is, they are not only good people, but they have a gift of leadership or the "charisma" needed to enable them to teach and to exhort and convince those who oppose the Gospel.

It is interesting that these are in essence the same qualifications that were laid out in the Old Testament for the elders who served under Moses. God's leaders were to be "able men, such as fear God, men of truth, hating covetousness" (Exod. 18:21).

Summation

The issue of Church Government is an issue that historically has distinguished one church from another. The names of various churches are based on several things: their founder (Lutheran, Wesleyan); their distinct doctrine (Baptist, Pentecostal); their belief about themselves (Assembly of God); or their form of church government (Presbyterian, Episcopal, Congregational, Independent). The fact that churches are named after government shows the importance of this area in people's minds.

The Government of the church can be the most important aspect of church life. It will affect: your ability to fulfill the will of God; your ability to reach the vision God has given you; and your ability to lead and be directed by the Holy Spirit. Wrong government can hinder God's will and direction.

There are four basic facts concerning church government:

1. **God has established government in His house (the Church).** And He stands behind it. With no government there is no order. There are those who rule in the house of God (Heb. 13:7, 17, 24; Rom. 12:8).

2. **God has a plan and pattern for government in His house.** Our pattern can come from various sources: the world system, religious tradition and the mind of regenerate man. Our pattern must come from God. God is a God of order and has a pattern and plan for everything that He does. God is very detailed and exact about how He wants things done. Example: David – ark of God – Divine order. Every structure that God ever commanded to be built, He provided the pattern (Noah's Ark, Moses' Tabernacle and Solomon's Temple). The glory of God can only fill that which is according to the pattern. The pattern cannot be violated if we are to experience the full blessing of God. The plan of God is never out of date.

   Exodus 40:34 *Then the cloud covered the tabernacle of meeting, and the glory of the Lord filled the tabernacle.*

3. **God identifies the rulers in His house as elders (1 Tim. 3:5; 5:17).** There are many forms of government that God could have chosen.
   - **Dictatorship** (Only as strong as the individual)
   - **Democracy** can be defined as judgment by the people. If church growth is happening the vote is controlled by the immature
   - **Central Control** (Headquarters with no understanding of local vision)
   - **Deacon Board** (Elected or approved by the people – not necessarily qualified).

God chose plurality of elders as His form of Government.
- Many elders (Acts 14:23; 20:17; 1 Tim. 5:17; James 5:14).
- One senior elder (Acts 12:17; 15:4-7, 12, 13, 22).

This government was patterned after the congregation in the wilderness.
- One – Episcopal – Moses
- Few – Presbytery – 70 Elders (Numbers 11:16-25)
- Many – Congregational – Rulers over 10, 50, 100 (Ex. 18:25)

4. **God determines the kind of individuals that are to be rulers in His House (I Tim. 3; Titus 1).**
   - They must be men of proven character.
   - They must be men of spiritual vision.
   - They must be men with their homes in order.
   - They must be men with the spiritual gifting for this ministry.

Discussion Questions:

1. How does church government affect the ability of a church to function?
2. What are the five forms of Church Government and which one is God's pattern?
3. What were the elders of the local church found doing in the New Testament that can be used as an example for us today?
4. Explain 'equality and headship' as referred to in team ministry.
5. What would be the four basic facts concerning church government?

Chapter 8

THE MEANING OF ELDERSHIP

Few offices have deteriorated more radically than that of the elder. Its original purpose has been obscured, its functions lost, and its purpose altered.

To understand the meaning of the office of elder, it is necessary to remember that the office was not created by the church but taken over from the practices of Israel. As Morris has written,

> The first Christians were Jews, and it is a reasonable inference that they took over the office of elder from the Judaism with which they were familiar. It will repay us accordingly to give some attention to the Jewish elders.
>
> These men were responsible for the administration of Jewish life. They had responsibilities in both what we would call civil and ecclesiastical affairs. Probably they made no hard and fast distinction between the two, for their law was the law of Moses which deals impartially with both. Moreover, their unit of organization was the synagogue congregation, and the synagogue, in addition to being a place for worship, was a place of instruction, a school. The Rabbis dealt with all manner of subjects. They did not confine themselves to what we would call religious matters, but laid down regulations for the conduct of civil affairs as well.
>
> The elders were elected by the community and held office for life. They were admitted to their functions by a solemn rite, which in New Testament times was apparently an act of enthronement. The laying on of hands does not appear to have been practiced at this time, and it probably did not make its appearance until the war of Bar Kochba or later ... The function of the elder was apparently centered on the law.

> They were to study it, expound it and deal with people who had offended against it.
>
> There are obvious similarities between this office and that of the first Christian elders. The importance of this similarity is heightened when we reflect that the Christian Church appears to have been regarded at first as a branch of Judaism. Her assemblies seem to have been modeled on the synagogue pattern. Any ten male Jews could form a synagogue. In fact one is called by this very name in James 2:2 and there is evidence that "The Christian congregations in Palestine long continued to be designated by this name" (J. B. Lightfoot, *Saint Paul's Epistle to the Philippians*, p. 192) ...These would supervise the affairs of the new society in the same way as Jewish elders looked after the synagogue.[28]

In order to understand the Hebrew background of the office, it is important to recognize its origin in the family and tribal structure of Israel. The elder, *first*, was what the name indicated, an older man in the position of authority. The term *elder* was comparative, so it could mean a man ruling over his household. This head of the household, or of a group of families, supervised the discipline and justice within his family, its education, worship, and economic support; he was also responsible for its defense against enemies.

Thus, very clearly, *law and order* were basic functions of the elder but in far more than in a police sense, in that it was the duty of the elder to train his charges into a way of life. The concern of the elder was thus religious, civil, educational, and vocational. He also provided for the welfare of his household.

Second, elders formed the basis of civil government. Since men who governed in so extensive a way their own households were

---

[28] Leon Morris, Ministers of God (London: Inter-Varsity Fellowship, 1964), p. 70 f.

best trained to govern, Moses turned to the elders, at the command of God, to form a group of seventy to rule Israel (Num. 11:16). These men governed under Moses and aided him in instructing the people in the implications of the law (Deut. 27:1). Local government was in the hands of elders (Deut. 19:12; 21:2; 22:15; 25:7; Josh. 25:4; Judges 8:14; Ruth 4:2). These elders are also referred to in the Gospels (Matt. 16:21; 26:47; Luke 7:3). In the New Testament era, some elders ruled in the Sanhedrin and were experts in the law, and others ruled in localities.[29]

Third, elders were rulers of synagogues, as Morris has indicated. Within the synagogue, the elder was the teacher, enforcer, and expert student of the law.

The fact that the elder ruled in church, state, and family in the Old Testament era did not make this office one institution. The fact of unity came not from the absorption of one institution into another, but in their common subordination to the law and their common use of the law.

The fact that the church took over the office of elder from Israel is an aspect of its claim to be the new and true Israel of God. The church was now God's true synagogue, and its people the new Israel. The purpose of the office was to create a new society, the Kingdom of God, to institute the new creation by means of the discipline of its law-word. The seal of God's approval on the church as the new Israel, and the elders as the new office-bearers of God's law, was the laying on of hands and the implied anointing of the Holy Spirit (1 Tim. 4:14).

The office of elder has, among its qualifications, the ability to teach, and the ability to rule (1 Tim. 3:2-5). Significantly, the tie to the origin of the office remains. The elder was originally and always a man who ruled a household; hence, in Israel, a ruler (and all rulers were in a real sense elders) had to be a family man, a man tested in authority and government. Paul restates this qualification as an inescapable fact, "For if a man know not how to rule his own

---

[29] W. E. Vine, *Expository Dictionary of N. T. Words*, p. 20 f.; J. A. Selbie, "Elder (in O. T.)," in James Hastings, *Dictionary of the Bible*, I, 676 f.

house, how shall he take care of the church of God?" (1 Tim. 3:5). The office of elder remains a family-centered society.

The government of the New Christian society was complicated by the fact of persecution. The offices of deacons and widows, created to function under the elders, had government as their function, the relief of the needy, ministering to the younger, education, etc. The elder as a teacher thus functioned in the early church on one sphere after another, in the church, in the family, in the area of welfare by delegation and supervision, in education, and, by their avoidance of civil courts, as civil government.

Precisely because the Roman courts were "unjust" (1 Cor. 6:1), the elders served as a court to judge controversies among Christians (1 Cor. 6:1-3). If a church member refused to heed a correction (Matt. 18:15-17), then he could be treated as "an heathen man and a publican" and taken, if need be to a civil court. Normally, the ungodly court is to be avoided even at a sacrifice (Matt. 5:40). No restriction against the use of courts exists in the Old Testament, because the courts there were either in the hands of the elders or reflected their influence. American courts, despite their corruption, have not lost their Christian character or Biblical law heritage.

Paul in 1 Corinthians 6:2 declares, "Do ye not know that the saints will judge the world?" Some, because of the reference to angels in verse 3, refer this judging to the world to come, but its true meaning is with reference to time and eternity. The word judge here has the Old Testament sense of *govern*. Moffatt translates it as *manage*. Manage does convey the meaning of a continuing government by the saints over the Kingdom of God, in time and in eternity.

One of the consequences of existing in a hostile world was that the church had to assume the function of a total society for its members. The elders or presbyters were central to this function. The *office* of elder began with the *family*. It retained not only the office but the concept of family in the new society of Christ. All true believers were members of the family of Christ. A congregation and a community of believers thus cares for its own, for "whoever has this world's good, and sees his brother have need, and shuts up his heart from him, how does the love of God abide in him?" (1 John 3:17). The literature of the early church underscores this position. At the same time, there was no toleration of indolence: "If any would not work, neither should he eat" (2 Thess. 3:10). Moreover, "If any provide not for his own, and especially for those of his own house, he has denied the faith, and is worse than an infidel" (1 Tim. 5:8). The goal of the elders and their teaching was thus to create a community of responsible believers, responsible for themselves and their household and for their fellow believers.

But this is not all. Because the saints were called to manage or govern the world, very quickly it became their purpose to move into positions of authority and power. The letters of Paul show clearly that prominent Romans were converted. The salutations include those "that are of Caesar's household" (Phil. 4:22). In the Puritan era, the pressure of the saints on every kind of office in church, state, school, and commerce was very extensive.

Law is equivalent to rule or reign: it is the expression of a rule or reign and the application of a sovereignty to the area of jurisdiction. The elders, as officers of a law, God's law, are thus called to apply the law of God to every sphere of life. It is the duty of the Christian home, school, and church to train elders who will apply the law of God to all the world. The elder is not governed by the church as a subordinate officer who is sent out as an imperial agent into the world. Rather, the elder governs in his sphere, even as the church in her area, each as imperial agents of Christ the King. At points, the elder is under the authority of the church, and at other points, independent of it.

The church calls out and ordains her elders, but there is little reason to limit the office to the church. Christians in education, civil government, the sciences, law, and other professions can constitute themselves as Christian bodies and examine and ordain men who will further the law and rule of God in their sphere. The eldership is a calling from God, and the church is one agency in which the calling is fulfilled. This was the form of the office in Israel, and there is no evidence of any changes in the nature of the office in the

New Testament. The fact that the very name of the office, *elder*, was retained emphasizes the continuity.

In Revelation, moreover, we meet with "four and twenty elders," symbolizing the fullness of the church of both the Old and New Testaments. The Jewish practice of enthronement of elders is echoed also, in that these elders "cast their crowns before the throne" (Rev. 4:10), indicating the supreme kingship of God. Elders were enthroned, an echo of the original calling of Adam to be a priest, prophet, and *king* over creation under God. The restoration of that kingly rule under Christ is the function of the elder, and it is a calling in every domain of life.

The concept of eldership or ministry was strongly revived by Luther with respect to the university and the professors. The professor's chair was the heir of the synagogue elder's chair, and there was a comparable enthronement. To this day, many professors are inducted into an endowed "chair" without realizing the meaning of that term. Rosenstock-Huessy pointed out that "The universities represented the life of the Holy Ghost in the German Nation."[30] The work of the Holy Spirit through the office and ministry of the elder was seen as manifested through the professor.

However, not until every legitimate calling is seen as an area of potential eldership and is brought under the rule of God's law-word by presbyters or elders serving God will the meaning of eldership be fully realized.

Discussion Questions:

1. In what ways is the office of the Jewish elder of the Old Testament the same as the office of the elder in the New Testament church?
2. What implication does the word 'judge' have for the saints given by Paul in 1 Corinthians 6:2?
3. Describe how a church community is like a family unit.

---

[30] Eugen Rosenstock – Huessy, *Out of Revolution, Autobiography of Western Man* (New York: William Morrow, 1938), p. 395.

4. Describe what the 'four and twenty elders' symbolize as mentioned in Revelation.
5. Where did the meaning of the professor's chair originate?

Chapter 9

PASTORAL LEADERSHIP

*"Therefore, I exhort the elders among you ...
shepherd [pastor] the flock of God."*
                                    1 Peter 5:1a, 2a

When most Christians hear of church elders, they think of an official church board, lay officials, influential people within the local church, or advisers to the pastor. They think of elders as policymakers, financial officers, fund raisers, or administrators. They don't expect church elders to teach the Word or be involved pastorally in the lives of people. The common view that people have is that elders assist their pastor; and through the senior pastor, elders establish a caring link with each person on the professional staff, whether assistant pastor; director of Christian education, evangelism ... But, even more important, elders help facilitate and strengthen the working relationship of the church staff.

Such a view, however, not only lacks scriptural support but flatly contradicts the New Testament Scriptures. One doesn't need to read Greek or be professionally trained in theology to understand that the contemporary, church-board concept of eldership is irreconcilably at odds with the New Testament definition of eldership. According to the New Testament concept of eldership, elders lead the church, teach and preach the Word, protect the church from false teachers, exhort and admonish the saints in sound doctrine, visit the sick and pray, and judge doctrinal issues. In biblical terminology, elders shepherd, oversee, lead, and care for the local church. Let us now consider the New Testament model for pastoral care by shepherd leaders.

Shepherd Elders

The biblical image of a shepherd caring for his flock – standing long hours ensuring its safety, leading it to fresh pasture and clear water, carrying the weak, seeking the lost, healing the wounded and sick – is precious. The whole image of the Palestine shepherd is characterized by intimacy, tenderness, concern, skill, hard work, suffering, and love. It is a subtle blend of authority and care. It is as much toughness as tenderness and as much courage as comfort.

The shepherd-sheep relationship is so incredibly rich that the Bible uses it repeatedly to describe God and His loving care for His people. In one of the most beloved of all the Psalms, David, the shepherd turned king, wrote: "The Lord is my shepherd, I shall not want. He makes me lie down in green pastures: He leads me beside quiet waters" (Psalm 23:1-2). The Bible also uses shepherd imagery to describe the work of those who lead God's people (Ezek. 34).

Thus when Paul and Peter directly exhorted the leaders to do their duty, they both employed shepherding imagery. It should be observed that these two giant apostles assigned the task of shepherding the local church to no other group or single person but the elders. Paul reminds the Asian elders that God, the Holy Spirit, placed them in the flock as overseers for the purpose of shepherding the church of God (Acts 20:28). Peter exhorts the elders to be all that shepherds should be to the flock (1 Peter 5:2). We, then, must also view apostolic, Christianized elders to be primarily pastors of a flock, not corporate executives, CEO's, or advisers to the pastor.

If we want to understand Christian elders and their work, we must understand the biblical imagery of shepherding. As keepers of sheep, New Testament elders are to protect, feed, lead, and care for the flock's many practical needs. Using these four, broad, pastoral categories, let us consider the examples, exhortations, and teachings of the New Testament regarding shepherd elders.

Protecting the Flock

A major part of the New Testament elders' work is to protect the local church from false teachers. As Paul was leaving Asia Minor, he summoned the elders of the church in Ephesus for a farewell exhortation. The essence of Paul's charge is this: guard the flock – wolves are coming:

> And from Miletus he sent to Ephesus and called to him the elders of the church ... "Be on guard for yourselves and for all the flock, among which the Holy Spirit has made you overseers, to shepherd the church of God which He purchased with His own blood. I know that after my departure savage wolves will come in among you, not sparing the flock; and from among your own selves men will arise, speaking perverse things, to draw away the disciples after them. Therefore be on the alert ..." (Acts 20:17, 28-31a)

According to Paul's required qualifications for eldership, a prospective elder must have enough knowledge of the Bible to be able to refute false teachers:

> For this reason I left you in Crete, that you might set in order what remains, and appoint elders in every city as I directed you, namely, if any man be above reproach ... holding fast the faithful word which is in accordance with the teaching, that he may be able ... to refute those who contradict (Titus 1:5, 6, 9).

The Jerusalem elders, for example, met with the apostles to judge doctrinal error: "And the apostles and the elders came together to look into this [doctrinal] matter" (Acts 15:6). Like the apostles, the Jerusalem elders had to be knowledgeable in the Word so that they could protect the flock from false teachers.

Protecting the flock is vitally important because sheep are defenseless animals. They are utterly helpless in the face of wolves, bears, lions, jackals, or robbers. Phillip Keller, writing from his wealth of experience as a shepherd and agricultural researcher in East Africa and Canada, explains how unaware and vulnerable sheep are to danger, even inevitable death:

> It reminds me of the behavior of a band of sheep under attack from dogs, cougars, bears, or even wolves. Often in blind fear or stupid unawareness they will stand rooted to the spot watching their companions being cut to shreds. The predator will pounce upon one then another of the flock raking and tearing them with tooth and claw. Meanwhile, the other sheep may act as if they did not even hear or recognize the carnage going on around them. It is as though they were totally oblivious to the peril of their own precarious position.

Guarding sheep from danger is clearly a significant aspect of the shepherding task. The same is true for church shepherds. They must continually guard the congregation from false teachers. Elders, then, are to be protectors, watchmen, defenders, and guardians of God's people. In order to accomplish this, shepherd elders need to be spiritually alert and must be men of courage.

Spiritually Alert

A good shepherd is always on the alert for danger. He knows the predator well and understands the importance of acting wisely and quickly. So too, shepherd elders must be spiritually awake and highly sensitive to the subtle dangers of Satan's attacks. It's hard, however, to be alert and ready to act at all times. That is why Paul exhorts the Asian elders "be on the alert" (Acts. 20:31). He knows the natural tendency of shepherds to become spiritually lazy, undisciplined, prayerless, and weary. The Old Testament proves that. The Old Testament prophets cried out against Israel's shepherds because they failed to keep watch and be alert to protect the people from savage wolves. Israel's leaders are vividly depicted by Isaiah as blind city watchmen and dumb dogs (Isaiah 56:9-12).

Shepherd elders must be watchful and prayerful. They must be aware of changing issues both in society and the church. They must continuously educate themselves, especially in the Holy Scripture, diligently guard their own spiritual walk with the Lord, and always pray for the flock and its individual members.

Who can calculate the damage done during the past two thousand years to the churches of Jesus Christ because of inattentive, naïve, and prayerless shepherds? Many churches and denominations that once stood for sound doctrine and life now reject every major tenet of the Christian faith and condone the most deplorable moral practices conceivable. How did this happen? The local church leaders were naïve, untaught, and prayerless and became inattentive to Satan's deceptive strategies. They were blind watchmen and dumb dogs, pre-occupied with their own self-interests and comforts. When their seminaries jettisoned the truths of the gospel and the divine inspiration of the Bible, they were asleep. They naively invited young wolves in sheep's clothing into their flocks to be their spiritual shepherds. Hence they and their flocks have been devoured by wolves.

Courageous

Shepherds must also have courage to fight fierce predators. King David was a model shepherd of outstanding courage. First Samuel records David's experiences as a shepherd protecting his flock from the lion and the bear (1 Samuel 17:33-37).

Courage such as David possessed is an essential leadership quality. An internationally known statesman was once asked by reporters, "What is the most important quality for a national leader to possess?" His answer: "Courage." This is true not only for political leaders, but for church elders as well. To discipline sin in the church (especially sin of prominent members or leaders), to confront internal strife, and to stand up to powerful teachers and theological luminaries who expound high-sounding false doctrines requires courage. Without courage to fight for the truth and the lives of God's people, the local church would be washed away by every new doctrinal storm or internal conflict.

There are many weak, immature, and unstable believers, so the elders must act as a wall of safety around the people, protecting them from the fearsome danger of savage wolves and other destructive influences. The hireling, on the other hand, "beholds the wolf coming, and leaves the sheep, and flees, and the wolf snatches them, and scatters them. He flees because he is a hireling, and is not concerned about the sheep" (John 10:12b). A good shepherd elder, like the "Chief Shepherd," however, is ready to lay down his life for the local flock. He will die before he allows wolves to devour the flock.

Feeding the Flock

Throughout the New Testament, extraordinary emphasis is placed on the centrality of teaching God's Word. Jesus, the Good Shepherd, was preeminently a teacher, and He commissioned others to teach all that He had taught (Matt. 28:20). To Peter He said, "Feed [teach] my sheep" (John 21:17). The apostles were teachers, and the early Christians steadfastly devoted themselves to teaching (Acts 2:42). Barnabas sought Paul to come to Antioch to help teach (Acts 11:25-26). Paul exhorted Timothy to give attention to the "public reading of Scripture, to exhortation, and teaching" (I Timothy 4:13). In the order of gifts in 1 Corinthians 12:28, the teaching gift is listed third, after apostle and prophet. So teaching is one of the greatest gifts a congregation should desire (1 Cor. 12:31).

Unlike modern board elders, all New Testament elders were required to be "able to teach" (1 Timothy 3:2). In the list of elder qualifications in his letter to Titus, Paul states, "[the elder must hold] fast the faithful word which is in accordance with the teaching, that he may be able both to exhort in sound doctrine and to refute those who contradict" (Titus 1:9). In an extremely significant passage on elders, Paul speaks of some elders who labor at preaching and teaching and who thus deserve financial support from the local church (1 Timothy 5:17-18).

Paul reminded the Ephesian elders that he had taught them and the church the full plan and purpose of God (Acts 20:27). Now it was time for the elders to do the same. Since the elders are commanded to shepherd the flock of God (Acts 20:28; 1 Peter 5:2), part of their shepherding task is to see that the flock is fed God's Word.

The importance of feeding sheep is evidenced by the fact that sheep are nearly incapable of feeding and watering themselves properly. Without a shepherd, sheep would quickly be without pasture and water, and would soon waste away. So, everything depends on the proper feeding of the sheep. Unless wisely fed they become emaciated and sick, and the wealth invested in them is squandered. When Ezekiel presents a picture of the bad shepherd, the first stroke of his brush is – "he does not feed the flock."

The Christian community is created by the Spirit's use of God's Word (1 Peter 1:23; James 1:18). The community also matures, grows, and is protected by the Word. Therefore, it is a scriptural requirement that an elder "be able both to exhort in sound doctrine and to refute those who contradict" (Titus 1:9). The elders protect, guide, lead, nourish, comfort, educate, and heal the flock by teaching and preaching the Word. Many pastoral needs of the people are met through the teaching of the Word. The failure of church elders to know and teach the Bible is one of the chief reasons doctrinal error floods churches today and drowns the power and life of the church.

Leading the Flock

In biblical language, to shepherd a nation or any group of people means to lead or to govern (2 Sam. 5:2; Psalm 78:71-72).

According to Acts 20 and 1 Peter 5, elders shepherd the church of God. To shepherd a local church means, among other things, to lead the church. To the church in Ephesus Paul states: "Let the elders who rule [lead, direct, manage] well be considered worthy of double honor" (1 Timothy 5:17a). Elders, then, lead, direct, govern, manage, and care for the flock of God.

In Titus 1:7, Paul insists that a prospective elder be morally and spiritually above reproach because he is "God's steward." A steward is a "household manager," someone with official responsibility over the master's servants, property, and even finances. Elders are stewards of God's household, the local church.

Elders are also called "overseers," which signifies that they supervise and manage the church. Peter uses the verb form of overseer when he exhorts the elders: "Therefore, I exhort the elders among you ... shepherd the flock of God among you exercising oversight" (1 Peter 5:1a, 2a). In this instance, Peter combines the concepts of shepherding and overseeing when he exhorts the elders to do their duty. Hence we can speak of the elders' overall function as the pastoral oversight of the local church.

Leading and managing a flock is important. Sheep must be led to fresh water, new pasture, and relief from dangerous summer heat. This often means traveling rugged roads and narrow paths through dangerous ravines. The sheep must also be made to rest. At evening, they must be brought into the fold. Thus shepherds must know how and where to lead their flock. They must use land and water supplies wisely, constantly planning for future needs and anticipating problems.

Management Skill

The same leading and managing principles involved in shepherding sheep also apply to shepherding the local church. A congregation needs leadership, management, governance, guidance, counsel, and vision. Hence all elders must be, to some measure, leaders and managers. The eldership must clarify direction and beliefs for the flock. It must set goals, make decisions, give direction, correct failures, affect change, and motivate people. It must evaluate, plan, and govern. Elders, then, must be problem solvers, managers of people, planners, and thinkers.

A healthy, growing flock of sheep doesn't just appear; it is the result of the shepherd's skillful management of sheep and resources. He knows sheep and is skillful in caring for them. A good shepherd elder knows people. He knows how sensitive they are. He knows their needs, troubles, weaknesses, and sins. He knows how they can hurt one another. He knows how stubborn they can be. He knows how to deal with people. He knows that they are to be slowly and patiently led. He knows when to be tough and when to be gentle. He knows peoples' needs and what must be done to meet those needs. He knows how to accurately assess the health and direction of the congregation. And when he doesn't know these things, he is quick to find answers. He loves to learn better skills and methods for managing the flock.

Since shepherd elders must lead and manage a congregation of people, the New Testament requires that all elder candidates evidence management ability by the proper management of their own households: "He [the prospect elder] must be one who manages his own household well ... but if a man does not know how to manage his own household, how will he take care of the church of God?" (1 Tim. 3:4-5). The Scripture also says that "the elders who rule [manage, lead, direct] well be considered worthy of double honor" (1 Tim. 5:17). So elders who manage the church well desire to be recognized for their leadership and management ability and service.

Hard Work & Caring for Practical Needs

Not only does leading and managing a flock demand skill and knowledge, it requires lots of hard work. Shepherding is hard and often uncomfortable work. Sheep don't take vacations from eating and drinking, nor do their predators vanish. Observe Jacob's description of his life as a shepherd: "Thus I was: by day the heat consumed me, and the frost by night, and my sleep fled from my eyes" (Gen. 31:40). Because a good shepherd must work hard, a self-seeking shepherd is, according to the biblical writers, a bad shepherd (Ezek. 34:2, 8). An idle, lazy shepherd is a disgrace and danger to the flock (Nah. 3:18; Zech. 11:17).

Pastoring God's flock requires a life of devoted work. That is why Paul exhorts believers to highly honor and love those who work hard at caring for the flock (1 Thess. 5:12; 1 Tim. 5:17). If a biblical eldership is to function effectively, it requires men who are firmly committed to our Lord's principles of discipleship. Biblical eldership is dependent on men who seek first the kingdom of God and His righteousness (Matt. 6:33), men who have presented themselves as living sacrifices to God and slaves to the Lord Jesus Christ (Rom. 12:1-2), men who love Jesus Christ above all else and willingly sacrifice self for the sake of others, men who love as Christ loved, men who are self-disciplined and self-sacrificing, and men who have taken up the cross and are willing to suffer for Christ.

To the Ephesian elders Paul said, "You yourselves know that these hands ministered to my own needs and to the men who were with me. In everything I showed you that by working hard in this manner you must help the weak and remember the words of the Lord Jesus, that He Himself said, 'It is more blessed to give than to receive'" (Acts 20:34-35). How do working men shepherd the church yet maintain family life: perseverance, hard work, and the power of the Holy Spirit.

In addition to the familiar, broad categories of protecting, feeding, and leading the flock, elders also bear responsibility for the practical care of the flock's many diverse needs. For example, James instructs sick members of the flock to call for the elders of the church: "Is anyone among you sick? Let him call for the elders of the church, and let them pray over him, anointing him with oil in the name of the Lord" (James 5:14). Paul exhorts the Ephesian elders to care for the weak and needy of the flock: "In everything I showed you that by working hard in this manner you must help the weak and remember the words of the Lord Jesus, that He Himself said, 'It is more blessed to give than to receive'" (Acts 20:35).

As shepherds of the flock, the elders must be available to meet whatever needs the sheep have. This means visiting the sick, comforting the bereaved; strengthening the weak; praying for all the sheep, even those who are difficult; visiting new members; providing counsel for couples who are engaged, married, or divorcing; and managing the many day-to-day details of the inner life of the congregation.

We must, however, balance what we have been saying about the elder's ministry with the parallel truth of every-member ministry. Although the elders lead and are officially responsible for the spiritual oversight of the whole church, they are not the total ministry of the church. They are not the ministers. Ministry is the work of the whole church. Ministry is not the work of one person or even one group of people.

The local church is not only a flock; it is also a body of Spirit-gifted, royal priests who minister to the Lord and His people. This, the care of the local body, is not the sole responsibility of the elders, but of all the members. Each member of Christ's body is equipped by the Spirit to minister to the needs of others. The elders are dependent upon the gifts and skills of others (some of whom may be more gifted than any of the elders in certain areas of ministry) for the overall care of the local church. Biblical elders do not want to control a passive congregation. They desire to lead an active, alive, every-member-ministering church.

Love for the Lord's People

The secret to caring for sheep is love. A good shepherd loves sheep and loves to be with them (2 Sam. 12:3). The best elders, likewise, are those who love people, love to be with them, and are fervently involved with them.

The loving heart of a true pastor is dramatically displayed in the life of Paul. Reminding the troublesome Corinthians of his deepest motives and feelings, Paul writes: "For out of much affliction and anguish of heart I wrote to you with many tears; not that you should be made sorrowful, but that you might know the love which I have especially for you" (2 Cor. 2:4). Paul's passion is clearly evident. Here is a Christian so committed to the well-being of other Christians, especially new Christians, that he is simply burning up inside to be with them, to help them, to nurture them, to feed them, to stabilize them, to establish an adequate foundation for them. Small wonder, then, that he devotes himself to praying for them when he finds he cannot visit them personally.

Elders' work is people-oriented work. If a body of elders lacks certain gifts or dynamic personalities, the elders' love for the people can compensate for such deficiencies. There is, however, no compensation for a lack of love and compassion on the part of the elders. Without love the eldership is an empty shell. Without love an elder is "a noisy gong," "a clanging cymbal," a spiritual zero (1 Cor. 13:1-2). So, like the Lord Jesus Christ, a good shepherd elder loves people.

Discussion Questions:

1. According to the New Testament, what do elders actually do?
2. Name two ways an elder can protect his flock.
3. How does an elder maintain a spiritual alertness?
4. What must an elder do to care for some practical needs of the flock?
5. What is the secret to caring for sheep?

Chapter 10

SHARED LEADERSHIP

"Let the elders who rule well be considered worthy of double honor, especially those who work hard at preaching and teaching."
1 Timothy 5:17

The New Testament provides conclusive evidence that the pastoral oversight of the apostolic churches was a team effort – not the sole responsibility of one person. Shared leadership is rooted in the Old Testament institution of the elders of Israel and in Jesus' founding of the apostolate. It is a highly significant and often overlooked fact that our Lord did not appoint one man to lead His Church. He personally appointed and trained twelve men. Jesus Christ gave the Church plurality of leadership. The Twelve comprised the first leadership council of the Church and, in the most exemplary way, jointly led and taught the first Christian community. The Twelve provide a marvelous example of unity, humble brotherly love, and shared leadership structure.

Shared leadership is also evidenced by the Seven who were appointed to relieve the twelve apostles of the responsibility of dispensing funds to the church's widows (Acts 6:3-6). The Seven were the prototype of the later deacons. There is no indication that one of the Seven was chief and the others were his assistants. As a body of servants, they did their work on behalf of the church in Jerusalem. Based on all the evidence we have, the deacons, like the elders, formed a collective leadership council.

The New Testament reveals that the pastoral oversight of many of the first churches was committed to a plurality of elders. This was true of the earliest Jewish Christian churches in Jerusalem, Judea, and neighboring countries, as well as many of the first Gentile churches. Note the following evidence:

- The elders of the church in Jerusalem united with the twelve apostles to deliberate over doctrinal controversy (Acts 15). Like the apostolate, the elders comprised a collective leadership body.

- James instructed the sick believer to "call for the elders [plural] in the church [singular]" (James 5:14).

- At the end of Paul's first missionary journey, he appointed a council of elders for each newly founded church: "And when they had appointed elders [plural] for them in every church [singular], having prayed with fasting, they commended them to the Lord in whom they had believed" (Acts 14:23). Note that here, as in James 5:15, the term *elder* is plural and the word church is singular. Thus each church had elders.

- When passing near the city of Ephesus during a hurried trip to Jerusalem, Paul summoned the "elders of the church," not the pastor, to meet for a final farewell exhortation (Acts 20:17, 28). The church in Ephesus was under the pastoral care of a council of elders. First Timothy 5:17 demonstrates beyond question that a plurality of elders led and taught the church in Ephesus: "Let the elders who rule well be considered worthy of double honor, especially those who work hard at preaching and teaching."

- When Paul wrote to the Christians at Philippi, he greeted "the overseers [plural] and deacons" (Phil. 1:1).

- At both the beginning and end of Paul's ministry, he appointed (or instructed others to appoint) a plurality of elders to care for the churches he founded or established (Acts 14:23; Titus 1:5). According to the Titus 1:5 passage, Paul did not consider a church to be fully developed until it had functioning, qualified elders: "For this reason I left you in Crete, that you might set in order what remains, and appoint elders in every city as I directed you" (Titus 1:5).

- When writing to churches scattered throughout the five Roman provinces of Pontus, Galatia, Cappadocia, Asia, and Bithynia in northwestern Asia Minor (1 Peter 1:1), Peter exhorted the elders to pastor the flock (1 Peter 1:5). This indicates that Peter knew that the elder structure of government was standard practice in these churches.

In addition to explicit statements regarding a plurality of elders, other examples of shared leadership exist throughout the New Testament (Acts 13:1; 15:35; 1 Cor. 16:15, 16; 1 Thess. 5:12, 13; Heb. 13:7, 17, 24). On the local church level, the New Testament plainly witnesses to a consistent pattern of shared pastoral leadership. Therefore, leadership by a plurality of elders is a sound biblical practice.

New Testament eldership is not, as many think, a high-status, board position that is open to any and all who desire membership. On the contrary, an eldership patterned on the New Testament requires qualified elders who must meet specific moral and spiritual qualifications before they serve (1 Tim. 3:1-7). Such elders must be publicly examined by the church as to their qualifications (1 Tim. 3:10). They must be publicly installed into office (1 Tim. 5:22; Acts 14:23). They must be motivated and empowered by the Holy Spirit to do their work (Acts 20:28). Finally, they must be acknowledged, loved, and honored by the whole congregation. This honor given by the congregation includes the giving of financial support to elders who are uniquely gifted at preaching and teaching, which allows some elders to serve the church in full or part time salaried positions (1 Tim. 5:17, 18). Thus a team of qualified, dedicated, Spirit-placed elders is not a passive, ineffective committee; it is an effective form of leadership structure that greatly benefits the church family.

The Benefits of a Council of Equals

Balancing people's weaknesses

Collective leadership can provide a church leader with critically needed recognition of and balance for his faults and deficiencies. We all have blind spots, eccentricities, and deficiencies. We all have what C. S. Lewis (1898-1963) called "a fatal flaw." We can see these fatal flaws so clearly in others, but not in ourselves. These fatal flaws or blind spots distort our judgment. They deceive us. They can even destroy us. This is particularly true of multitalented charismatic leaders. Blind to their own flaws and extreme views, some talented leaders have destroyed themselves because they have no peers to confront and balance them and, in fact wanted none.

In a team leadership structure, different members complement one another and balance one another's weaknesses. If one elder has a tendency to act too harshly with people, the others can temper his harshness. If some members fear confrontation with people, others can press for action. Elders who are more doctrinally oriented can sharpen those who are more outreach- or service-oriented, and the outreach- or service-minded elders can ignite the intellectually oriented members to more evangelism and service.

I believe that traditional, single-church pastors would improve their character and ministry if they had genuine peers to whom they were regularly accountable and with whom they worked jointly. Most pastors are not multitalented leaders, nor are they well suited to singularly lead a congregation effectively. They have personality flaws and talent deficiencies that cause them and the congregation considerable vexation. When placed in a council of qualified pastors, however, a pastor's strengths make important contributions to the church and his weaknesses are covered by the strengths of others.

Lightening the work load

Shared pastoral leadership also helps to lighten a very heavy work load. If the long hours, weighty responsibilities, and problems of shepherding a congregation of people are not enough to overwhelm a person, then dealing with people's sins and listening to seemingly endless complaints and bitter conflicts can crush a person. Even the mighty Moses wilted to near death under the pressures of leading the people of Israel (Num. 11). Certainly every shepherd who has sought to do his duty according to Scripture has felt, at one time or another, like Moses.

To make matters worse, the single-pastor system of leadership is often ruthlessly cruel and unfair to pastors. Many overworked pastors are alone and isolated, with the church board and congregation serving as a multitude of ringside critics. This is one reason why there are so many "short-term" pastors in churches. Many other pastors stay in the same church but are ineffective because they suffer from severe battle fatigue. In a multiple-elder system of leadership, however, the heavy burdens of pastoral life are shared by a number of qualified, functioning, shepherd elders. A team ministry provides pastors for each pastor, men whom one can expect full encouragement and help.

Finally, plurality of leadership allows each shepherd elder to function primarily according to personal giftedness rather than being forced to do everything and then being criticized for not being multi-gifted.

Providing accountability

English historian Lord Acton (1834-1902) said, "power tends to corrupt, and absolute power corrupts absolutely." Because of our Christian beliefs in the reality of sin, Satan, and human depravity, we should understand well why people in positions of power are easily corrupted. In fact, the better we understand the biblical doctrine of sin, the stronger our commitment to accountability will be. The collective leadership of a biblical eldership provides a formal structure for genuine accountability.

Shared leadership provides close accountability, genuine partnership, and peer relationships – the very things imperial pastors shrink from at all costs.

Shared leadership also provides the local church shepherd with accountability for his work. Left to ourselves, we so mainly do what we want to do, not what we should do or what is best for others. This is especially true if we face tense, confrontational situations with erring members. Most people will avoid unpleasant confrontation at all costs. Thus church leaders need the loving encouragement and close accountability that team leadership provides so that they will accomplish their duties promptly and responsibly.

First Among a Council of Equals: Leaders Among Leaders

An extremely important but terribly misunderstood aspect of biblical eldership is the principle of "first among equals." Failure to understand the concept of "first among equals" (1 Tim. 5:17) has caused some elderships to be tragically ineffective in their pastoral care and leadership. Although elders act jointly as a council and share equal authority and responsibility for the leadership of the church, all are not equal in their giftedness, biblical knowledge, leadership ability, experience, or dedication. Therefore, those among the elders who are particularly gifted leaders and /or teachers will naturally stand out among the other elders as leaders and teachers within the leadership body. That is what the Romans called *primus inter pares*, meaning "first among equals," or *primi inter pares*, meaning "first ones among equals."

The principle of "first among equals" is observed first in our Lord's dealings with the twelve apostles. Jesus chose twelve apostles, all of whom He empowered to preach and heal, but He singled out three for special attention – Peter, James, and John ("first ones among equals"). Among the three, as well as among the Twelve, Peter stood out as the most prominent ("first among equals"). Consider the following facts:

- Among the twelve apostles, Peter, James, John, and sometimes Andrew are "first ones among equals." On key occasions Jesus chose only Peter, James, and John to accompany Him to witness His power, glory, and agony (Luke 8:51; 9:28; Mark 14:33).

- Among the three, as well as the Twelve, Peter is unquestionably first among his equals. In all four lists of the apostles' names, Peter's name is first (Matt. 10:2-4; Mark 3:16-19; Luke 6:14-16; Acts 1:13). Matthew actually refers to Peter as "the first" (Matt. 10:2). By calling Peter "the first," Matthew means "first among his equals." We must not, in reaction to Roman Catholicism's mistaken elevation of Peter, underestimate Peter's outstanding leadership among the Twelve. The Gospel writers don't.

- In all four Gospels, Peter is indisputably the prominent figure among the Twelve. Outside of Jesus, Peter is mentioned most often as speaking and acting. If you doubt this, look up the name Peter in a Bible concordance, then look up the names of the other apostles. You will immediately see Peter's prominence among the Twelve in the four Gospels and in Acts.

- Jesus charges Peter to "strengthen your brothers" (Luke 22:32). Jesus acknowledged Peter as first among his brothers, the natural leader and motivator. He knew that they would need Peter's leadership to help them through the dark days immediately following their Lord's departure.

- The book of Acts richly demonstrates Peter's leadership. Among the Twelve who jointly shared the leadership of the first church (Acts 2:14, 42; 4:33, 35; 5:12, 18, 25, 29, 42; 6:2-6; 8:14; 9:27; 15:2-29), Peter is the chief spokesman and natural leader throughout the first twelve chapters of Acts (Acts 1:15; 2:14; 3:1 ff; 4:8 ff; 5:3 ff; 5:15, 29; 8:14-24; 9:32-11:18; 12:3 ff; 15:7-11; Gal. 2:7-14). Some scholars even divide the book of Acts according to its two central figures: the acts of Peter (Acts 1-12) and the acts of Paul (Acts 13-28). Many sound, evangelical Bible commentators interpret Christ's statement in Matthew 16:18 to mean that Peter is the rock and that upon him Christ would build His Church (but not exclusively upon him according to other passages such as Ephesians 2:20). They view the book of Acts as the record of that promise fulfilled (especially Acts 10:1-11:18).

- In Paul's letter to the Galatians, Paul speaks to James, Peter, and John as the acknowledged "pillars" of the church in Jerusalem (Gal. 2:9; see also Gal. 2:7-8).

As a natural leader, the chief speaker, the man of action, Peter challenged, energized, strengthened, and ignited the group. Without Peter, the group would have been less effective. When surrounded by eleven other apostles who were his equals, Peter became stronger; more balanced, and was protected from his impetuous nature and his fears. In spite of his outstanding leadership and speaking ability, *Peter possessed no legal or official rank or title above the other eleven. They were not his subordinates. They were not his staff or team of assistants. He wasn't the apostles' "senior pastor."* Peter was simply first among his equals and that by our Lord's own approval.

The "first among equals" leadership relationship can also be observed among the seven who were chosen to relieve the apostles in Acts 6. Philip and Stephen stood out as prominent figures among the five brothers (Acts 6:8-7:60; 8:4-40; 21:8). Yet, as far as the account records, the two held no special title or status above the others.

The concept of "first among equals" is further evidenced by the relationship of Paul and Barnabas on their first missionary journey. Paul and Barnabas were both apostles (Acts 13:1-3; 14:4; 15:36-39; 1 Cor. 9:1-6), yet Paul was first between the two because he was "the chief speaker" and dynamic leader (Acts 13:13; 14:12). Although Paul was plainly the more gifted of the two apostles, he held no formal ranking over Barnabas; they labored as partners in the work of the gospel. A similar relationship seems to have existed between Paul and Silas, who was also an apostle (1 Thess. 2:6).

Finally, the "first among equals" concept is evidenced by the way in which congregations are to honor their elders. Paul wrote specific instructions concerning elders to the church in Ephesus: "Let the elders who rule well be considered worthy of double honor, especially those who work hard at preaching and teaching. For the Scripture says, 'You shall not muzzle the ox while he is threshing,' and 'The laborer is worthy of his wages'" (1 Tim. 5:17, 18). All elders must be able to teach the Word, but not all desire to work fully at preaching and teaching. Those who are gifted in teaching and spend the time to do so should be properly acknowledged by the local church. They should receive double honor.

This doesn't mean, however, that elders who are first among their equals do all the thinking and decision-making for the group, or that they are the pastors while the others are merely elders. To call one elder "pastor" and the rest "elders" or one elder "the clergyman" and the rest "lay elders" is to act without biblical precedence. To do so will not result in a biblical eldership. It will, at least in practice, *create a separate, superior office over the eldership, just as was done in the early second century when the division between "the overseer" and "elders" occurred.*

The advantage of the principle of "first among equals" is that *it allows for functional, gift-based diversity within the eldership team without creating an official, superior office over fellow elders.* Just as the leading apostles, such as Peter and John, bore no special title or formal distinctions from the other apostles, elders who receive double honor form no official class or receive no special title. The differences among the elders are functional, not formal.

Discussion Questions:

1. Give two quintessential examples of team ministry that Jesus gave us to follow.
2. Name three scriptural incidences that give us evidence of plurality of elders.
3. What was Paul's measure for a fully developed church? Read Acts 14:23; Titus 1:5 to answer.
4. What are the four required qualifications of elders before they serve the church?
5. Describe the benefits of a council of equals.

Chapter 11

QUALIFIED LEADERSHIP

"An overseer, then, must be above reproach."
1 Timothy 3:2a

In a letter to a young presbyter named Nepotian, dated A.D. 394, Jerome (A.D. 345-419) rebuked the churches of his day for their hypocrisy in showing more concern for the appearance of their church buildings than the careful selection of their church leaders: "Many build churches nowadays; their walls and pillars of glowing marble, their ceilings glittering with gold, their altars studded with jewels. Yet to the choice of Christ's ministers no heed is paid."[31]

A similar error is repeated by multitudes of churches today. Many churches seem oblivious to the biblical requirements for their spiritual leaders as well as to the need for the congregation to properly examine all candidates for leadership in light of biblical standards (1 Tim. 3:10). This failure was dramatically highlighted when a leading evangelical journal in America brought together five divorced pastors and asked them to share their feelings, experiences, and views on divorce and the ministry. The journal's staff published the forum because they believed the growing problem of divorce among ministers needed to be faced openly and honestly. In fact, the article claimed that a recent survey of divorce rates in the United States showed that pastors had the third highest divorce rate – exceeded only by that of medical doctors and policemen![32]

The pastors' thoughts on divorce were presented in the journal through an open forum format. Along with the forum, the journal published the responses of seven well-known evangelical

---

[31] Jerome, "Letters 52," in *The Nicene and Post-Nicene Fathers*, 14 vols., Second Series, eds. Philip Schaff and Henry Wace (repr. Grand Rapids: Eerdmans, n.d.), 6: 94. (Hereafter cited as *The Nicene and Post-Nicene Fathers*.)
[32] "A Biblical Style of Leadership?" *Leadership 2* (Fall, 1981): 119-129.

leaders to the divorced pastors' comments. What is astounding about the article is that not one of the seven leaders mentioned the biblical qualifications for leadership outlined in 1 Timothy or Titus! This article reveals a widespread ignorance within the Christian community concerning Scripture's vigorous insistence on God's qualifications for local church leaders. It also demonstrates that churches and denominations have substituted their own standards for the biblical ones.

The Need for Qualified Shepherd Elders

The most common mistake made by churches that are eager to implement eldership is to appoint biblically unqualified men. Because there is always a need for more shepherds, it is tempting to allow unqualified, unprepared men to assume leadership in the church. This is, however, a time-proven formula for failure. A biblical eldership requires biblically qualified elders.

The overriding concern of the New Testament in relation to church leadership is for the right kind of men to serve as elders and deacons. The offices of God's Church are not honorary positions bestowed on individuals who have attended church faithfully or who are senior in years. Nor are they board positions to be filled by good friends, rich donors, or charismatic personalities. Nor are they positions that only graduate seminary students can fill. The church offices, both eldership and deaconship, are open to all who meet the apostolic, biblical requirements. The New Testament is unequivocally emphatic on this point:

- To the troubled church in Ephesus, Paul insists that a properly constituted Christian church (1 Tim. 3:14, 15) must have qualified, approved elders (1 Timothy 3:1-7).

- Paul also insists that prospective elders and deacons be publicly examined in light of the stated list of qualifications. He writes, "And let these [deacons] also [like the elders] first be tested [examined]; then let them serve as deacons if they are beyond reproach" (1 Timothy 3:10; 5:24-25).

- When directing Titus in how to organize churches on the island of Crete, Paul reminds Titus to appoint only morally and spiritually qualified men to be elders. By stating elder qualifications in a letter, Paul establishes a public list to guide the local church in its choice of elders and to empower it to hold its elders accountable (Titus 1:5-9).

- When writing to churches scattered throughout northwestern Asia Minor, Peter speaks of the kind of men who should be elders. He exhorts the elders to shepherd the flock "not under compulsion, but voluntarily, according to the will of God; and not for sordid gain, but with eagerness; nor yet as lording it over those allotted to your charge, but proving to be examples to the flock" (1 Peter 5:2-3).

It is highly noteworthy that the New Testament provides more instruction on the qualifications for eldership than on any aspect of eldership. Such qualifications are not required for all teachers or evangelists. One may be gifted as an evangelist and be used of God in that capacity, yet be unqualified to be an elder. An individual may be an evangelist immediately after conversion, but Scripture says that a new convert cannot be an elder (1 Tim. 3:6). There are three critically important reasons why God demands these qualifications of church elders.

First, the Bible says that an elder must be of irreproachable moral character and capable in the use of Scripture because he is "God's steward," that is, God's household manager (Titus 1:7). An elder is entrusted with God's dearest and most costly possessions, His children. He thus holds a position of solemn authority and trust. He acts on behalf of God's interest. No earthly monarch would dare think of hiring an immoral or incapable person to manage his estate. Nor would parents think of entrusting their children or family finances to an untrustworthy or incompetent person. So, too, the

High and Holy One will not have an unfit, unqualified steward caring for His precious children.

As stewards of God's household, elders have access to people's homes and the most intimate details of their lives. They have access to the people who are most vulnerable to deception or abuse. They also have the greatest influence over the doctrinal direction of the church. Therefore, church elders must be men who are well-known by the community, have proven integrity, and are doctrinally sound.

Second, local church elders are to be living examples for the people to follow (1 Peter 5:3). They are to model the character and conduct that God desires for all His children. Since God calls His people to "be blameless and innocent, children of God above reproach in the midst of a crooked and perverse generation" (Phil. 2:15), it is necessary that those who lead His people be morally above reproach and model godly living.

John MacArthur, well-known radio preacher and author, echoes this point when he writes: "Whatever the leaders are, the people become. As Hosea said, 'Like people, like priest' (4:9). Jesus said, 'Everyone, after he had been fully trained, will be like his teacher' (Luke 6:40). Biblical history demonstrates that people will seldom rise above the spiritual level of their leadership."[33] Because people are like sheep, shepherd elders have an extraordinary powerful impact on the behavior, attitudes, and thinking of the people:

- If the elders have a contentious spirit, the people will inevitably become contentious (1 Tim. 3:3; Titus 1:7).

- If the elders are inhospitable, the people will be unfriendly and cold (1 Tim. 3:2; Titus 1:8).

---

[33] John MacArthur, Jr., *Different by Design: Discovering God's Will for Today's Man and Woman* (Wheaton: Victor, 1994), p. 114.

- If the elders love money, the people will become lovers of money (1 Tim. 3:3).

- If the elders are not sensible, balanced, and self-controlled, their judgment will be characterized by ugly extremes, which will cause the people to be extreme and unbalanced (1 Tim. 3:1-2; Titus 1:8).

- If the elders are not faithful, one-woman husbands, they will subtly encourage others to be unfaithful (1 Tim. 3:2; Titus 1:6).

- If the elders do not faithfully hold to the authority of the Word, the people will not hold to it (Titus 1:9).

Much of the weakness and waywardness of our churches today is due directly to our failure to require that church shepherds meet God's standards for office. If we want our local churches to be spiritually fit, then we must require our shepherds to be spiritually fit.

Third, the biblical qualifications protect the church from incompetent or morally unfit leaders. Some people push themselves into positions of church leadership to satisfy their unholy egos. Others are sadly deceived about their own ability and character. And some are evildoers who are motivated by Satan to infiltrate and ruin churches. The public, objective, God-given qualifications for church leadership protect the congregation from such unfit people.

These observable, objective standards for elders are especially important when churches must deal with dominating, stubborn church leaders who are incapable of truly seeing their sins or heresies and yet must be discharged from office. The elder qualifications empower each congregation and its leaders with the right and the objective means to hold back or remove unfit men from leadership. To refuse to remove a sinful or doctrinally unsound elder, however, is willful disobedience to God's Word that will eventually undermine the moral and spiritual vitality of the whole church as well as the integrity of the leadership council. The refusal to remove an erring elder will also damage the church's credibility and gospel witness before an unbelieving community, which is a matter of utmost concern to Paul (1 Tim. 3:7). Thus the God-given standards for elders are essential for protecting the local church's spiritual welfare and evangelistic witness.

Today churches most need men of Christlike character to be in spiritual leadership. The best laws and constitutions are impotent without men who are "just," "devout," "sensible," "self-controlled," "forbearing," "uncontentious," "and faithful to sound doctrine." These are precisely the qualities that God requires of those who lead His people.

The Qualifications for Shepherd Elders

When we speak of the elder's qualifications, most people think these qualifications are something different from those of the clergy. The New Testament, however, has no separate standards for professional clergy and lay elders. The reason is simple. There are only two offices – elders and deacons. From the New Testament perspective, any man in the congregation who desires to shepherd the Lord's people and who meets God's requirements for the office can be a pastor elder.

As the lists show (1 Timothy 3:2-7; Titus 1:6-9; 1 Peter 5:1-3), God does not require wealth, social status, senior age, advanced academic degrees, or even great spiritual gifts of those who desire to shepherd His people. We do the congregation and the work of God a great disservice when we add our arbitrary requirements to God's qualifications. Man-made requirements inevitably exclude needed, qualified men from the pastoral leadership of the church.

To be faithful to Holy Scripture and God's plan for the local church, we must open the pastoral leadership of the church to all in the church who are called by the Holy Spirit (Acts 20:20) and meet the apostolic qualifications. Although such a plan may be abhorrent to the clerical mind-set, it represents an authentic, apostolic mind-set. According to the New Testament, the elders of the church are all the men of the local church who desire to lead the flock and are scripturally qualified to do so. The Scriptural qualifications can be divided into three broad categories relating to moral and spiritual character, abilities, and Spirit-given motivation.

MORAL AND SPIRITUAL CHARACTER

Most of the biblical qualifications relate to the candidate's moral and spiritual qualities. The first and overarching qualification is that of being "above reproach." What is meant by "above reproach" is defined by the character qualities that follow the term. In both of Paul's lists of elder qualifications, the first specific character virtue itemized is, "the husband of one wife." That means that an elder must be above reproach in his marital and sexual life.

From the beginning, God sternly warned His people against the corrupt sexual practices of the heathen nations. He commanded His people to be holy and separate from the nations, to be faithful to the marriage covenant, and to be sexually pure. In the eighteenth chapter of Leviticus, Moses details all the sexual sins of the godless nations that would soon surround Israel. God warns His people against the practice of such sins: "Do not defile yourselves by any of these things [depraved sexual practices]; for by all these the nations which I am casting out before you have become defiled … Thus you are to keep My charge, that you do not practice any of the abominable customs which have been practices before you, so as not to defile yourselves with them; I am the Lord your God" (Lev. 18:24, 30). The need for purity was taught to the new community as well. Paul writes, "But do not let immorality or any impurity or greed even be named among you, as is proper among saints" (Eph. 5:3).

One of Satan's oldest, most effective strategies for destroying the people of God is to adulterate the marriages of those who lead God's people (Num. 25:1-5; 1 Kings 11:1-13; Ezra 9:1-2). Satan knows that if he can defile the shepherd's marriage, the sheep will follow. The specific marital and family qualifications God requires for elders are meant to protect the whole church. So the church must insist that its leaders meet these qualifications before serving and while serving. If the local church does not insist on these requirements, the people will sink into the toxic wasteland of today's sexual and marital practices.

Tragically, many major Christian denominations have learned nothing from the Old Testament about the certain results of accommodating secular standards of sexual behavior. In nearly every major Christian denomination, God's laws regarding marriage, divorce, sexuality, and gender differences are being discarded and replaced with an acceptance of the most corrupt human practices. Among Christian leaders, adultery and other sexual sins are at epidemic levels. Among the major denominations, clergy divorce and remarriage is hardly an issue. As Time magazine aptly describes today's religious landscape, "Denominations that once would not tolerate divorced ministers now find themselves debating whether to accept avowed lesbian ones."[34]

The other character qualities stress the elders' integrity, self-control, and spiritual maturity. Since elders govern the church body, they must be self-controlled in the use of money, alcohol, and in the exercise of their pastoral authority. Since they are to be models of Christian living, they must be spiritually devout, righteous, lovers of good, hospitable, and morally above reproach before the non-Christian-community. In pastoral work, relationship skills are preeminent. Thus shepherd elders must be gentle, stable, sound-minded, and uncontentious. Angry, hot-headed men hurt people. So an elder must not have a dictatorial spirit or be quick-tempered, pugnacious, or self-willed. Finally, an elder must not be a new Christian. He must be a spiritually mature, humble, time-proven disciple of Jesus Christ.

---

[34] Richard N. Ostling, "The Second Reformation," *Time* (November 23, 1992). P. 54.

ABILITIES

In the catalogs of elder qualifications, three requirements address the elder's abilities to perform the task. He must be able to manage his household well, provide a model of Christian living for others to follow, and be able to teach and defend the faith.

Able to Manage the Family Household Well

An elder must be able to manage his household well. The Scripture states: "He must be one who manages his own household well, keeping his children under his control with all dignity (but if a man does not know how to manage his own household, how will he take care of the church of God?)" (1 Tim. 3:4-5). The Puritans referred to the family household as the "little church." This perspective is in keeping with the scriptural reasoning that if a man cannot shepherd his family, he can't shepherd the extended family of the church.

Managing the local church is more like managing a family than managing a business or state. A man may be a successful businessman, a capable public official, a brilliant office manager, or a top military leader but be a terrible church elder or father. Thus a man's ability to oversee his household well is a prerequisite for overseeing God's household.

What about single men or married men who have no children? Can these men be elders? Most definitely (1 Cor. 7:8-35)! The qualification regarding marriage and children should not be construed as commands to marry and have children. Rather, because most men are married and have children, the Scripture sets forth God's standard for church leaders who are husbands and fathers. Setting standards for married men who have children is quite a different issue from commanding marriage and fatherhood, which is not always a matter of choice. Single men and childless, married men can certainly be pastor elders. When they lack experience because of their unmarried or childless status, their fellow elders what are married and have children can fill in the gap.

Single and childless men have a unique contribution to make to the flock and the eldership team. Of course the sexual conduct and home management of single and childless men must be above reproach, just as it must be above reproach for married men who have children.

Able to Provide a Model for Others to Follow

An elder must be an example of Christian living that others will want to follow. Peter reminds the Asian elders "to be examples to the flock" (1 Peter 5:3b). If a man is not a godly model for others to follow, he cannot be an elder even if he is a good teacher and manager. Like Peter, Paul also recognized the importance of modeling Christ. He did his utmost to model Christ and expected the people to follow:

- Brethren, join in following my example, and observe those who walk according to the pattern you have in us (Phil. 3:17).

- Be imitators of me, just as I also am of Christ (1 Cor. 11:1).

- For you yourselves know how you ought to follow our example, because we did not act in an undisciplined manner among you … but in order to offer ourselves as a model for you, that you might follow our example (2 Thess. 3:7, 9b).

- I exhort you, therefore, be imitators of me (1 Cor. 4:16; cf. Gal. 4:12; 1 Thess. 1:5-6; 1 Tim. 4:12; Titus 2:7).

The greatest way to inspire and influence people for God is through personal example. Character and deeds, not official position or title, is what really influences people for eternity. Today men and women crave authentic examples of true Christianity in action. Who can better provide the week-by-week, long-term examples of family life, business life, and church life than local church elders? This is why it is so important that elders, as living imitators of Christ, shepherd God's flock in God's way.

Able to Teach and Defend the Faith

An elder must be able to teach and defend the faith. It doesn't matter how successful a man is in his business, how eloquently he speaks, or how intelligent he is. If he isn't firmly committed to historic, apostolic doctrine and able to instruct people in biblical doctrine, he does not qualify as a biblical elder (Acts 20:28ff; 1 Tim. 3:2; Titus 1:9).

The New Testament requires that a pastor elder "[hold] fast the faithful word which is in accordance with the teaching" (Titus 1:9a). This means that an elder must firmly adhere to orthodox, historic, biblical teaching. Elders must not be chosen from among those who have been toying with new doctrines. Since the local church is "the pillar and support of the truth" (1 Tim. 3:15b), its leaders must be rock-solid pillars of biblical doctrine or the house will crumble. Since the local church is also a small flock traveling over treacherous terrain that is infested with "savage wolves," only those shepherds who know the way and see the wolves can lead the flock to its safe destination. An elder, then, must be characterized by doctrinal integrity.

It is essential for an elder to be firmly committed to apostolic, biblical doctrine so "that he may be able to exhort in sound doctrine and to refute those who contradict" (Titus 1:9b). This requires that a prospective elder has applied himself for some years to the reading and study of Scripture, that he can reason intelligently and logically discuss biblical issues, that he has formulated doctrinal beliefs, and that he had the verbal ability and willingness to teach others. There should be no confusion, then, about what a New Testament elder is called to do: he is to teach and exhort the congregation in sound doctrine and to defend the truth from false teachers. This is the big difference between board elders and pastor elders. New Testament elders are both guardians and teachers of sound doctrine.

For this reason, God's book, the Bible, is to be the prospective elder's continual course of study. The Bible is God's complete training manual for all spiritual leaders. Paul reminds Timothy that "from childhood you have known the sacred writings which are able to give you the wisdom that leads to salvation through faith in Christ Jesus" (2 Tim. 3:15). Paul further states that "all Scripture is inspired by God [God-breathed], and profitable for teaching, for reproof, correction, for training in righteousness; that the man of God may be adequate, equipped for every good work" (2 Tim. 3:16-17). Thus a man is unequipped for the shepherding task if he has not been schooled in God-breathed Holy Scripture. A shepherd who doesn't know the Bible is like a shepherd without legs; he can't lead or protect the flock.

How are prospective elders to be educated in God's book? First, if raised in godly, Christian homes, they will have had years of instruction in doctrine and holy living from the most effective teachers in the world, their mothers and fathers (Deut. 6:7; 11:19; Prov. 1:8; 4:1-5; Eph. 6:4; 1 Thess. 2:11; 1 Cor. 14:35; 2 Tim. 1:5; 3:15).

Second, if the local church fulfills its role as a school for teaching apostolic doctrine, prospective elders will have been taught God's Word by gifted teachers. The Bible says that the local church is "the pillar and support of the truth" and "the household of God" (1 Tim. 3:15). This is why Paul charges Timothy to "give attention to the public reading of Scripture, to exhortation and teaching" (1 Tim. 4:13). Timothy was also to teach "faithful men, who will be able to teach others" (2 Tim. 2:2b). When Timothy departed from Ephesus, he expected that "faithful men," like the Ephesian elders, would teach future teachers and pastor elders who in turn would teach others.

Furthermore, the local church is not only a place to learn Scripture; it is the very best place to learn the skills required for shepherding people. It is in the local church that leaders learn to apply God's book to real-life situations. Thus the local church is to be God's school for the spiritual development of His children and the learning of Scripture (Acts 2:42; 11:26).

Third, a prospective elder learns the great truths of God through the consistent reading and study of Scripture and the ministry of the Holy Spirit (1 Cor. 2:12ff; 1 Thess. 4:9; 1 John 2:27). There is no substitute for a disciplined, persistent encounter with God through personal study of and meditation on Holy Scripture. In addition to studying Scripture, a growing Christian should be reading sound doctrinal material written by godly teachers of the Word.

Sadly, however, many churches (and Christian homes) have no vision for serious teaching or training in Scripture and doctrine. Other churches simply do not have the means to train their leaders; they are struggling to survive as a church body. Yet serious-minded believers hunger for in-depth teaching of the Scriptures. That is why Bible schools and seminaries will always be needed. Although there are problems with religious institutions that breed doubt in the authority of Scripture or reinterpret the Bible to agree with the spirit of the age, a good, Bible-believing and teaching school can provide excellent, in-depth training in Scripture.

I must warn, however, against the arbitrary requirement that many denominations impose on their shepherds to earn a master's degree before they are allowed to serve as a church pastor. God does not require advanced academic degrees as a qualification for spiritual leadership. When we set up formal academic standards, we professionalize the government of the church and create, at least in practice, a pastoral office that is separate from the eldership. We do not have God's authorization to establish such standards.

Do not forget that our Lord and Master, Jesus Christ, was not formally trained in a rabbinical school, although such training was available and very much prized in His day. Despite His lack of formal schooling in religion, however, Jesus was eminently educated in Scripture. Indeed, the people were so amazed by Jesus' knowledge and teaching as an untrained layman that they commented: "How has this man become learned, having never been educated?" (John 7:15b). The same observation was made of Jesus' close disciples: "as they observed the confidence of Peter and John, and understood that they were uneducated and untrained men, they were marveling, and began to recognize them as having been with Jesus" (Acts 4:13).

Unfortunately, many Christian people today are so clergy dependent that they can't imagine how men and women without formal theological training and the degrees that go with it can know the Bible and teach it effectively. We must remember that degrees are required in the world of business and academia but they are not required to minister in the household of God. Some people who are not able to go to school are taught by Christ through the Holy Spirit. They are educated in His Word and thus, according to God's standards, are qualified to lead and teach His people.

Spirit-Given Motivation for the Task

An obvious but not insignificant qualification is the shepherd's personal desire to love and care for God's people. Paul and the first Christians applauded such willingness by creating a popular Christian saying: "If any man aspires to the office of overseer, it is a fine work he desires to do" (1 Tim. 3:1). Peter, too, insisted that an elder shepherd the flock willingly and voluntarily (1 Peter 5:2). He knew from years of personal experience that the shepherding task can't be done by someone that views spiritual care as an unwanted obligation. Elders who serve grudgingly or under constraint are incapable of genuine care for people. They will be unhappy, impatient, guilty, fearful, and ineffective shepherds. Shepherding God's people through this sin-weary world is far too difficult a task – fraught with too many problems, dangers, and demands – to be entrusted to someone who lacks the will and desire to do the work.

A true desire to lead the family of God is always a Spirit-generated desire. Paul reminded the Ephesian elders that it was the Holy Spirit – not the church or the apostles – who placed them as overseers in the church to shepherd the flock of God (Acts 20:28). It was the Spirit who called them to shepherd the church and who moved them to care for the flock. The Spirit planted the pastoral desire in their hearts. He gave the compulsion and strength to do the work and the wisdom and appropriate gifts to care for the flock. The elders were His wise choice for the task. In the church of God, it is not man's will that matters but God's will and arrangement. So the only men who qualify for eldership are those whom the Holy Spirit gives the motivation and gifts for the task.

A biblical eldership, then, is a biblically qualified team of shepherd leaders. A plurality of unqualified elders is of no benefit to the local church. It is better to have no elders than the wrong ones. The local church must in all earnestness insist on biblically qualified elders, even if such men take years to develop.

Discussion Questions:

1. What are four points that the New Testament mentions concerning eldership?
2. Name the three important reasons why God demands specific qualifications for the leadership of elders.
3. What abilities must the elder have?
4. Give several scriptures that support the concept of elders requirement of being an example to the flock.
5. What would you consider to be the most important quality a leader should have for the office of elder?

Chapter 12

SERVANT LEADERSHIP

"If I then, the Lord and Teacher, washed your feet, you also ought to wash one another's feet. For I gave you an example that you also should do as I did to you"

John 13:14-15

Jesus Christ lived and taught the principles of life, humility, oneness, prayer, trust, forgiveness, and servanthood. After His ascension into heaven, the twelve apostles put these principles into practice by working together humbly and lovingly as a leadership team. Thus they became the first model of collective servant leadership.

Jesus' Teaching on Servant Leadership

Just as Christianity influenced the Roman empire, the Greco-Roman world also affected the course of Christianity. Renowned church historian and professor of Christian missions Kenneth Scott Latourette (1884-1968), when citing pagan influences on early Christianity, states that the Roman concepts of power and rule corrupted the organization and life of the early churches. He observes that "the Church was being interpenetrated by ideals which were quite contrary to the Gospel, especially the conception and use of power which were in stark contrast to the kind exhibited in the life and teaching of Jesus and in the cross and the resurrection."[35] This, Latourette goes on to say, proved to be "the menace which was most nearly disastrous" to Christianity.[36]

---

[35] Kenneth Scott Latourette, *History of Christianity*, 2 vols., 2nd ed. (New York: Harper & Row, 1975), 1:269.
[36] Ibid., 261.

I believe it is more accurate to say that the conceptual and structural changes that occurred during the early centuries of Christianity proved disastrous. Christianity, the humblest of all faiths, degenerated into the most power-hungry and hierarchical religion on the face of the earth. After the emperor Constantine elevated Christianity to the status of a state religion in A.D. 312, the once-persecuted faith became a fierce persecutor of all its opposition. An unscriptural clerical and priestly cast that was consumed by the quest for power, position, and authority arose. Even Roman emperors had a guiding hand in the development of Christian churches. The pristine character of the New Testament church community was lost.

When we read the Gospels, however, we see that the principles of brotherly community, love, humility, and servanthood are at the very heart of Christ's teaching. Unfortunately, like many of the early Christians, we have been slow to understand these great virtues and especially slow to apply them to church structure and leadership. Because love, humility, and servanthood are pivotal to authentic Christian leadership and the inner life of the Christian community, however, let us briefly survey our Master's teaching on the subject.

Matthew 11:29: Gentle and Humble. Contrasting Himself with the harsh, self-absorbed religious leaders of His day, Jesus called out to the people, "Take my yoke upon you, and learn from Me, for I am gentle and humble in heart." Through this significant statement, Jesus tells us who He is as a person: He is gentle and humble. Too many religious leaders, however, are not gentle nor are they humble. They are controlling and proud. They use people to satisfy their fat egos. But Jesus is refreshingly different. He truly loves people, selflessly serving and giving His life for them. He expects His followers – especially the elders who lead His people – to be humble and gentle like himself.

Mark 9:33-35: Humble Servants of All. On the first recorded occasion when the disciples discussed which of them was the greatest, Jesus, the master teacher, answered their age-old question by means of this now-famous paradoxical statement: "If anyone wants to be first, he shall be the last of all, and servant of all." Here Jesus begins to transform His disciples' thinking about personal greatness. He declares that true greatness is not achieved by striving for prominence over others or by grasping for power, but by exhibiting a humble, self-effacing attitude of service to all – even to the lowliest people.

Charles Colson, who served as Special Counsel to the President of the United States from 1969 to 1973, knows from personal experience the magical enticement of power and high position. He skillfully describes the difference between the worldly view of power and position and the Christian view: "Nothing distinguishes the kingdom of man from the kingdom of God more than their diametrically opposed views of the exercise of power. One seeks to control people, the other to serve people; one promotes self, the other prostrates self; one seeks prestige and position, the other lifts up the lowly and despised."[37]

Colson's wise warning to Christian leaders bears repeating: "Power is like saltwater; the more you drink the thirstier you get. The lure of power can separate the most resolute of Christians from the true nature of Christian leadership, which is service to others. It's difficult to stand on a pedestal and wash the feet of those below."[38]

Mark 10:35-45: Sacrifice, Service, and Suffering. In the most blatant display of selfish ambition and total disregard for the good of their ten colleagues, James and John ask Jesus to give them the two most prominent seats in His kingdom: "Grant that we may sit in Your glory, one on your right, and one on Your left." Their request immediately stirs bad feelings among the other apostles, as selfish ambition always does. Mark records that "the ten began to feel indignant with James and John."

---

[37] Charles Colson, *Kingdoms in Conflict* (Grand Rapids: Zondervan, 1987), p. 274.
[38] Ibid., p. 272.

Contrary to the glory of James and John were seeking for themselves, Jesus calls the Twelve, in verses 38-45, to "sacrifice, service and suffering."[39] John Stott, author and former rector of All Souls' Church in London, insightfully contrasts the attitudes of James and John with those of Jesus who walked the way of the Cross:

> Yet the world (and even the church) is full of Jameses and Johns, go-getters and status-seekers, hungry for honor and prestige, measuring life by achievement, and everlastingly dreaming of success. They are aggressively ambitious for themselves.
>
> This whole mentality is incompatible with the way of the cross. "The Son of Man did not come to be served, but to serve, and to give …." He renounced the power and glory of heaven and humbled himself to be a slave. He gave himself without reserve and without fear, to the despised and neglected sections of the community. His obsession was the glory of God and the good of human beings who bear his image. To promote these, he was willing to endure even the shame of the cross. Now he calls us to follow him, not to seek great things for ourselves, but rather to seek first God's rule and God's righteousness.[40]

Matthew 23:1-12: The Humble Shall Be Exalted. No one understands religious pride like Jesus Christ does. In Matthew 23, Jesus exposes the awful pride, petty selfishness, self-superiority, legalism, and deception of religious hypocrites who love to exalt themselves:

> "And they love the place of honor at banquets, and the chief seats in the synagogues, and respectful greetings in the market places, and being called by men, Rabbi. But do

---

[39] John R. W. Stott, *The Cross of Christ* (Downers Grove: Inter Varsity, 1986), p. 288.
[40] Ibid., pp. 286, 287.

not be called Rabbi; for One is your teacher, and you are all brothers" (Matt. 23:6-8).

"But the greatest among you shall be your servant. And whoever exalts himself shall be humbled; and whoever humbles himself shall be exalted" (Matt. 23:11-12).

The religious leaders about whom Jesus spoke separate and exalted themselves above the people. They sought for themselves special titles, cloths, and treatment – the chief seats among their fellow men. They loved high-profile, public ministry. They loved the limelight and celebrity status. In marked contrast, Jesus prohibited His disciples from using honorific titles, calling one another Rabbi, exalting themselves in any way that would diminish their brotherly relationship, or usurping the unique place that Christ and the Father have over each believer.[41]

---

[41] The modern array of ecclesiastical titles accompanying the names of Christian leaders – reverend, archbishop, cardinal, pope, primate, metropolitan, canon, curate – is completely missing from the New Testament and would have appalled the apostles and early believers. Although both the Greeks and Jews employed a wealth of titles for their political and religious leaders in order to express their power and authority, the early Christians avoided such titles. The early Christians used common and functional terms to describe themselves and their relationships. Some of these terms are "brother," "beloved," "fellow-worker," "laborer," "slave," "servant," "prisoner," "fellow-soldier," and "steward."

Of course there were prophets, teachers, apostles, evangelists, leaders, elders, and deacons within the first churches, but these terms were not used as formal titles for individuals. All Christians are saints, but there were no "Saint John." All are priests, but there was no "Priest Philip." Some are elders, but there is no "Elder Paul." Some are overseers, but there was no "Overseer John." Some are pastors, but there was no "Pastor James." Some are deacons, but there was no "Deacon Peter." Some are apostles, but there was no "Apostle Andrew."

Rather than gaining honor through titles and positions, New Testament believers received honor primarily for their service and work (Acts 15:26; Rom. 16:1, 2, 4, 12; 1 Cor. 16:15, 16, 18; 2 Cor. 8:18; Phil. 2:29, 30; Col. 1:7; 4:12, 13; 1 Thess. 5:12; 1 Tim. 3:1). The early Christians referred to each other by personal names (Timothy, Paul, Titus), the terms "brother" or "sister," or by describing an individual's spiritual character or work:

- Stephen, a man full of faith and of the Holy Spirit (Acts 6:5);

Despite our Lord's repeated teaching on humility, we must concur with Andrew Murray (1828-1917), the beloved writer and missionary statesman from South Africa, that humility is still a neglected virtue among many Christians:

> When I look back on my own religious experience, or on the Church of Christ in the world, I stand amazed at the thought of how little humility is sought after as the distinguishing feature of the discipleship of Jesus. In preaching and living, in the daily activities of the home and social life, in the more special fellowship with Christians, in the direction and performance of work for Christ – how much proof there is that humility is not esteemed the cardinal virtue.[42]

Luke 22:24-27: One Who Serves. As unbelievable as it may sound in light of Christ's clear and repeated teaching, the disciples again argued during the Passover meal as to which one of them was regarded as the greatest (Luke 22:24). Again, we witness our Lord patiently teaching them not to think and act like worldly leaders:

> "The kings of the Gentiles lord it over them; and those who have authority over them are called 'Benefactors.' But not so with you, but let him who is the greatest among you become as the youngest, and the leader as the servant. For who is greater, the one who reclines at the table, or the one who serves? Is it not the one who reclines at the table? But I am among you as the one who serves" (Luke 22:25-27).

- Barnabas, a good man, and full of the Holy Spirit and of faith (Acts 11:24);
- Philip the evangelist (Acts 21:8);
- Greet Mary, who has worked hard for you (Rom. 16:6).

[42] Andrew Murray, *Humility* (Springdale: Whitaker, 1982), p. 7.

Sadly, the same competitive, self-seeking spirit exhibited by the disciples is alive today. Perhaps its most common form is expressed by the question, "Who has the largest church?" David Prior, in his book, *Jesus and Power*, illustrates the carnal striving among churches because of envy and pride over which is bigger and better:

> This rivalry among his disciples was a constant thorn in the side of Jesus. It was endemic in the church at Corinth (cf. 1 Cor. 3:1-15). It is frequently found today among and within large evangelical congregations which strive to be larger, better and more famous than each other. The very size of these congregations often produces an envious attitude among not-so-large churches, and attitude which reveals precisely the same competitive spirit in those churches also. During the last twenty years, I have been a member of four congregations with attendances which happen to have been much higher than most in the neighborhood. Being an Anglican, these four have all been Anglican churches. One of the most difficult obstacles to overcome has been the unholy combination of pride-in-numbers in the local church on the one hand, and envy-at-success in the diocese on the other. Competitiveness is a cancer. Jesus recognized it as completely hostile to the reality of power which he was teaching and demonstrating."[43]

John 13:3-17: Washing One Another's Feet. That same Passover evening when disciples questioned who among them was the greatest, Jesus illustrated the humble, servant role that is so basic to His ministry and to the ministry of those who follow Him. He demonstrated that role by washing His disciples' feet:

---

[43] David Prior, *Jesus and Power* (Downers Grove: InterVarsity Press, 1987), p. 82.

> And so when He had washed their feet, and taken His garments, and reclined at the table again, He said to them, "Do you know what I have done to you? You call Me teacher and Lord; and you are right, for so I am. If I then, the Lord and the Teacher, washed your feet, you ought to wash one another's feet" (John 13:12-14).

Here we see that the symbol of our Lord is the servant's towel, not the cleric's robe. If our beloved Teacher and Lord stooped in love to wash His disciples' feet, then we should gladly stoop to minister to the needs and restoration of our fellow brothers and sisters. Only when we learn what it means to wash one another's feet and clothe ourselves in humility will we have any hope of living together in peace and unity.

John 13: 34-35: Love. The secret to a good eldership team, a healthy church, and all relationships with our brothers and sisters is Christ's new commandment:

> "A new commandment I give to you, that you love one another, even as I have loved you, that you also love one another. By this all men will know that you are My disciples, if you have love for one another" (John 13:34-35).

Thus we are to love one another with the same intensity as Christ loved us.

Three Lessons

Our Lord's repeated instruction on love, humility, and servanthood, teaches us three important lessons. First, God hates pride. In the list of seven sins that God especially hates, pride is at the top (Prov. 6:16-19). Proverbs says, "Everyone who is proud in heart is an abomination to the Lord" (Prov. 16:5a). Those are strong words. The Scripture also says, "When pride comes, then comes dishonor, but with the humble is wisdom" (Prov. 11:2). James echoes a similar thought in his writings: "God is opposed to the proud, but gives grace to the humble" (James 4:6). God hates pride so much that He gave Paul a thorn in the flesh to keep him from exalting himself and to force him to be dependent on his Creator (2 Cor. 12:7-10).

One of the awful things about pride is that it deceives us. We may think we are serving God and others, but in reality we are serving ourselves only. John Stott is certainly right when he says, "Pride is without doubt the chief occupational hazard of the preacher."[44] The proud church leader is an offense to the gospel of Jesus Christ, a prime target for the Devil and – no matter how talented and indispensable he may think himself to be – an unfit leader of God's people.

Second, Christ's persistent teaching on love and humility servanthood demonstrates how difficult it is for people to understand and implement this principle. Pride and selfishness continually strive to dominate and deceive the human heart. Tragically, many Christians are more comfortable with Plato's Republic and its tough-minded, singular leadership style than with Jesus' style of humble-servant leadership. The past two thousand years of Christian history show that we have advanced little in our understanding of Christ's core teaching. Many of the scandalous divisions, ugly power struggles, wounded feelings, and petty jealousies in our churches and personal relationships exist because pride and selfishness motivate much of our thinking and behavior. The church leader who doesn't understand the Christlike spirit of humility, love, and servanthood is doomed to perpetuate fighting and division.

Third, our Lord's repeated teaching shows that humility, servanthood, and love are essential qualities of the Christian Church. They express the mind and disposition of Christ: "Having this attitude in yourselves which was also in Christ Jesus, who ... taking the form of a bond-servant ... humbled Himself" (Phil. 2:5, 7, 8).

---

[44] John R. W. Stott, *Between Two Worlds: The Art of Preaching in the Twentieth Century* (Grand Rapids: Eerdman, 1982), p. 320.

Every local church is to be a servant community that is identified by Christ's love. Thus Christian leaders must be servant leaders, not unholy, worldly big shots.

The Pauline Example of Servant Leadership

If you can't imagine how a strong, gifted leader can also be a loving, humble servant, consider the life of Paul. The once unyielding, proud Pharisee became the loving, gentle servant of Jesus (2 Cor. 10:1). God had gifted Paul with giant intellectual powers and indomitable zeal. He had also given him extraordinary authority. Yet after his conversion, Paul viewed his giftedness and authority as a means of building up and protecting others, not as a means of controlling and gaining prominence or material advantage for himself (2 Cor. 10:8; 2 Cor. 1:24).

Paul's restraint in his use of authority is a remarkable example of his humble, servant spirit. Paul would rather suffer than risk wounding his children in the faith (2 Cor. 1:23-2:4; 13:7). He would rather appeal than command, choosing to deal with people in love and gentleness rather than "with a rod" (1 Cor. 4:21; 2 Cor. 10:1-2; 13:8-10; Gal. 4:20). Although he used his authority and powers when needed to stop false teachers, his patience with erring converts was extraordinary. He is so identified with his converts that their discipline, weakness, and humiliation became his (2 Cor. 11:29; 12:21; Gal. 4:12). He would lower and sacrifice himself so that he might raise others in faith and maturity (2 Cor. 11:7, 21; 13:9). He sacrificed all personal gain and advantage for others (1 Cor. 10:33). In everything, his converts' spiritual welfare was foremost in his mind.

As a humble servant, Paul avoided self-promotion and self-exaltation. He always promoted Christ, never himself: "For we do not preach ourselves but Christ Jesus as Lord, and ourselves as your bond-servants for Jesus sake" (2 Cor. 4:5). Consider the following example of his humble service: Although he lived in Corinth for a year and a half, he never once mentioned to his new converts his extraordinary experiences of being taken up to the third heaven to hear "inexpressible words, which a man is not permitted to speak" (2 Cor. 12:4). He revealed his heavenly experience some four years later only when he was compelled to do so because the proud Corinthians had fallen prey to the boasting of false teachers (2 Cor. 12:1-13). He didn't speak of his heavenly experience prior to that time because he knew the Corinthians would have falsely idolized him. Paul wanted them to exalt Christ, not himself.

The Corinthians' sinful propensity to idolize powerful teachers and form groups around them is addressed in the first four chapters of 1 Corinthians. There Paul says, "So then let no one boast in men" (1 Cor. 3:21a; cf. 4:6, 7). Paul reminds the Corinthians that he and Apollos are servants, not their gods: "What then is Apollos? And what is Paul? Servants through whom you believed even as the Lord gave opportunity to each one. I planted, Apollos watered, but God was causing the growth. So then neither the one who plants not the one who waters is anything, but God who caused the growth" (1 Cor. 3:6-7).

Paul's servant display of his apostolic authority was, however, misunderstood by many Christians, which shows how difficult it is to understand godly humility. Some of them even considered him to be weak and cowardly (1 Cor. 4:18-21; 2 Cor. 10:1-11). But, as the life of Jesus Christ clearly demonstrates, humility is not weakness or cowardliness. Jesus was humble and gentle, yet He taught vast crowds, faced grueling intellectual debate, taught with great authority, and confronted with scorching criticism the hypocritical, religious clerics of His day. In righteous anger, He took a whip and drove the money changers out of the temple. Humility is not a symptom of weakness or incompetence, but of true self-understanding, godly wisdom, and self-control.

The humble servant, Paul, was a strong, brave warrior and leader for Christ. He served God and cared for His people with all his might and zeal. During his life he faced many conflicts, debates, and struggles. The man who could say that he "served the Lord with all lowliness of mind" handed over an impenitent believer to Satan for the destruction of his flesh, struck the false teacher Elymus with blindness, rebuked Peter and Barnabas for their hypocrisy, and stood bravely before Roman courts and judges. Despite the many problems he confronted, Paul consistently responded to his brethren in humility and love. He knew that acting in pride would make things worse and divide God's people. That is one reason why Paul's letters, as well as those of Peter, John and James, are supersaturated with commands concerning love, patience, kindness, prayer, forgiveness, gentleness, and compassion.

Elders as Servant Leaders

Elders are to be servant leaders, not rulers or dictators. God doesn't want His people to be used by petty, self-serving tyrants. Several elders have chosen a life of service on behalf of others. Like the servant Christ, they sacrifice their time and energy for the good of others. Only elders who are loving, humble servants can genuinely manifest the incomparable life of Jesus Christ to their congregations and a watching world.

A group of elders, however, can become a self-serving, autocratic leadership body. Thus Peter, using the same terminology as Jesus, warns the Asian elders against abusive, lordly leadership: "nor yet as lording it over those allotted to your charge, but proving to be examples to the flock" (1 Peter 5:3). With similar concern, Paul reminds the Ephesian elders of his example of humility. In Acts 20:19, he describes his manner of "serving the Lord with all humility" and implies that they, too, must serve the Lord in the same manner. Because of pride's lurking temptation, a new Christian, the Scripture says, should not be an elder: "And not a new convert, lest he become conceited and fall into the condemnation incurred by the devil" (1 Tim. 3:6).

In addition to shepherding others with a servant spirit, the elders must humbly and lovingly relate to one another. They must be able to patiently build consensus, compromise, persuade, listen, handle disagreement, forgive, receive rebuke and correction, confess sin, and appreciate the wisdom and perspective of others – even those with whom they disagree. They must be able to submit to one another, speak kindly and gently to one another, be patient with their fellow colleagues, defer to one another, and speak their minds openly in truth and love. Stronger and more gifted elders must not use their giftedness, as talented people sometimes do, to force their own way by threatening to leave the church and take their followers with them. Such selfishness creates ugly, carnal power struggles that endanger the unity and peace of the entire congregation.

Conflict among elders is a serious, all-too-common problem. It is appalling how little regard some Christian leaders have for the sacredness of the unity of the body of Christ and how quickly they will divide the body in order to get their own way. In the end they may get their own way, but it is not God's way.

The solution to the problem, however, is not to revert to one-man rule or to leave the church. That is the easy way out. The Christian solution is to humble oneself, love as Christ loved, wash one another's feet, repent, submit, pray, turn from pride, shun impatience, and honor and love one another. I firmly believe that if elders were to spend as much time praying for one another as they do complaining about one another that most of their problems and complaints would disappear. That is the kind of eldership God wants the elders to exemplify for His people.

Elders must understand that the agonizing frustrations, problems, and conflicts of pastoral life are the tools God uses to mold them into the image of the Good Shepherd, the Lord Jesus Christ. If they respond to these difficulties in obedience and faith, they will be molded into Christ's image. And few things in life are more thrilling than to know that one is being transformed into a Christlike pastor.

The humble-servant character of the eldership doesn't imply, however, an absence of authority. The New Testament terms that describe the elders' position and work – "God's stewards," "overseers," "shepherd," "leading" – imply authority as well as responsibility. Peter could not have warned the Asian elders against "lording it over those allotted to your charge" if they had no authority. As shepherds of the church (Acts 20:28-31), the key issue is the attitude in which elders exercise that authority.

Following the Christian model, elders must not wield the authority given them in a heavy-handed way. They must not use manipulative tactics, play power games, or be arrogant and aloof. They must never think they are unanswerable to their fellow brethren or to God. Elders must not be authoritarian, which is incompatible with humble servanthood. J.I. Packer, noted author and professor of theology at Regent College in Vancouver, Canada, defines authoritarianism and describes its evils:

> Exercise of authority in its various spheres is not necessarily authoritarian. There is a crucial distinction here. Authoritarianism is authority corrupted, gone to seed. Authoritarianism appears when the submission that is demanded cannot be justified in terms of truth or morality.... Any form of human authority can degenerate in this way. You have authoritarianism in the state when the regime uses power in an unprincipled way to maintain itself. You have it in churches when leaders claim control of their followers' consciences. You have it in academic work at high school, university or seminary when you are required to agree with your professor rather than follow the evidence of truth for yourself. You have it in the family when parents direct or restrict their children unreasonably. Unhappy experiences of authority are usually experiences of degenerate authority, that is, of authoritarianism. That such experiences leave a bad taste and prompt skepticism about authority in all its forms is sad but not surprising.
>
> Authoritarianism is evil, anti-social, anti-human and ultimately anti-God (for self-deifying pride is at its heart), and I have nothing to say in its favor.[45]

---

[45] J.I. Packer, *Freedom and Authority* (Oakland: International Council on Biblical Inerrancy, 1981), p. 8.

When we consider Paul's example and that of our Lord's, we must agree that biblical elders do not dictate, they direct. True elders do not command the consciences of their brethren, but appeal to their brethren to faithfully follow God's Word. Out of love, true elders suffer and bear the brunt of difficult people and problems so that the lambs are not bruised. They bear the misunderstanding and sins of others so that the assembly may live in peace. They lose sleep so that others may rest. They make great personal sacrifices of time and energy for the welfare of others. They see themselves as men under authority. They depend on God for wisdom and help, not on their own power and cleverness. They face the false teachers' fierce attacks. They guard the community's liberty and freedom in Christ so that the saints are encouraged to develop their gifts, to mature, and to serve one another.

In summary, using Paul's great love chapter, we can say that a servant elder "is patient ... is kind, and is not jealous ... [a servant elder] does not brag ... [a servant elder] is not arrogant, does not act unbecomingly ... does not seek [his] ... own ... [a servant elder] is not provoked, does not take into account a wrong suffered, does not rejoice in unrighteousness, but rejoices with the truth; [a servant elder] bears all things, believes all things, hopes all things, endures all things" (1 Cor. 13:4-7).

Discussion Questions:

1. What pagan influences corrupted the early church?
2. In your own words describe Jesus' message to his Apostles and elders for serving? Use Matthew 23:11-12 to answer.
3. Jesus prohibits His disciples from using honorific titles. How then does the New Testament acknowledge their leaders?
4. What are three important lessons Jesus teaches us about love, humility and servanthood?
5. Define humility as it should reflect within an elder's life.

Chapter 13

DISCIPLINED LEADERSHIP

Church discipline is almost unheard of in today's church world. Confronting another church member about his or her sinful lifestyle is not only neglected, the very thought of it is despised by most church members.

It is interesting that the only time Jesus talked directly about the local church was in the context of discipline (Matthew 18:15-20). He seemed to indicate that there would be problems in the church, and that these problems would not go away by themselves. He actually gave a rather specific procedure by which such confrontation was to take place.

What would happen in the natural family without discipline? There would be chaos. Selfishness would be the rule of the day. People would function on the basis of feelings rather than principle. There would be a tendency to only do what had to be done to get by. Sounds a little like some churches!

The church is to be more than a loosely-knit group of followers. It is to be a disciplined army on the march against the powers of darkness. Followers are to become disciples. Disciples are to become warriors. Warriors are to become overcomers.

When Jesus commissioned His followers, He gave them some tall orders. If you examine all of the charges that Jesus gave His followers between His resurrection from the dead and His ascension into heaven, you will find the church's marching orders for all of the church age. Putting all of the verses together, we will arrive at a multifaceted commission. The disciples were to:

- Be witnesses (Acts 1:8)

- Preach the Gospel or evangelize (Mark 16:15-20)

- Preach repentance and remission of sins (Luke 24:27)

- Make disciples (Matthew 28:19-20)

- Baptize the disciples (Matthew 28:19-20)

- Teach the disciples (Matthew 28:19-20)

- Feed the lambs (John 21:15)

- Tend the sheep (John 21:15)

This list is obviously more involved then simply "getting people saved," getting them to tithe, and getting them to attend the services of the church. God's goal is that His people be a disciplined army pressing forward and reclaiming that which the enemy has taken away.

The Foundation for Discipline in the Local Church

The foundation for discipline in the church comes from two important instructions given to us by Jesus Himself. Jesus gave a commission to the church that involves making followers of Christ into "disciplined ones."

> **Matthew 28:19-20** Go therefore and make disciples of all the nations, baptizing them in the name of the Father and of the Son and of the Holy Spirit, teaching them to observe all things that I have commanded you; and lo, I am with you always, even to the end of the age." Amen.

Obviously, if the followers of Jesus are going to be entrusted with the keys of the Kingdom and the awesome responsibility of storming the "gates of Hades," they will have to be a disciplined group. In addition, when Jesus referred specifically to the local church, He gave clear instructions as to how to handle difficulties that arise between members of the church.

> **Matthew 18:15-18** "Moreover if your brother sins against you, go and tell him his fault between you and him alone. If he hears you, you have gained your brother. But if he will not hear, take with you one or two more, that 'by the mouth of two or three witnesses every word may be established.' And if he refuses to hear them, tell it to the church. But if he refuses even to hear the church, let him be to you like a heathen and a tax collector. Assuredly, I say to you, whatever you bind on earth will be bound in heaven, and whatever you loose on earth will be loosed in heaven.

He was implying that accepting Christ as Lord and Savior would not solve everyone's problems for all time, but that the church would need a process by which those who professed to be believers actually lived like believers.

One of the greatest indictments against the church today is that members of the church do not live like true Christians. Some church members have a terrible testimony in the business world. Some church members have as much trouble with lying, immorality, divorce, cheating on the job and covetousness as nonbelievers. As long as there is no difference in the lives of those who profess Christ, the church will be powerless to affect the commands of Christ and fulfill their commission.

Why Discipline is Often Neglected

Discipline in the church is a very neglected aspect of modern day pastoral ministry. It is neglected primarily because of four things: fear, ignorance, lack of true covenantal love for the sheep, and lack of faith on the part of church leaders.

Fear

Church discipline is neglected because of fear of various sorts. The first fear that must be overcome is a fear of confrontation in general. No one enjoys confrontation. It seems that people would rather talk to anyone else about someone's problem than the person who is directly involved. No one likes to tell someone that what they are doing is wrong and that they need to change. We don't like the uneasy feeling that comes with such confrontation. We would rather pray in private, tell someone else or simply "let it go." Jesus was willing to become uncomfortable for our betterment. We must be willing to lay our personal lives and preferences down for others for their betterment as well.

A second fear that will hinder us from our biblical responsibility to exercise discipline and accountability toward another believer is the fear of being unpopular among people. We all have a desire to be liked by others. We can be afraid that if we confront someone regarding an issue in their life, they will hate us forever (2 Chron. 18:7). Every time we speak into someone's life, we run this risk. But we have to be willing to put our relationship on the line for others to save them from themselves. If a person was about to be hit by a speeding car, we would not think of our personal popularity as we pushed them out of danger even if in our exuberance we bruised them in the process. Sometimes people do not appreciate our actions until much later.

A third fear that pastors can have if they discipline a member of the church is the fear the church will become divided or polarized over the discipline. They fear that members of the church will try to defend or take up the cause of the person being disciplined. This is a realistic fear. People tend to be extremely tolerant of certain kinds of sin and often want to extend more grace to people then they really ought to have. People tend to have fewer facts at their disposal, which inhibits their ability to render accurate judgment. Perhaps they feel that if they side with the person being disciplined, it will go better for them if they ever get into a similar situation.

Just like a child in a family can get upset with the parents because they discipline a sibling, members of the church can take up the cause of sinning members. The reality that these things happen does not change the fact that the church needs pastoral care or that parents are responsible to discipline their children. Failure to discipline will not produce spiritual health in people's lives any more than failure to discipline will produce health in the home.

A fourth fear that can hinder the pastor is a fear of reaction outside of the church or in the local community. We do not want to get a reputation for church discipline. It is amazing how many people in a small community can be aware of what is going on in a local church even though they have never attended any of its gatherings. The pastor and leaders of a church are trying to get people interested in the church, not drive them away.

Pastors and leaders need to realize that they already have a reputation in the community. Actually, if pastors and leaders do not discipline their members who are sinning, the message will also reach the community. It is interesting that the unsaved community seems to have a pretty good idea of what a Christian should look like. If they are aware of someone who is openly living in a way that is against the teachings of Christ, they know something is wrong. If the person involved is a member in good standing in a local church and nothing is being done to confront the sin in this person's life, the community knows something is wrong. In such a case the church itself will lose its testimony, and the community will have little or no respect for its leaders.

Finally, pastors and leaders can be hindered by a fear of a lawsuit against them or the local church. There is no question that we are living in a society with litigation frenzy. People are suing for everything imaginable. If we are not careful we will be afraid to do anything because of a potential lawsuit. We hear the horror stories where other local churches have lost thousands of dollars over such suits.

The court systems of our day do not always sympathize with pastors over their biblical mandates, especially when they render judgment concerning things that are not illegal and are openly practiced in society by "consenting adults." The court systems in the days of the early church were not always sympathetic to the commands of Jesus as the disciples preached the Gospel openly. But at some point, for the sake of the higher commission, we must stand and declare with the disciples of Jesus, "We must obey God rather than men" (Acts 4:20-21; 5:29).

Certainly we need to use wisdom in exercising any form of discipline and take all of the appropriate precautions even to the point of consulting legal counsel ourselves, but we cannot cease to do what God has clearly commanded us to do because of the fear of man. We must fear God more than man. If we do not, we will never be able to take the Gospel into a hostile world.

Ignorance

In addition to fear, ignorance can keep us from exercising biblical discipline. We can have ignorance of the necessity of discipline, thinking that if we love God, are sincere as leaders, and pray about it, everything will work out in the end. The sad fact is that is why God gave leaders to the church. Leaders are the answer to such prayers. We are often asking God to do things that He has commanded us to do. We are waiting for Him to act, and He is waiting for us to act.

We assume at times that if we pray hard enough, then God will do the work for us. Unfortunately, in many cases the parties being prayed for are not listening to the Holy Spirit. If they were, they would be ready to return to Him. They are in reality ignoring the Holy Spirit Whom they cannot see, and they need someone that they can see to get in front of them and tell it like it is.

In addition to our ignorance concerning the importance of discipline, we can also dwell in ignorance regarding the practice of discipline in the church. It is possible to grow up in the modern church and never see discipline administered in a godly way. Many times when we have seen discipline administered, it was practiced in an unbiblical way or a vindictive way that did not produce good fruit and did not lead to restoration.

We cannot choose to remain in ignorance because we have had some negative experiences. We must be willing to see the heart of God and be instructed in His ways. Fortunately He has given us clear guidelines for this important area of church life.

Lack of Covenantal Love

Too often we relate to people out of a sense of self-preservation. Pastoral ministry involves a daily laying down of one's life for others. This is the model of Jesus. In order to fulfill the commands of Jesus in the area of discipline, we must have a love for people that goes beyond the positive feelings that they produce in us or what they can do for us personally.

We have to ask God to place His love in us. His love is a covenant love that reaches beyond self interest to a realm that is sacrificial and purposeful in relationship. It is the Lord's covenantal love that motivates Him to discipline His children. It is because He cares so much about us and our future together that He is willing to do whatever it takes to bring us to a place of prosperity (Heb. 12:6-7).

Christ has demonstrated this kind of love in that while we were sinners He set His affections on us. He cared so much for us that He was willing to do whatever it took to see us restored to God.

Lack of Faith

It must be extremely difficult for a farmer who has planted an orchard to go out the first time and prune the trees that he has so faithfully planted, watered, and nurtured into a place of fruit bearing. Will he damage or even kill the tree? It certainly looks like he is attacking it. However, because of what he has been taught in the gardening manual he is willing to take the risk for the sake of the promise of "more fruit."

Discipline is part of the fruit bearing process in people's lives. As pastors and leaders we can neglect it because we do not have the spirit of faith that we need to trust the gardening manual of God's Word. We are afraid that we might kill the tree.

If you have ever seen a fruit tree that is old but has never been pruned, you will fully understand what I am talking about. A tree left to itself will become sickly, and what fruit it does produce will be virtually inedible.

We must have faith as parents that as we follow God's instruction manual in the rearing of our children, they will turn out in a way that will bring glory to God. We must have the same faith in God's instruction manual for building the church. Discipline will not kill the church; it will improve it and bring it into the realms of greater fruitfulness.

Reasons for Church Discipline

Church discipline will help the church to be strong. It counteracts the spirit of lawlessness of our age. It evidences a standard of biblical conviction for living that the Christian is commanded to uphold. It has the potential for bringing about change and growth in the individual's life when nothing else will. It helps the individual member to deal with sin in himself that by himself he has been unable to eliminate. It underscores the value of righteousness as the basis for all relationships in the body.

In addition, it prohibits the leavening influence of sin from gaining a foothold in other members of the congregation. When sin is left to sit in the congregation, others will be tempted to do outwardly what they have only been tempted to do inwardly. When leaders fail to deal with obvious areas of sin in the church, their silence becomes tacit approval of the activity in question.

No Discipline Will Create Problems

Churches that fail to exercise any discipline end up having serious problems over the long term. Without church discipline there is no clear standard of right and wrong among the congregation. Without church discipline sinning members go on sinning, destroying their own potential fruitfulness in God. Without church discipline the spiritual life of the body as a whole becomes greatly weakened, spiritual vitality and life seep out, and a progressive, spiritual stagnation sets in. Without church discipline confidence and respect for the church leadership is lost.

Discipline Involves More Than Excommunication

Often when we talk about the subject of church discipline, it is easy for our minds to go directly to the ultimate form of discipline, that is, excommunication. In reality, excommunication is only a small part of discipline as it relates to the church. In fact if more attention were to be paid to the other issues of discipline, perhaps there would be little or no need for excommunication.

There are many biblical admonitions to leaders regarding how they are to relate to their people in areas of discipline. These admonitions deal more with the regular or daily life of the church. Some of the main words used in this area include reprove, rebuke, admonish, correct, judge, or warn. These have nothing to do with cutting an erring member off from fellowship. They have to do with the ongoing spiritual tune-up that every believer needs from time to time. To some degree every believer has a responsibility to every other believer. Members of the church are to be each other's keepers.

Important Words Used in Connection with Leadership Ministries

Reproving

Paul wrote to Timothy who was the pastor of the church at Ephesus that he was to reprove or convince (Gk, *elenko*) with all authority (2 Tim. 4:2). He gave the same admonition to Titus who was also a pastor (Titus 2:15). The word that he used here literally means "to convict, to expose, to bring to light, to admonish, to correct, to call to account, to show one his fault (demanding an explanation), to chasten, to punish."

This is the same word that Jesus used when he exhorted brothers and sisters in the church who felt that they were sinned against. Jesus instructed them to go to the offending party and show them their fault or demand an explanation (Matt. 18:15). Jesus did not say if someone has offended you, tell everyone else about it including the pastor of the church. He encouraged believers or members of the covenant community to go to the person in private in an attempt to resolve the issue.

Jesus indicated that this kind of reproof was a measure of His love (Rev. 3:19). This kind of reproof is the measure of a true friend (Prov. 27:6). This kind of reproof is part of our responsibility to each other as covenant partners (Luke 3:19; John 3:20; 8:9, 46; 16:8; 1 Cor. 14:24; Eph. 5:11, 13; 1 Tim. 5:20; 2 Tim. 3:16; Tit. 1:9, 13; Heb. 12:5; James 2:9).

Rebuking

A second word that indicates a form of discipline in our relationships in the local church is the word rebuke (Gk. *epitimao*). This word is a little stronger than the word described above. It means "to tax with a fault, rate, chide, reprove, censure severely."

Jesus used this word in respect to our interpersonal relationships. In Luke 17:3 He said, "If your brother sins against you, rebuke him; and if he repents, forgive him." Paul instructed Timothy that this type of activity was part of what leaders do in pastoring a church (2 Timothy 4:2, See also Matt. 12:16; 16:22; 17:18; Luke 9:55; Jude 9).

Admonishing

A third word that is used in the New Testament relating to leaders and their people is the word admonish (Gk. *noutheteo*). This word means "to admonish, warn or exhort." Paul indicated that such warning or admonition was a major part of the function of elders in relation to their pastoral duties (1 Thess. 5:12). Paul tells pastors that they are to warn the unruly (1 Thess. 5:14). He tells leaders to reject those who do not respond to two or three admonitions (Titus 3:10).

Pastors see people all of the time who are living beneath their potential and are doing things that will hurt them in the long run. Often in the counseling ministry, pastors work with people who are resistant to come under the authority of God's Word and change their negative life patterns. Part of the counselor's duty is to warn people of the consequences of such resistance (Acts 20:31; Rom. 15:14; 1 Cor. 4:14; 10:11; Eph. 6:4; Col. 1:28; 3:16).

Correcting

A fourth word that carries within it the concept of discipline is the word correct (Gk. *epanorthosis*). This means "to correct, to restore to an upright state, to raise up again, to reform, to restore, to reestablish" (2 Tim. 3:16).

This word highlights the fact that the purpose of all discipline is to bring about restoration of the believer to God's intended purpose. It also points out the fact that sometimes people need assistance in coming back to an upright position. This is what covenant relationship means. This is how true brothers and sisters respond to each other in the Body of Christ (Gal. 6:1-2). When one of our company falls, we reach out to pick him or her up. We do not shoot our wounded.

Judging

A controversial word that enters into this concept of discipline in the local church is the word judge (Gk. *krino*). How many times, when someone is involved in some sort of confrontation, don't we hear the phrase, "Who are you to judge?" Or we hear people say, "Judge not, least ye be judged!"

Many believers have the concept that in the church we have no right to make judgments when it comes to the behavior of others, because, "No one knows the heart." Nothing can be further from the truth. They are correct when it comes to judging the world or the unbeliever (1 Cor. 5:12-13), because that is the work of the Holy Spirit (John 16:8).

However, when it comes to members of the local church, we are required to make judgments. Leaders especially must do so if they are going to be able to fulfill their responsibilities to their congregations.

The word judge means "to separate, put asunder, to select, to approve, to determine, decree, to judge, to pronounce an opinion concerning right and wrong, to rule, to govern, to preside over with power of giving judicial decisions." Pastors and leaders who refuse to make judgments will face a multitude of problems that will continue to mount up because problems do not just go away by themselves (I Cor. 6:2-31; 14:29).

Key Biblical Verses Concerning Church Discipline

As you read through the pages of the Bible, it is clear that God has a lot to say about the area of discipline. As with most truths in the Bible, there are key passages that deal very specifically with this subject. Let's take a closer look at some of these key texts.

Matthew 18:15-22

These verses give us the only passage where Jesus dealt directly with the local church. It is interesting that Jesus did not have any unrealistic expectations concerning the local assembly. He indicated that there would be problems. He said, "If your brother *sins* against you..." Perhaps we could say *"when* your brother sins against you." If you live with people long enough, offenses will come.

The word Jesus used for "sin" here is the word meaning "to miss the mark." We all have experienced times of weakness where we fail in some area of personal relationship. Thankfully Jesus understood this and gave us guidelines as to how to function in the event that such things happened.

Jesus said that when an offense occurs, the responsibility is on the offended party to go to the offender alone and "show him his fault." The Greek word here is *"elenko,"* which means to bring it out in the open, point out the fault, and perhaps even demand an explanation. Sometimes the problem was simply the result of bad communication. In this case it can be cleared up easily and quickly. In this case perhaps no one else needs to be drawn into it.

Jesus goes on in this passage to give us a process for situations where the results are not so positive. We will discuss this process later because it is so absolutely essential if we are to find success in the area of church discipline. Suffice it to say at this point that the process is gradual, attempts are made to keep the problem as private as possible, and the extent of the discipline is totally dependent upon the response of the person being disciplined.

1 Corinthians 5:1-13

In 1 Corinthians 5, Paul is addressing a serious problem in one of the churches that he personally fathered. He is concerned because a member of the church is living in open sin and no one seems to be too terribly concerned. In fact, it is clear that the people in the church are rather proud of their tolerance and absence of a "judgmental spirit" (vss. 1-2).

Paul lets them know in no uncertain terms that their tolerance is ungodly and that he doesn't have to know all of the details to know that something serious needs to be done both to save this man and to preserve the congregation from further pollution.

Paul gives several specific instructions to the church. They were facing a drastic situation, and it would call for drastic measures (Matt. 5:29). He instructed them that this man should be "taken away from among you" (vs. 2); that they should "deliver such a one to Satan for the destruction of the flesh (vs. 5); that they should "purge out the old leaven" (vs. 7); that they were not to "keep company with sexual immoral people" in the church (vs. 9); that they were "not even to eat with such a person" (vs. 11) and that they were to "put away . . . that wicked person" (vs. 13).

All of this is pretty serious. But Paul's concern is for the rest of the church. He knows that if the church leaders do not take their responsibility to judge those who profess to be believers (vs. 12), and they continue to tolerate sin in the congregation, it will eventually affect other believers (vs. 6-8).

2 Corinthians 2:5-11

Evidently, the leaders of the church "saw the light" and followed through on the discipline that Paul had recommended to them. Paul referred to this discipline in his second letter to the church at Corinth and described this action as "the punishment which was inflicted by the majority" (2 Cor. 2:6). In other words this discipline was an action of the entire church.

Unfortunately, the church that had been so tolerant of sin among them now had gone to the other end of the discipline spectrum. Now, after their discipline had accomplished its intended purpose and the man actually repented, they did not want to receive the disciplined man back into the congregation. Paul had to challenge them now to reaffirm their love to this man (vs. 8). He gave great instructions to them on how to receive someone back into fellowship and how to see them restored. He told them to forgive, comfort, and receive this man back so that Satan would not win in this situation.

It is so typical among God's people. We tend to like extremes. It is so easy for us to swing from one end of the spectrum to the other. We can be all law or all grace. Somehow Jesus was able to be full of grace and full of truth all at the same time. All discipline should be mixed with grace. All grace should be tempered by truth.

Romans 16:17-18

Paul makes it clear in Romans 16 that discipline does not always involve areas of moral impurity or disorderliness. Sometimes discipline may be called for when someone is sowing discord in a local church by the persistent teaching and dissemination of false doctrine. He encouraged the believers in the Roman church to "note those who cause divisions and offenses, contrary to the doctrine which you learned" (vs. 17). He spoke of those who used "smooth words and flattering speech" to deceive individuals who were not grounded in truth.

Paul makes reference to an initial posture toward these people by encouraging people to "note them" and "avoid them" (vs. 17). It is clear, however, from later passages that should people persist in sowing division, it could lead to more severe measures.

2 Thessalonians 3:6-16

Paul seems to be referring to the same kind of scenario when he writes to the believers in Thessalonica. He instructs the church to "withdraw from every brother who walks disorderly and not according to the tradition which he received from us" (vs. 6). Here Paul seems to be talking about issues of lifestyle. He speaks of people who are lazy and refuse to work, who are disorderly in behavior, and who are busybodies (vs. 11).

He goes on to challenge them to use his epistle to bring some adjustment to these people, and if they do not respond, the leaders should "note" them and "not keep company with" them. This is all with the intent that they might be "ashamed" (vs. 14), repent, and change their behavior. The church leaders are cautioned, in this case, not to treat these individuals as enemies but to admonish them as fellow Christians.

1st Timothy 1:20

Paul writes to Timothy about a couple of men by the names of Hymenaeus and Alexander. We do not know too much about the situation of these men. They were most likely leaders who had been discipled by Paul. They seem to have rejected the faith and a good conscience and refused to respond to Paul's personal admonitions. Paul, in a sense, had given up on them to realize that these men would not respond to his leadership in their lives. As a last resort Paul had delivered them to Satan "that they may learn not to blaspheme" (vs. 20).

Just exactly what Paul meant by this is uncertain from this passage alone. Other passages in the New Testament seem to suggest some form of church discipline or excommunication. In any event it is important that whatever this action entailed, it was for the purpose of bringing about change in the lives of the disciplined parties.

Titus 1:10-13

When writing to Titus who was also pastoring a church, Paul makes reference to those who are insubordinate, idle talkers and deceivers who are teaching false doctrine and undermining the work of God. These individuals are evidently using their teaching as a way to gain disciples to themselves and make a living by what they are doing.

Paul indicates that these individuals should be rebuked "sharply" (vs. 13). The word "sharply" used here means "abruptly, curtly, or severely with uncompromising hardness." Paul understood that there were certain individuals who were doing damage to the local church. Paul could be very direct with such people.

The thing to note here is that when it came to the protection of the Bride of Christ, the church, Paul was very motivated. It is one thing when someone has a diverse opinion about something. But when these individuals insist on disseminating their opinions in a way that brings harm to others or leads others astray, they must be stopped. Paul told Titus that sometimes you have to "rebuke with all authority" (Titus 2:15).

Titus 3:10-11

It is necessary that it is in what have been called the "pastoral" epistles of Paul that we find so many admonitions about how to deal with problem people. Sometimes we have the idea that to be "pastoral" is to be conciliatory to everyone so as not to be offensive. The truth is that one of the instruments in the hands of the shepherd was the rod. This rod was used to defend the flock against those who would do harm whether it was from outside the flock or inside the flock (Acts 20:29-30).

Paul warns Titus of "divisive" men. He instructs Titus to warn a divisive person once, then warn him a second time. If he does not respond, have nothing to do with him (vs. 10). Paul indicates that such people who do not respond are "warped and sinning, being self-condemned" (vs. 11).

The Purpose of Discipline and Confrontation

Discipline that takes place in the local church is purposeful. It is never vindictive. It is never self-serving. In fact it takes a lot of courage and love to exercise biblical discipline. The exercise of discipline is redemptive in nature. Yet it is important to see that as leaders we must realize that there is more at stake than the individual that is being disciplined. There are three main concerns that must be kept in balance as discipline is administered. First of all, we must have a deep love for the individual who is at fault. Second, we must do what is best for the entire local church. Third, we must remember that God has some issues in this situation as well.

Discipline as it Relates to the Individual

Discipline has an important place in the life of the members of any family. In the same way, every believer needs some discipline or accountability in his or her life. Discipline in the life of the individual has a nine-fold purpose. For the sake of space I will simply list these with biblical references. Discipline is applied . . .

1. To keep people from going astray (Ps. 119:67; Hosea 7:11-12; Jer. 10:23-24; Prov. 10:17; I Cor. 5:5).

2. To keep people from the calamity of the wicked (Ps. 94:12; 1 Cor. 11:32).

3. To bring people closer to God (Isa. 26:16).

4. To make people wise (Prov. 22:15).

5. To bring people to a place of abundant life (Heb. 12:9).

6. To help people deal with sin and grow in righteousness in areas where they have been personally unsuccessful (Hebrews 12:9-12).

7. To teach people the right ways of God (Ps. 119:71).

8. To produce greater fruitfulness in the lives of people (John 15:2).

9. To restore the repentant believers (Gal. 6:1; 2 Cor. 2:7-10).

Discipline as it Relates to the Local Church

Discipline is not just about the individual who is involved in the problem. It is very much about the rest of the local church as well. It may even have implications to the entire Body of Christ.

For this reason, discipline has a purpose as it relates to the church. I will also simply list these purposes with biblical references. Discipline is applied . . .

1. To bring the church to maturity (Ep. 4:12-16; 1 Cor. 3:1).

2. To deter others from similar sins (1 Tim. 5:20; Titus 3:10).

3. To protect the reputation and witness of the church and its leaders (1 Cor. 5:1).

4. To protect the church from further contamination (1 Cor. 5:6-7).

5. To prove that leaders love and care (2 Cor. 7:12).

6. To affirm each member's responsibility to be his brother's keeper (Heb. 3:13).

7. To cut emotional ties with unrepentant Christians (1 Cor. 5:11).

Discipline as it Relates to God

Discipline in the local church is also very much about God. The local church is not only God's representative to the community, but it has a responsibility to reflect back to God His heart. In other words we have a responsibility to handle the situation at hand the way God would handle it. We cannot be more gracious than God is. We cannot be more tolerant than God is. We must function in a way that is consistent with who God is. Discipline has a purpose as it relates to God. Discipline is applied . . .

1. To affirm the authority of God and His Word in our lives (2 Cor. 2:9).

2. To maintain the honor of God (Rom. 2:24).

3. To maintain the purity of the Scriptures (Titus 1:10-11).

The Kinds of Sins that are to be Disciplined by the Church

It should be obvious by now that discipline takes on many different forms and has many different degrees depending on the severity and scope of the issues involved. Bill Gothard in his advanced seminar described three areas that should lead to discipline by church leaders. Those three categories are as follows:

- Irresolvable disputes between members (Matt. 18:15; 1 Cor. 5:11)

- Persistent teaching of false doctrine (Titus 1:9-11; 3:10-11; Rom. 16:17)

- Continuing immorality and disorderliness (2 Thess. 3:6; 1 Cor. 5:11)

The thing that all of these areas have in common is a persistence on the part of the disciplined person to continue in sin even after the initial confrontation. People who are in the place of discipline are in full control. If they respond to discipline, there will be healing and restoration. If they persist in their sin, there will be further steps of increasing severity.

The Levels of Discipline (Matthew 18:15-20)

In Matthew 18, Jesus describes a process for discipline in the church. While there is some debate over the actual steps and how they should be applied, it is clear that it is God's intention that the church should be a place of unity where conflicts are laid to rest and the power of God can be released.

Private

The first observation that we can make from Jesus' instruction is that privacy is always attempted. In other words, God is not interested in embarrassing anyone. The first step involves believer to believer where the situation can be handled as privately as possible (Note: A possible exception to this is dealing with those in leadership who have been found to be guilty of a sin of disqualification (1 Tim. 5:19-20).

We often miss this step in the process. In general, members of the congregation are reluctant to confront another member whom they see sinning. Unfortunately, as a result, small issues become large issues. Pastors must teach their people that we are a covenant community that shares in a mutual accountability and that we are our brothers' keepers. Most people who are sinning are not doing so in the purview of leaders in the church. When they are around leaders in the church, they are at their best. Often it is the members of the congregation who will first see the problem.

If the people of God would follow Jesus' first step and go to another brother and sister alone, perhaps there would not be as much need for more serious discipline to be applied.

Semi-Private

It is clear, however, that if sinning members of the church will not respond to the gentle admonition of another believer, the situation will progress to another level. Two or three others may have to be brought into the situation. The whole idea is to get others involved to exert more pressure on the erring brother or sister to repent and change.

Who should be brought in at this level? I do not believe that we should grab any three people in the church that we can find to bolster our case. If our goal is restoration, we should seek to include people who have the most power and influence in the life of the erring party. Perhaps we would choose a close friend of the party, a parent, an official church leader, or some other key individual in the person's life. The goal is to get them to do the right thing.

Public

Once the person being disciplined responds in a biblical way, the need for further levels of discipline is eliminated. However, if the erring party refuses to respond at any level, the circle of those involved widens. At this point there is some disagreements as to what is meant by "tell it to the church." It is my view that the next step would be to tell it to the leadership team or the elders of the church. The elders are the official authority of the church, and as such they are responsible for all affairs that affect the well-being of the local assembly.

The elders at this stage may make an official confrontation of the situation. If the person still remains obstinate, a formal declaration of discipline may have to be made, and the entire congregation will have to be brought into the process.

This, of course, is the most severe form of discipline and hopefully will rarely need to be exercised, especially if the other forms of discipline are faithfully administered.

Prerequisites for Effective Church Discipline

Before a local church can begin to discipline at this level, there must exist the proper climate for that discipline. Elders and other church leaders cannot "all of a sudden" step up in this area. Too often pastors and church leaders read books or attend conferences where they are challenged to make some changes or implement some programs. The pastor comes home with great resolve to put into practice all that he has been taught.

Unfortunately, the people in the local church have not read those same books or have been to those same meetings. They do not know what is coming and may resist change because that change has not been properly sown into their hearts.

It can be much like parents who attend a seminar on childrearing and realize they have been inconsistent and have not disciplined their children in a biblical way. They cannot come home and immediately implement all they have received. They must talk to the children, repent of their past negligence, and instruct them regarding how it is going to be in the future. Only then can they proceed on the enlightened path.

The same is true in the local church. If church leaders have been negligent in the areas of church discipline, they need to repent to their congregations, teach and lay the foundation for biblical discipline, and gradually implement the truth at all levels, especially the early levels.

Before pastors and leaders can exercise discipline in the local church, there must be the establishment of a biblical standard in the life of the church. If leaders are not living holy lives, if there are not true biblical standards of right and wrong, it is hypocritical and ultimately arbitrary to discipline issues in the congregation.

Before pastors and leaders can exercise discipline in the local church, leaders must teach the membership concerning discipline. I know that we do not like to preach on the subject of discipline in the church. We are trying to get people to come to our churches, not drive them away. Somehow the subject of discipline does not look good on the church reader board in the front lawn of the facility. However, people must have truth to draw upon if we are to expect right behavior. I heard one pastor say one time that if my people are not responding in the way that I think they should, it is because I have not taught them properly.

Before pastors and leaders can exercise discipline in the local church, the leadership must be willing to set the example in all areas of living. Parents who are violating the law will not have the respect of their children and will lose the moral authority to discipline. The same is true in the local church. Pastors and leaders must lead by example. They must be willing to live by the preached standard, and they must demonstrate that they accept the authority of Christ in their personal lives.

Before pastors and leaders can exercise discipline in the local church, they must be committed to all the levels of confrontation, especially the first level. It is wrong to jump directly to the ultimate level of excommunication when other levels of confrontation have not taken place in a timely manner. In some cases, I think we actually owe our people an apology for not taking our pastoral charge seriously and neglecting to confront them sooner.

Excommunication

Excommunication is the most serious form of discipline in the local church. It is exercised when all else fails. Excommunication is the public removal of a church member from membership and a severing of fellowship with the believing community.

What effectively takes place in excommunication is that when a person refuses to respond to the earthly authorities in their life, they are referred up to the higher authority. God has divested His authority in the local church. If people will not respond to that authority, God will step in Himself.

It is not unlike a woman who is having trouble with her children not responding to her or not submitting to her attempts at discipline. She may say, "Wait until dad gets home!" Of course no dad wants to come home to that situation, but the principle is the same. Jesus is the head of the church. If you don't respond to His ordained leaders, you will answer directly to Him. There is no question that God has a "bigger stick" than church leaders when it comes to discipline.

In excommunication the sinning member is placed outside of the spiritual covering of the church. The sinning member is turned over to God for direct discipline. Since God fully respects the authority of the local church, it is the official action of the church that initiates this ultimate stage of discipline.

When a person is placed outside of the church, they not only come under the direct auspices of God, but the covering or protection that they had previously experienced by being rightly related to authority is removed, exposing them in a fresh way to the attacks of Satan.

People need to know that God cares enough about His people that He will use any means that He can to bring them back. And God has things at His disposal that earthly leaders do not. It is a fearful thing to fall into the hands of the living God.

I heard about one person who was excommunicated by a church for perpetual immorality. He had violated his marriage covenant and was seeing another woman. The day following his public excommunication, he was in a car accident, he lost his job, and a couple of other calamities occurred. He came back to the elders the next day pleading to be restored. He is living in right relationship with his family today. Excommunication works! It does not always work that fast, but it accomplishes what it is intended to. It works especially well if the congregation does its part in the process.

The Congregation's Part in Excommunication

What is the congregation's part in the excommunication process? Actually, the congregation plays a vital role. If they do not cooperate with the discipline, they can undermine and prolong the process. But their cooperation will ensure that the greatest possible pressure is exerted on the offending party.

The congregation has three parts to play in the process. First of all, they are to refuse to fellowship with the sinning member. This withdrawal of fellowship is designed to put pressure on the person and help him to understand what he is losing by persisting in his sin. If the congregation continues to treat the person like everything is normal, it takes the teeth out of the discipline.

I heard of an incident that happened many years ago about a man in a church who was behaving badly toward his wife and family. He was an avid hunter, and many of the people in his church, including some key leaders, enjoyed going hunting with him because he always got his catch. Because of the man's hunting prowess, these leaders tended to overlook his less-than-Christian lifestyle, and the man had little or no motivation to change his behavior.

Finally, one of the leaders realized what they were doing. They were in essence caring more about their hunting than they were about this man and his family. They decided to confront the situation in a different way than they had done in the past. They determined that they would no longer fellowship with this man or hunt with him until he made some significant changes. It worked! The man had also loved to be with these Christian friends. When his friends cut him off, it put the kind of pressure on him that he needed to make some serious changes in his life.

The second responsibility of the congregation is to urge and implore the offending party to repent. The Bible teaches that we are to treat the person like a heathen. This does not mean that we refuse to speak to them. We are friendly, but when we speak to them, we only have one aim in our conversation and that is to implore them to repent. This is not the same as fellowship. This is not the same as hanging out together. This is taking every opportunity to speak truth into the life of the disciplined member, keeping the pressure on them until they do the right thing.

The third responsibility of the congregation is to pray for the disciplined member that they might see the light, repent, and be restored. As you can see, the members of the congregation must be on board with the discipline because they have such a powerful role in its effectiveness. Therefore, it is essential to determine before someone is disciplined whether or not the discipline is for something that is generally considered to be wrong by the congregation.

Restoring the Repentant Member

Ideally, the day will come when all of this pressure produces the desired fruit and the erring member repents and turns his life back to God. When there is sufficient evidence that true repentance has taken place, the Bible makes it clear that this repentance should be cause for great rejoicing. Now is the time for the congregation to do their part to open their arms of comfort to the person, forgive him both privately and publicly, and reaffirm love to this individual (2 Cor. 2:6-8).

The Attitude of a Restorer

Throughout this process, the attitudes of those who are handling the issues of discipline are critical to its overall success. The leaders of the church are not to be judgmental, vindictive, or harsh in their approach to sinning members. On the contrary, the Bible is very clear about the attitudes that must be possessed by those enforcing discipline. These attitudes involve six aspects:

1. The restorer must be motivated by love (Heb. 12:6; Rev. 3:19; Eph. 4:15; 2 Thess. 3:15).

2. The restorer must function with gentleness (1 Thess. 2:1-9; Ps. 141:5).

3. The restorer must have a spirit of meekness, recognizing that except for the grace of God we would all be in trouble (Gal. 6:1-2).

4. The restorer must be ready to extend mercy and forgiveness (2 Cor. 2:6-8).

5. The restorer must have the heart of a father (1 Thess. 2:10-12; 1 Cor. 4:14-16).

6. The restorer must reprove in wisdom (Prov. 25:2).

   Proverbs 25:12 Like an earring of gold and an ornament of fine gold is a wise rebuker to an obedient ear.

Practical Steps of Church Discipline

The following thoughts represent a good, practical process for the leaders of the church.

1. Thoroughly investigate charges (Matt. 18:16; 1 Tim. 5:19; Deut. 13:14; 19:18; Prov. 25:9; 18:13).

2. Work with parents and other authority figures whenever possible.

   a. Parents still have much influence (Deut. 4:9; Prov. 23:22).
   b. Parents can give background information.
   c. Parents should be first to get involved (Eph. 6:1; Deut. 21:20).

3. Prepare the church for public discipline.

   a. In teaching
   b. In prayer, fasting and self-examination (2 Cor. 7:11)
   c. In reminding them of the purpose and place of discipline in the church

4. Inform the church (Matt. 18:17).

   a. Read a prepared and approved (lawyer and leadership) statement. Statement should be brief, factual, and project no malice.

    b. The church should be called to continued prayer for and appeal to the sinning members.
    c. Scriptural love, not avoidance, should be followed.

5. Be ready to restore the person when repentant (2 Cor. 2: 7-11).

Public Announcement

"It has come to the attention of the board that a member of our church must be dealt with by church discipline.

The church board has carefully and thoroughly investigated the facts, and has confirmed that discipline is necessary.

The parents and the board have appealed to the one who has sinned. All attempts have so far been rejected.

Scripture now instructs us to inform the church so that the united prayer and obedience of the members to the scriptural steps of discipline may be used of God to bring this person to repentance and to a life of victory over sin.

Before naming this person we are asking each member to set aside a time of personal self-examination, confession of sin, and commitment to God's instructions of church discipline and restoration.

We are doing this so that Satan will be given no opportunity to bring confusion or division on this matter and that God may be free, because of our obedience, to accomplish His purpose in the life of the one who has sinned."

Conclusions about Discipline

If a church is to grow and prosper from generation to generation, that church must determine to exercise spiritual discipline relative to its membership.

Discipline is an important aspect of the church. Discipline is a demonstration of faithfulness (Ps. 110:75; Prov. 27:5-6). It is for the purpose of restoration and salvation (James 5:19-20; 2 Thess. 3:15). Discipline is a means of instruction (Ps. 94:12). It is designed as a means of grace, not of destruction. Discipline is important for the protection of the rest of the church body. It is gradual and totally dependent on attitude and response of the person being disciplined. Discipline is designed as an evidence of love, not of hate or of fear.

Discussion Questions:

1. What eight verses of scripture give an account of the great commission?
2. What problems do churches have when discipline is neglected?
3. What will keep us from exercising discipline in the church besides fear?
4. Describe what leaders are to do to discipline the church. Name at least four.
5. Pick and comment on a Bible verse that directs the leaders to discipline the church.

Chapter 14

HOW AN ELDERSHIP FUNCTIONS

Let's take a look at some of the foundational criteria that needs to be present for a good functioning eldership.

- **A strong conviction concerning the biblical basis for eldership.** Conviction will carry you through the rough times.

- **A strong conviction that the biblical qualifications for eldership are applicable for the church today (I Tim. 3; Tit. 1).** (See Position Paper on "Qualifications for Spiritual Leadership"). This is the only thing that makes eldership work.

- **There could also be a commitment to wait until these qualities emerge.** Here are some of the qualities that you should look for in a good team member. Is he:

    o Faithful - Behind the scenes – job, husband, father, menial tasks

    o Teachable - Do they receive instruction – are they adjustable?

    o Mature - Are they viewed as standing out?

    o Diligent - Hard workers – not slothful or lazy.

    o Willing.

    o Lover of People.

- o Full of Faith - They should not be overly negative. How are they taking challenges in their personal life?

- o Cooperative – Knowing how to flow with others.

- o Self-motivated – Should not have to jump start them.

- o Gatherer – Do people like to be around them?

- o Loyal to Friends – Should have long-term friendships. Lover of God and His Word - Are they worshippers? Do they exhort from the Word?

- **A commitment to the principle of unity (Acts 1:14; 2:1; 4:23-24, 32-33; see also 1 Cor. 1:10; 3:1-4).** Elders must be of the same mind and judgment – which comes through communication and teaching. You cannot divide the church, if you cannot divide the eldership.

Elder's Governance Process Policies

These Elders' Governance Process Policies have been prepared by the Elders of Master Builder Ministries, in collaboration with Senior Pastor Ronald L. Bernier. The leadership of Master Builder Ministries has always believed that the purpose of church government is to facilitate ministry. That principle is echoed in these policies, which are designed to both instruct and guide individuals entrusted with the responsibility of governing the church.

These policies reflect the best efforts, sincere deliberations and prayerful agreement of the Elders and Senior Pastor. It is our hope and expectation that this remains a living document, based on leadership's continuing sensitivity to the leading of the Holy Spirit.

Perhaps they can serve as a guide for your own ministry.

Master Builder Ministries' Purpose Statement

Our purpose is to establish a community of people who gratefully embrace and faithfully demonstrate the life-changing message of Jesus Christ to impact every area of life. We desire to bless our neighborhoods locally and the specific nations of the world as God directs by planting churches, equipping leaders, assisting the poor, caring for the sick and educating the children. We pursue this by celebrating God's presence (WORSHIP), assimilating God's family (FELLOWSHIP), educating God's people (DISCIPLESHIP), demonstrating God's love (MINISTRY) and communicating God's word (EVANGELISM).

Master Builder Ministries
Elders' Governance Process Policies

Governance Process Policy #1: *Global Governance Purpose*
Intent: **To define the purpose of the Elders**

The Elders of Master Builder Ministries, along with the Senior Pastor, act as a governing body on behalf of the members of the church. We are accountable to God, to the members of Master Builder Ministries, and to one another for our decisions and actions.

Our purpose is:
1) To ensure that the church's purpose is consistently affirmed and effectively accomplished.
2) To facilitate and support the ministries of the church with the appropriate use of resources.
3) To ensure that the church develops and maintains a healthy balance among its core values (Worship, Fellowship, Discipleship, Ministry and Evangelism).
4) To develop and administer church policies that address issues concerning moral behavior, discipline and other matters related to church health.

5) To avoid engaging the church in unacceptable situations or actions that would detract from or subvert its mission, local vision or direction.

Governance Process Policy #1a: *Global Governance Purpose – Church*
Intent: **To define the role of the Elders in relation to the church**

The Elders of Master Builder Ministries are responsible for:

1) Ensuring that those functions of Elders explicitly defined in the New Testament are fulfilled, including:
   a. Examining matters that are brought before them and providing counsel and direction *(Acts 15:6)*.
   b. Seeing that the people of the church are properly cared for and taught
      (I Timothy 3:1-7)
   c. Praying for the sick *(James 5:14)*.
   d. Leading by example *(I Peter 5:3)*.

The Elders, along with the Senior Pastor, are responsible for:

1) Developing and implementing assessment tools to ensure church health and balance.
2) Ensuring that the church's resources are aligned with its purpose.
3) Developing and enforcing policies that define acceptable/non-acceptable practices for church members.
4) Developing and enforcing policies that define a discipline process for church members.
5) Calling Membership Meetings.

Governance Process Policy #1b: *Global Governance Purpose -- Staff*
Intent: **To define the role of the Elders in relation to the church staff**

The Elders of Master Builder Ministries will interact with the church staff according to the following guidelines:

1. The Senior Pastor is the only member of the church staff who has a direct reporting relationship with the Elders.
    a. The Senior Pastor deliberates with the Elders on all issues (except those related to the Elders' direct oversight of the Senior Pastor, i.e. evaluation, etc.) and is a voting board member
2. No reporting relationship exists between any individual Elder or the Elders' board and any other member of the church staff.
3. Any concerns, questions, etc. the Elders have about a staff member shall be addressed to the Senior Pastor.
4. The focus and purpose of any communications between the Elders and church staff members shall be to encourage and support the Staff and to provide a discerning ear for their questions and concerns.

Governance Process Policy #1c: *Global Governance Purpose – Calling Membership Meetings*
Intent: **To define the purpose of meetings of members of the church**

The Elders of Master Builder Ministries are responsible for setting the date and calling the Annual Meeting of members of the church. The Elders will establish the agendas for and preside over all Annual Meetings of the members.

Every registered member of Master Builder Ministries will receive notice about the Annual Meeting.

Agenda items for the Annual Meeting will include, but is not limited to:
   1) Recognition and affirmation of all Elders.

2) Affirmation by the Elders of the church's purpose and goals for the year.
3) Affirmation by the Elders of the leadership of the Senior Pastor.
4) A financial status report.

The Elders also may call special meetings, as needed. Every registered member of Master Builder Ministries will receive notice about any special meeting called. The Elders will establish the agendas for and preside over all special meetings of the members.

Governance Process Policy #2: *Governing Style*
Intent: **To define the governance culture of the Elders**

The Elders of Master Builder Ministries will govern with a commitment to:

1) Reflect Biblical principles in words and actions.
2) Discern and follow the leading of the Holy Spirit.
3) Model humility, integrity, faith and unity.
4) Deliberate in many voices but speak with one voice.
5) Support and affirm the Senior Pastor.
6) Actively seek new ideas and best practices in governance and leadership, and to be open to learning from others.
7) Maintain an awareness of and sensitivity to the needs of the "silent" – the unchurched.
8) To foster church health and growth by aligning people to God's purpose and leading them from:
    a. The community (indifferent/non-religious)
    b. To the crowd (connected and/or occasional attendees).
    c. To the congregation (members and/or regular attendees).
    d. To the committed (members and ministry participants).

e. To the core (committed members/leading in ministry).

Governance Process Policy #2a: *Governing Style -- Meetings*
Intent: **To define how the Elders will conduct meetings**

The Elders of Master Builder Ministries will conduct their meetings guided by the following principles:

1) Dependent upon God's grace and the wisdom of the Holy Spirit, we will always incorporate prayer as a vital part of our meetings.
2) Discussions will be characterized by mutually respectful attitudes and language.
3) We will actively seek to discern truth in any matter that comes before us.
4) We may deliberate with many viewpoints, but will work to achieve agreement on all matters.
5) No individual's role or opinion is more important than that of any other. All are co-equal in service, governance, and deliberation.
6) We may request input from individuals who have particular expertise on any matter we are deliberating.
7) All matters discussed will be considered strictly confidential. By agreement, a decision on any matter may be communicated to individuals or to the church.

Governance Process Policy #2b: *Governing Style – Achieving Agreement*
Intent: **To define how the Elders will reach agreement for their decisions**

The Elders of Master Builder Ministries will deliberate with many voices and viewpoints, but will work to achieve agreement on all matters and ultimately speak with one voice. This is particularly important when a decision will have significant impact, such as in a policy or practice area.

In reaching agreement, the Elders and Senior Pastor are guided by the following principles:

1) We believe a leading from God will be characterized by unity in the Spirit.
2) We believe we should discern God's leading as a group.
3) We believe a leading from God will not contradict Scripture or policies.

If agreement is not initially reached on an issue, the following process will be used:

1) Any decision/action will be postponed until there has been sufficient time for further prayer, reflection, and discussion.
2) We will re-visit the issue, again seeking unity.
3) The steps of prayer, reflection and discussion will be continued until it is clear that agreement can or cannot be reached.

If full agreement cannot be reached, the matter will be decided by no less than a ¾ majority vote of all the Elders.

Statements made by any Elder after a decision shall reflect the agreement reached.

Governance Process Policy #2c: *Governing Style* – Role of the Facilitator of the Elders' Board
Intent: **To define the role of the Facilitator of the Elders' Board**

The Facilitator of the Elders' Board will be selected annually by vote of the Elders at their first meeting immediately following the appointment of new Elders and prior to the Annual Meeting of members.

The Facilitator's role is an administrative function only. The position does not confer any privileges that are not available to all Elders.

The Facilitator will:
1) Schedule Elders' meetings.
2) Set agendas for Elders' meetings.
3) Moderate Elders' meetings.
4) Make ministry assignments to the Elders.
5) Serve as the Elders' liaison with the Senior Pastor.
6) Schedule the Elders' annual planning retreat.
7) Moderate the Annual Meeting and special meetings of members

Governance Process Policy #3: *Elders' Job Description*
Intent: **To define the specific ways in which the Elders will accomplish the purpose of governance and perform their "job"**

The Elders' and Senior Pastor's governance purpose will be accomplished by developing and adhering to the following four interdependent sets of governing policies:

1) *Elder Process Policies* – these policies shall describe how the Elders self-administrate and create policy.
2) *Elder to Pastor Relationship Policies* – these policies shall describe how the Elders and the Senior Pastor interact/interface together. These policies shall define the relationship between the Elders and Senior Pastor, as well as a methodology by which the following can be consistently and reliably achieved: open two-way communication, project/problem initiation and resolution, Elder policy administration and Senior Pastor evaluation.
3) *Pastor Requirement Policies* – these policies shall tell the Senior Pastor what must be done to fulfill the church's

purpose. This may include specific requirements relating to each of the church's core values

4) *Senior Pastor Restriction Policies* – these policies shall directly inform the Senior Pastor what practices, methods, and procedures cannot be engaged in to accomplish the church's mission, caring for people, overseeing funds, providing for the staff, moral standings, etc.

These policies shall form the essence or total set of governing policies and shall establish the parameters within which the Elders and the Senior Pastor will accomplish their role of governance in the church.

The Elders shall perform their "job" by overseeing the whole of the church in the following three broad areas:

1. *Affirming Church Direction* – as the Senior Pastor and staff develop plans, budgets, programs, and directions, these broad-scale initiatives shall be presented to the Elders for affirmation and/or counsel. The Elders may give counsel, incorporate the initiative into Elder policies or reject the initiative, as may be appropriate, given its policy responsibilities.

2. *Establishing Firm Foundations* – certain global issues extend beyond the scope of Elder policy administration and beyond the authority of the Senior Pastor and require the articulation of a "church" position. The Elders and Senior Pastor shall judiciously select which issues are to be studied and develop a "position paper" or "white paper" to articulate the church's position on the specific global issue in question.

3. *Overseeing Church Health* – the Elders shall oversee church health by ensuring that the church is consistently creating health and restoring health in its members. This shall require

the Elders to effectively address any issues that may adversely impact the health of the church.

    a. *Creating Health*: the Elders shall pursue answers to the following questions in this area: Is the culture healthy (caring and loving)? Is the teaching effective and balanced (addressing all five core values)? Are the programs serving the needs of the church and the community? Are the finances of the church being utilized in a way that serves the development and ministries of the church? Are budget expectations/forecasts realistic and on target? Etc.

    b. *Restoring Health*: the Elders shall pursue answers to the following questions in this area: is there a problem that needs addressing? Is church discipline required? Do adjustments need to be made to church finances? Etc.

Governance Process Policy #3a: *Elders' Job Description – Qualifications*
Intent: **To define the qualifications an individual must have to serve as an Elder**

To serve as an Elder of Master Builder Ministries, an individual must meet the qualifications outlined for elders in the New Testament (the books of Timothy and Titus). See also position paper on "Spiritual Qualifications of Ministry."

In addition, he must:

1) Be an active member of Master Builder Ministries for a minimum of three years.
2) Be at least 30 years old.
3) Demonstrate a clear understanding of and support for the church's purpose.

4) Demonstrate competence in leadership/service in ministry to the church.
5) Work as a "team player," able to relate effectively with other Elders and the Senior Pastor.
6) Be intelligent, communicative, assertive, and mentally and emotionally healthy.
7) Model character that is honest, humble, teachable, patient and reliable.
8) Be recognized as one who is able to discern, provide wise counsel, share knowledge and expertise.
9) Demonstrate a commitment to spiritual disciplines.

Governance Process Policy #3b: *Elders' Job Description – Selection/Appointment Process*
Intent: **To define how Elders are selected and appointed, and the term of service in the office**

Master Builder Ministries will have 3-8 Elders in office at any given time. The Elders and the Senior Pastor will determine the number serving, based on the needs of the Church.

The term an Elder is to serve is implicit in the church's perspective that the Eldership is to be a long-term, unified, maturing, inspiring, and stable governing body to the church. To that end, Elders serve without a term limit. However, Master Builder Ministries does not believe that eldership is a lifetime commitment or responsibility.

Using the qualifications outlined in Governance Process Policy #3a and their discernment, the Elders will, as needed, invite selected candidates to consider appointment to the Eldership. Any individual so invited must have the unanimous consent of all existing Elders.

The Senior Pastor will serve as an Elder.

Prior to new appointments, the Elders will send a letter to Church members with the names of all new candidates. Church members will have 30 days to submit confidential comments about any candidate; any comments received will be evaluated by the Elders.

All new and continuing Elders will be presented to the Church at the Annual Meeting of members for recognition and affirmation.

Once, selected, Elders will serve with an annually renewable term. Near the end of each one-year term, every Elder will complete a self-evaluation and will be evaluated by all other Elders. The evaluation process is designed to determine if each Elder believes that he is called to continue to serve in the office and maintains a full commitment to the Church's purpose.

Appointments to the Eldership are continued with the unanimous consent of all other Elders.

Should any Elder object to the re-appointment of an individual, a cause discussion shall ensue. If resolution cannot be reached, such an appointment will be made only if a majority of the Elders believe the cause is without merit.

If the above action takes place and the Elder's appointment is continued with less than a unanimous vote, this shall be considered to be a significant breach in the unity of the Elders. The Elders shall then make the restoration of unity their highest priority using all the tools available to them through these Governance Policies.

Any Elder may relinquish the position at any time for personal reasons, or at the unanimous request of the other Elders.

Governance Process Policy #3c: *Elders' Job Description – Reappointment*
Intent: **To define how Elders may resign from office**

Any Elder may relinquish the position at any time for personal reasons.

An Elder (with the exception of the Senior Pastor) who accepts a position on the church staff will be required to resign from the Eldership prior to the effective date of the staff appointment. The appropriate period of time to pass between the resignation and the staff appointment will be determined by the Senior Pastor in consultation with the Elders. If the former Elder subsequently leaves the staff position, reappointment to the office of Elder is not automatic.

Regardless of the reason for any Elder's resignation, the reappointment of any former Elder must follow the selection/appointment process described in Governance Process Policy #3b.

Governance Process Policy #3d: "Once and Elder, Always an Elder"
Intent: **To define the concept of "Once an Elder, Always an Elder"**

Master Builder Ministries does not believe that the role of Elder requires a lifetime commitment or responsibility to be active in that church government office. However, we recognize that once an individual has been appointed to and served in that office, he gains a unique understanding of and sensitivity to the life of the church that is likely to endure long after the term of office has passed.

We hold all who have served in the office of Elder in the highest regard for their gifting and commitment to serve the church, and recognize these individuals may provide valuable insights, observations, and discernment.

By unanimous consent, the Elders may choose to share information about specific and critical church government matters with former Elders, soliciting their prayers and any other assistance deemed necessary.

Governance Process Policy #3e: *Elders' Appointment of Treasurer*
Intent: **To define the appointment, role, and responsibilities of the Treasurer**

The church regards money as a gift from God and His people. The financial objective of the church is to raise and use money to develop and fulfill the church's purpose and to keep the church moving toward its strategic goals.

The Elders, in consultation with the Senior Pastor, shall appoint a Treasurer.
The Treasurer serves a three-year renewable term with no term limits.

The Treasurer shall be a volunteer and member of the church. The Treasurer shall serve as a member of the Board of Directors. The Treasurer shall not be an Elder. The Treasurer shall have skills associated with financial management, accounting and be an effective communicator.

The Treasurer shall work on behalf of the members of the church and serves the Elders as an internal auditor and advisor. The Treasurer shall act as an advocate for church health by insuring the church's financial integrity.

The Treasurer shall have full and free access to all financial records and receipts of the church. The Treasurer shall receive a full explanation of financial policies and procedures upon request.

The Treasurer may bring any matter of financial concern to the Elders or the Board of Directors without the consent of the Senior Pastor. The Senior Pastor may bring concerns about the Treasurer to the Board of Directors or the Elders without the consent of the Treasurer.

The Treasurer in serving the Elders:

1) Reviews the budget and receives regular financial reports to review for fiscal soundness and consistency with the church's financial goals.
2) Advises the Elders of both strategic opportunities to improve the church's overall financial position as well as potential financial pitfalls that may endanger the church's health.
3) Ensures that policies and procedures are in place that will maintain the church's financial integrity.
4) Responds to members who request information regarding the church's finances and signs the annual statements issued to donors.
5) As appropriate, develops relationships with financial institutions, firms and agencies as a key representative of the church.
6) Insures that the church's financial records are submitted to an independent CPA for annual review, or as further directed by the board of directors.
7) With the consent of the Elders can develop assistants as necessary to fulfill this job description.
8) Participates as a member of the Board of Directors in any actions requiring Board action as defined in the By-laws.

The Treasurer may be removed for any reason by a ¾ majority vote of the Elders.

Governance Process Policy #4: *Senior Pastor*
Intent: **To define the role of the Senior Pastor**

The Elders delegate the authority, leadership, management function, and accountability necessary for the operation of the church to the Senior Pastor.

The Senior Pastor is accountable to God, to the Elders, and to the membership of the church for achieving the church's purpose.

The Elders will set appropriate limitations policies for the Senior Pastor that will serve as the ethical and practical boundaries within which he may exercise judgment when determining operating practices, methods, and personal and professional conduct.
Only those decisions made by the Elders as a body are binding upon the Senior Pastor.

The Senior Pastor is authorized to use reasonable interpretations of the church's purpose and within the parameters of the limitations policies, to make decisions, take action, establish practices and develop activities.

The Elders will support the Senior Pastor's continuing personal and professional development by encouraging mutually productive relationships with peers in healthy local churches, as well as providing opportunities for the Senior Pastor to seek out new ideas and best practices from within and outside of the church.

The Elders will evaluate the performance of the Senior Pastor on an annual basis, according to the guidelines of the performance evaluation policy.

Governance Process Policy #4a: *Senior Pastor -- Elders*
Intent: **To define the role of the Elders in relation to the Senior Pastor**

The Elders of Master Builder Ministries are responsible for:

1) Developing and administering the process for the recruitment and selection of the Senior Pastor.
2) Developing the executive limitations policies for the Senior Pastor.
3) Providing on-going support and affirmation of the leadership and vision of the Senior Pastor.
4) Conducting an annual evaluation of the Senior Pastor.

5) Approving the total compensation package for the Senior Pastor.
6) Disciplining and/or dismissing the Senior Pastor.

Governance Process Policy #4b: *Senior Pastor – Limitations*
Intent: **To define the appropriate ethical boundaries for the decisions and actions of the Senior Pastor**

The Senior Pastor is the most recognizable public representative of the church; much of the church's image and credibility depends upon the personal and professional conduct demonstrated by the Senior Pastor in public and private interactions. The professional and personal conduct of the Senior Pastor must meet the Bible's highest ethical and moral standards.

The Senior Pastor must ensure that:

1) The church's purpose is continually advanced with integrity.
2) The church's core vales are maintained and promoted in a healthy, balanced way.
3) The resources and assets of the church are not unnecessarily risked, inadequately maintained, or used in any improper way.
4) All funds distributed or used meet the requirements of the auditing standards of the church, as established by the Elders.
5) Staff members are treated in a fair, respectful and ethical manner.
6) The Elders are kept informed about major developments which may affect the church.

Governance Process Policy #4c: *Senior Pastor – Ends Policy*
Intent: **To define the ends policies to be achieved by the Senior Pastor**

The Senior Pastor is the primary ministry leader of the church and reports to the Elders. In this role, he develops, oversees, and directs the church's spiritual development, ministries, and resources. He leads the church to fulfill its mission and realize its purpose. He is the shepherd of the flock and its principle teacher.

To accomplish these responsibilities the Senior Pastor:

1. Develops a balanced approach and ministry program for developing and implementing the five core values within the church, with the goal of enabling members to live the core values in their own lives.
2. Develops and implements an annual ministry plan that demonstrates direction and understanding of the following framework for ministry:
    a. **Ideal** – a long-term perspective reflecting the full implementation of the church's vision. What are the ideals we are moving toward?
    b. **Actual** – an assessment on the current state of the church and the community. What is actually happening today both within and outside of the church?
    c. **Real** – a one-year look at what steps need to be taken so that the church will move closer to the Ideal. What is achievable and necessary in the next year to move the church a step closer to the Ideal?
3. Develops a budget in support of the annual ministry plan (with consideration given to the Ideal) and oversees its implementation.
4. Develops and participates in relationships with ministry leaders and thought leaders outside of Master Builder Ministries to enable the church to remain culturally relevant to those in the community the church is called to reach and the members it is called to serve.

Governance Process Policy #4d: *Senior Pastor – Performance Evaluation Process*

Intent: **To define the performance evaluation process for the Senior Pastor**

The Senior Pastor will be evaluated annually to determine how effectively he has led the church in executing purpose, as well as the progress that has been made in aligning the church with its core values.

This performance evaluation will include an assessment of how effectively the Senior Pastor has advanced the ends policies, including an assessment of how he has:

1) Managed the church's human and financial/physical resources.
2) Developed productive relationships with staff.
3) Fostered growth in church membership.
4) Increased member participation in the purpose of the church.

Governance Process Policy #4e: *Financial Consultants to the Senior Pastor*

Intent: **To define how the Senior Pastor may use financial consultants**

The church regards money as a gift from God and His people. The financial objective of the church is to raise and use money to develop and fulfill the church's purpose and to keep the church moving toward its strategic goals.

The Senior Pastor, in consultation with the Elders, may seek counsel on any financial matter where he believes that the expertise and advice of skilled financial consultants (volunteer or compensated) will help maximize church resources to fulfill the church's purpose. In no case, however, is the Senior Pastor able to abdicate his responsibility before the Elders for the financial solvency and effectiveness of the church.

The following areas outline some, but not all, of the ways in which the Senior Pastor may use the services and counsel of financial consultants:

1) To review the budget for fiscal soundness and consistency with the church's financial goals.
2) For evaluation and advice on strategies and tactics to fulfill the church's ministry plan through effective financial planning and management.
3) To assist in:
   a. staff salary determination and execution
   b. input to the development of procedures and policies
   c. approaches to accounting practices
   d. collection of offerings, fund raising, etc.
4) To develop relationships with potential and actual "key donors" to build and maintain their confidence in the church's ministry plans, financial practices, and operating effectiveness.

Governance Process Policy #5: *Board of Directors*
Intent: **To define the purpose of the Board of Directors**

The Board of Directors shall function to ensure that the legal and financial responsibilities and obligations of the church are met with integrity.

The Board of Directors shall consist of the Elders, the Senior Pastor and Treasurer.

The Board of Directors shall operate under the authority of the Corporation's By-Laws.

The Board of Directors shall have no authority to reverse, modify, or adapt any provisions that have been expressly granted to the Elders or to the Senior Pastor in the Elders' Governance Process Policies.

The Elders shall not be able to supercede the Board of Directors in matters of legal and financial responsibility or obligation.

The Board of Directors shall meet annually and at other times as necessary, according to the provisions established in the By-Laws.

Discussion Questions:

1. What are four qualities that should be looked for in a good team member?
2. Fill in the blank; "You cannot divide the church, if you cannot divide the _____."
3. What five things are pursued in the Master Builder Ministries' Purpose Statement?
4. In your own estimation what is the most important purpose of the Elders?
5. Name the four agenda items for the Annual Meeting that elders preside over for the members.

Chapter 15

APPOINTMENT OF ELDERS

Acts 14:23 *"So when they had appointed elders in every church, and prayed with fasting, they commended them to the Lord in whom they had believed."*

According to 1 Timothy 3:1 and Titus 1:7, a local church should have overseers. By definition, overseers supervise the activities of the church. In 1 Timothy 5:17, the elders are the ones who "rule" the local church. The word "rule" is the Greek word *prohistemi*, which means lead, manage, or direct. So in vitally important matters such as selecting, examining, approving, and installing prospective elders or deacons, the overseers should direct the entire process. (In all New Testament cases of initial elder or deacon appointment, the apostles or an apostolic delegate initiated and supervised the appointment process. See Acts 6:1-6; 14:24; Titus 1:5.) If the elders do not oversee the appointment process, disorder and mismanagement will ensue, and people will be hurt. Moreover, if the elders do not take the initiative, the process will stagnate. The elders have the authority, position, and knowledge to move the whole church to action. They know its needs, and they know its people. So they can, intentionally or not, stifle or encourage the development of new elders. The reason some churches can't find new elders is that no one is really looking for them.

Although the New Testament provides no example of elders appointing elders, perpetuation of the eldership is implied in the elders' role as congregational shepherds, stewards, and overseers. Perpetuating the eldership is a major aspect of church leadership responsibility. It is absolutely vital to the ongoing life of the church that the leaders recognize the Spirit-given desire of others to shepherd the flock.

For this reason, a good eldership will be praying and looking for capable men to join them and will be conscientiously training and preparing men for future leadership. What Paul told Timothy applies to the eldership: And the things which you have heard from me in the presence of many witnesses, these entrust to faithful men, who will be able to teach others also" (2 Tim. 2:2). Ideally, long before the church examines a prospective elder, he will have prepared himself and been trained by the elders and watched by the congregation. When this has occurred, the process of examining and approving the candidate moves quickly and in an orderly fashion.

Elements in the Appointment Process: Desire, Qualification, Selection, Examination, Installation, and Prayer

It is commonly thought that Acts 6:1-6 provides the model for all the stages in the process of appointing deacons or elders. Acts 6, however, is the account of the original establishment of the seven; it doesn't tell us how the group perpetuated itself, assuming it continued to exist after the great persecution of Acts 8. If the group did continue to function (and the need for it certainly didn't disappear), did the seven ask the congregation to select new members and have the apostles lay hands on them, or did they simply replace themselves? Was the group always required to have seven members, or could there be six or ten? Was there a fixed time each year when the church selected new replacements for the seven? We don't know the answers to these questions, and the same is true concerning the elders. Even if, in Acts 14:23, Paul and Barnabas followed the model of Acts 6, we still don't know exactly how the Galatian elders perpetuated themselves after the apostles left.

The New Testament says very little concerning such detailed procedures as appointing elders. In the same way, the New Testament is amazingly silent regarding specific procedures for administering the Lord's Supper and baptism. Exact procedures for these activities are left to the discretion of the local church. Even under the Mosaic Law, which prescribed detailed regulations, for every area of life, matters such as the appointment and organization of elders were left to the people's discretion. God expects His saints to use the creativity and wisdom He has given to organize all such matters within the revealed guidelines of His Word. He expects His people to do so in a way that exemplifies the gospel's truth and the true nature of the Church. I concur with Neil Summerton, who captures the biblical spirit when he writes:

> It is characteristic of Technological Man of the twentieth century to worry abnormally about the precise mechanism of selection. But biblically of much greater importance is its manner and spirit. Be we ever so precise about the *modus operandi,* it will be of no avail if the mechanism still succeeds in choosing the wrong people. For this reason it may not matter much whether selection of elders is by church planters, the existing elders, or the congregation as a whole, so long as all are certain that the outcome is the choice of God.

Although the New Testament doesn't provide a blueprint for the process of elder appointment, it specifies certain key elements. Let us consider the elements of desire, qualifications, selection, examination, installation, and prayer.

PERSONAL DESIRE

The Bible says, "If any man aspires to the office of overseer (eldership), it is a fine work he desires to do" (1 Tim. 3:1b). The first matter to consider in appointing elders is the candidate's personal desire. The desire to be an elder is not sinful or self-promoting, if it is generated by God's Spirit. Paul reminded the Ephesian elders that it was the Holy Spirit who had placed them in the church as elders (Acts 20:28). This means, among other things, that the Holy Spirit planted in the hearts of the elders the desire and motivation to be shepherd elders. In a similar way, Peter addresses the need for an elder to shepherd God's flock with a willing heart (1 Peter 5:2). So the starting point is a Spirit-given desire to be a shepherd of God's people.

A Spirit-given desire for pastoral eldership will naturally demonstrate itself in action. It cannot be held in. A man who desires to be a shepherd elder will let others know of his desire. That is one way in which the congregation and elders can know of a prospective elder. The knowledge of this desire will prompt the elders to pray and to encourage such desire through appropriate training and leadership development. More important, the person with a Spirit-created motivation for the work of eldership will devote much time, thought, and energy to caring for people and studying the Scriptures. There is no such thing as a Spirit-given desire for eldership without the corresponding evidence of sacrificial, loving service and love for God's Word. Eldership is a strenuous task, not just another position on a decision-making board. In fact, the stronger a man's desire for eldership, the stronger will be his leadership and love for people and the Word.

So before a man is appointed to eldership, he is already proving himself by leading, teaching, and bearing responsibility in the church. In 1 Thessalonians 5:12, Paul reminds the congregation of its responsibility to acknowledge and recognize those in the congregation who work hard at leading and instructing others: "But we request of you, brethren, that you appreciate those who diligently labor among you, and have charge over you in the Lord and give you instruction." One way the congregation and elders acknowledge a man's diligent labors is to recommend and encourage him to prepare for eldership. So it ought to be clearly known in the church that "if any man aspires to the office of overseer, it is a fine work he desires to do."

MORAL AND SPIRITUAL QUALIFICATIONS

The New Testament is positively emphatic that only morally and spiritually qualified men can serve as elders. So, in addition to his subjective desire to be a shepherd elder, Scripture demands that a candidate for eldership meet certain objective qualifications (1 Tim. 3:1-7; Titus 1:5-9). Since we have previously explored in detail the biblical qualifications for elders, I refer you back to *"Qualification for Spiritual Leadership: Expanding on the Qualifications Delineated in the Constitution of Master Builder Ministries, a New Testament Church"* in the appendix at the back of this book.

SELECTION AND EXAMINATION

The actual selection of elders can be done by the congregation, especially in the case of a new church (Acts 6:3), or it can be done by the existing elders, or by a combination of both.

Exactly how the congregation in Jerusalem selected seven of its men for the task of distributing funds to its widows is not explained (Acts 6:3). It would not have been difficult for the congregation to organize itself for such selection, however. From its earliest days, the nation of Israel was organized into precisely defined, manageable groups for the purpose of expediting communication, war, service, and travel (Ex. 13:18; 18:13-27; 36:6; Num. 2:2 ff; 7:2; 1 Kings 4:7). Congregational decisions and operations were conducted primarily through representatives or heads of clans and towns (compare Lev. 4:13 with 4:15; Ex. 3:15, 16; compare Ex. 4:29 with 4:31; Ex. 19:7, 8; Deut. 21:1, 2, 6-9). So it is possible that the Jewish congregation in Jerusalem was already organized into manageable units (Acts 12:12, 17; 15:4, 6, 22; 21:17, 18). Such organization would enable issues to be decided and information to be passed along quickly. We should not conclude that this account proves that each member had one equal vote in selecting the seven. These were Jews, not Gentiles, so they were accustomed to having representative leaders, such as elders, act on their behalf (Acts 15:6-22; 21:18).

Closely associated with selecting prospective elders is the examination of their moral and spiritual fitness for office. Since the qualifications for eldership are to be taken seriously by the local congregation, it follows that a formal, public examination of a prospective elder's qualifications is necessary. This is exactly what 1 Timothy 3:10 states: "And let these (deacons) also (like the elders) first be tested; then let them serve as deacons if they are beyond reproach." First Timothy 5:24,25 also teaches that an assessment of character and deeds is necessary in order to avoid appointing the wrong people as elders or overlooking qualified men: "The sins of some men (prospective elders) are quite evident, going before them to judgment (human examination); for others, their sins follow after. Likewise also, deeds that are good are quite evident, and those which are otherwise cannot be concealed."

Although the elders are to take the lead in all church procedures, this does not mean that the congregation is passive. Biblical elders want an informed, involved congregation. Biblical elders eagerly desire to listen to, consult with, and seek the wisdom of their fellow believers. The prospective elder or deacon will serve the congregation, so the people must have a voice in examining and approving their prospective elders and deacons. The context in which 1 Timothy 3:10 appears lays out general instructions for the whole church (1 Tim 2:1-3:16), not just for the elders. Therefore, everyone in the church is to know the biblical qualifications for church elders and is obligated to see that the elders meet those qualifications. Some people in the congregation may have information about the prospective elder or deacon that the elders do not have, so their input in the evaluation process is absolutely essential, regardless of how that process is carried out in detail.

If objections or accusations are voiced as to a candidate's character, the elders should investigate to determine if the accusations are scripturally based. If not, the objections or accusations should be dismissed. No candidate should be refused office because of someone's personal bias. Members of the congregation must give scriptural reasons for their objections. This examination process is not a popularity contest or church election. It is an assessment of a candidate's character according to the light of Scripture. If even one person in the congregation has a verified scriptural objection, the prospective elder should be declared unfit for office – even if everyone else approves. *God's standards alone, not group popularity, govern God's house.*

During a meeting (or several meetings) with the prospective elder, the elders should inquire about the candidate's doctrinal beliefs, personal giftedness, ministry interests, family unity, moral integrity, and commitment of time. Remember, one of the qualifications for eldership is "that he may be able to exhort in sound doctrine and to refute those who contradict" (Titus 1:9b), so time needs to be allotted to examine the prospective elder regarding his knowledge and ability to use his Bible to counsel people and direct the church. For example, the candidate should be able to open the Bible and answer questions such as "What does the Bible teach about divorce and remarriage?" "Where in the Bible does it teach Christ's divine nature?" "What is the gospel message?" What does the Bible say about male-female roles?" What does the Bible say about church discipline?" and many more.

Opportunity must be provided for members of the congregation, either verbally or in written form such as through an elder-evaluation survey, to express freely their questions, doubts or approval of a candidate for eldership. Since God's Word provides an objective, public standard, everyone is responsible to see that God's requirements for eldership are followed.

Finally, the elders, acting as the chief representatives and stewards of God's household, will formally state, in full consultation with the church, their approval, rejection, reservations, or counsel concerning the prospective elder.

INSTALLATION

After the examination process, individuals nominated to office shall be confirmed by a unanimous decision of the elders (or by the policy that your church constitution stipulates). The candidate should soon thereafter be publicly installed into office. The word "first" in 1 Timothy 3:10, informs us that there is an order to observe when appointing elders or deacons. The text reads, "And let these also *first* be tested; *then* let them serve as deacons" (italics added). A prospective elder's or deacon's character must first be examined. Only after he is shown to be biblically qualified can he be installed into office.

The New Testament provides little detailed instruction about the elder's public installation into office, and the Old Testament says nothing about it. In contrast, there was an elaborate and detailed ceremonial procedure for installing the Old Testament priest. There were special sacrifices to be offered, special washings, ceremonial garments, prescribed actions on certain days, and anointing with holy oil (Ex. 28:40-29:41). No one could deviate even slightly from these prescribed laws.

New Testament elders and deacons, however, are not anointed priests like Aaron and his sons (Lev. 8:12). Elders and deacons are not appointed to a special priestly office or holy clerical order. Instead, they are assuming offices of leadership or service among God's people. *We should be careful not to sacralize these positions more than the writers of Scripture do.* The New Testament never shrouds the installation of elders in mystery or sacred ritual. There is no holy rite to perform or special ceremony to observe. Appointment to eldership is not a holy sacrament. Appointment confers no special grace or empowerment, nor does one become a priest, cleric, or holy man at the moment of installation. The vocabulary of the New Testament is carefully chosen to communicate certain concepts and beliefs, and its writers chose to express simple appointment to office. Therefore, to speak of ordaining elders or deacons is as confusing as speaking of ordaining judges or politicians.

The New Testament indicates that elders were formally installed into office by the laying on of hands and prayer. Within the context of his instructions on elders (1 Tim. 5:17-25), Paul's reference to the laying on of hands must mean appointment to office: "Do not lay hands upon anyone too hastily and thus share responsibility for the sins of others" (1 Tim. 5:22). Thus Paul thought of Timothy as formally appointing new elders for the church in Ephesus by the laying on of hands. If the term "appointed" in Acts 14:23 is a summary description of the full process that is explained in Acts 6, then hands were laid on the Galatian elders by Paul and Barnabas. Certainly the laying on of hands was practiced frequently by Paul (Acts 9:17; 13:3; 14:3; 19:6, 11; 28:8; 2 Tim. 1:6), and from 1 Timothy 4:14 we know that the church elders laid their hands on Timothy as he was about to begin his travels and work with Paul.

The first Christians were not adverse to simple, public ceremony for appointing or commissioning fellow members to special positions or tasks (Acts 6:6, 13:3; 1 Tim. 4:14). For important events such as the appointment of elders, some kind of public, official recognition of new elders would be necessary. The formal installation of an elder before the congregation by the laying on of hands and prayer (or any other means) would signal the start of the new elder's ministry. It would say to the new elder, "You now officially begin your responsibilities. You are now a member of the church's eldership team. The pastoral care of the flock rests on your shoulders and on the shoulders of fellow elders." It would say to the people, "Here is a new pastor elder to care for you and your family." So formal installation is an official starting point. Furthermore, the formal installation of an elder by the laying on of hands would communicate to the new elder the approval, blessing, prayers, recognition, and fellowship of the church.

Regarding the laying on of hands, the New Testament provides few instructions (1Tim. 5:22). It is not a prescribed practice such as baptism or the Lord's Supper, nor is it restricted to a particular person or group within the church (Acts 9:12; 13:3). So the precise significance of the laying on of hands in specific situations is difficult to determine. We do know that the imposition of hands, like fasting, was practiced by the first Christians because it was useful and a blessing to all. Because of the confusion and superstition surrounding the laying on of hands, many churches avoid its use entirely. This is tragic because the laying on of hands can be a meaningful, precious expression of blessing, approval, and partnership. Christians are free, then, to use the laying on of hands if they desire, or to refrain from practicing it if it creates misunderstanding or division.

PRAYER

Finally, all procedures concerning this important decision must be bathed in patient prayer. The church and its leaders must pray for spiritual insight, guidance, and unbiased judgment. They must desire God's will and God's choice, not their own. God said, of Israel, "They have set up kings, but not by Me; They have appointed princes, but I did not know it" (Hos. 8:4a). May God not say the same of us.

Sadly, too many churches expend the least amount of time and effort possible when selecting and examining prospective elders or deacons. A friend told me that in his church the pastor invites all the members to assemble in the church basement once a year, after a Sunday-evening service, to select and elect deacons. After everyone gathers in front of the blackboard, the chairman of the deacons asks for nominations to the diaconate. Several names are suggested and quickly voted on. The new deacons are than installed, and the pastor closes the meeting in prayer. The entire process takes half an hour. There is no consideration of scriptural qualifications, no prayer, and no time to fully examine the nominated deacons. For many, it is a simple matter of, "We have to replace outgoing members of the board. We have a quota to maintain."

Thoughtless, lazy, and prayerless procedures such as those described above weaken our churches and demean the eldership and deaconship. Evaluating an elder's or deacon's fitness for office should be done thoughtfully, patiently, and biblically. The Scripture clearly states that no one is to be appointed to office in a hurried, thoughtless manner: "Do not lay hands upon anyone too hastily" (1 Tim. 5:22a).

Discussion Questions:
1. What are the six elements in the appointment process of elders?
2. Who has the authority to make sure that new elders will be appointed?

Chapter 16

RELEASING GIFTS AND MINISTRIES

The church must be a place where people can get a vision for their lives and discover the purpose for which they were created. Not only must they receive this vision, but they must also be developed, mentored, and given opportunities for the release of these gifts and ministries.

Part of this process involves making people aware of God's purpose in their lives. Another part is to help define spiritual gifts and biblical ministries so that people can measure themselves accordingly.

The church of today needs the supernatural element embodied in the gifts of the Spirit. The church needs the word of wisdom, the word of knowledge, healing, miracles, prophecy, and the other gifts if it is going to do the works of Christ on the earth. The church needs all of the ministries of Christ functioning in our day if the church is going to complete the ministry of Christ. The church needs apostles, prophets, evangelists, pastors, teachers, showers of mercy, healers, intercessors, encouragers, and givers.

It is clear from the New Testament that if the commission that Christ gave to the church is to be fulfilled, the church must not only preach the doctrine of the church as the Body of Christ, but it must see the Body of Christ fully released to function. We must be clear in our day that the work Christ began two thousand years ago will be completed by His church or His Body. Christ's Body is not merely composed of the leadership of the church but includes every single member of the church. Every single member of the church must be activated toward the goal of committed fulfillment.

The Initiation of the Body of Christ

When Christ ascended into heaven, He ascended to become the Head of the church, which is His Body (Col. 1:19). After His resurrection from the dead He ascended to the Father having completed His assignment. In doing so He received from the Father the promise of the Holy Spirit and in turn poured out that Spirit upon the waiting disciples (Acts 2:1-4; 33). When He did this, He gave of the grace and gifts that were in Him to those who would make up His Body (Eph. 4:11-13).

What happened in the natural realm on the Day of Pentecost in Acts 2 was symbolic of what was taking place in the spiritual realm. As one studies the language of Acts 2, it is apparent that several things occurred. There was a great sound, there was a manifestation of fire, and there was the miracle of speaking with other tongues. Each sign had its own significance.

The manifestation of fire is of particular interest in this context. The original language seems to indicate that this was a "distributing fire." This is picked up in various translations of this passage. The NIV says, "They saw what seemed to be tongues of fire that separated and came to rest on each of them." J.B. Phillips says, "Before their eyes appeared tongues like flames, which separated off and settled above the head of each one of them." Moffatt says, "They saw tongues like flames distributing themselves, one resting on the head of each."

It appears that what they saw was a manifestation of fire, which appeared above them. This major manifestation of fire then broke up into smaller tongues of fire that rested on the head of each of them until the whole of the fire was distributed.

What an incredible image! And what a perfect picture of that which is described for us in Ephesians 4:11-13. Jesus had ascended on high as the fullness of the Godhead bodily. Jesus was the fullness of grace and truth as He walked on the earth among us (John 1:14; 3:33-35). He was the embodiment of all ministry and divine function. But if He was to complete His ministry on earth, the Holy Spirit would have to be sent to His followers, and the gifts and ministries that were in Him would have to be dispensed to them.

The fullness that was in Jesus is represented by the manifestation of fire in the Upper Room. The individual flames that came to rest on the head of each one represents the measure or part of Christ's ministry that was given to each one.

This is an accurate picture of what was taking place in the spiritual realm. When Christ ascended to the Father, He dispensed the fullness that was in Him to the individual members of the church. No one person has experienced the fullness, but each member of the Body of Christ has received a portion of Christ's ministry to the world.

As a result of this, Christ is able to continue His powerful ministry on the earth. The only difference is that now Christ functions through the church, which is His Body. Christ was the apostle, the prophet, the evangelist, the pastor, the teacher, the shower of mercy, the healer, the comforter, the encourager, the giver, the helper, and the intercessor. He had it all. Now He has given an aspect of His ministry (our own personal flame) to each believer who has been born of the Spirit.

In this present age, if we want to experience Christ's ministry in one of these areas, we must experience it through those who have received Christ's ministry gift in that particular area. It is only when we rightly relate to the Body of Christ that we can experience the fullness that is in Christ.

The Body of Christ comprises unity in diversity. There is one body, but many members. There is one vine, but many branches. There is one army, but many soldiers. There is one temple, but many living stones. There is one family, but many children (sons). There is one sheepfold, but many sheep.

Each member of the Body has a place in that Body, a place to function (Rom. 12:1-8; 1 Cor. 12:1-31). There is no such thing as a nonfunctioning member. Regardless what some may think, regardless of our natural understanding, everything was made with purpose and design.

God, not man, has set the members in the Body (1 Cor. 12:18). No one got to see a list of options before they were born to decide what they wanted to be when they came into the world. God has assigned ministries to people as it has pleased Him (1 Cor. 12:11). We must believe that God knows exactly what He is doing and that He does all things well.

Releasing the Body to Function

Pastors and church leaders must place a high priority on releasing others into ministry. Sometimes we have exalted the leadership ministries listed in Ephesians 4 above the other ministries of the body. Sometimes we have functioned as if God's purposes were going to be accomplished when the ministry of these leadership gifts were fully activated and the people released their leaders to function fully.

The opposite is actually the case. The purposes of God are going to be realized when the leadership ministries rise up and serve the other ministries in the Body of Christ in maturing, training, and releasing them to function fully. The leaders are the ones that God has ordained to train, build up, equip, and release into ministry with the goal that every single member of the church is doing what God has indeed called them to do.

It is not difficult to see the mentality of the leadership of churches where I go to visit them. Do the leaders see the people as those who exist for them? Are the people in their minds a platform for the release and full expression of their personal ministry? Or, do the leaders see themselves as existing for the sake of the people? Do they see themselves as the ones who are to lay their lives down? Do they see their primary function being to strengthen the hands of the members of their church so that they can fully function as God has ordained?

Until there is a major shift in the philosophy of many in leadership of the church today, the purposes of God are going to be hindered by a lack of spiritual manpower. It is going to take the full ministry of Christ to accomplish the task, and that full ministry will not be experienced until every member is indeed functioning in his or her God-ordained place.

Without this the church will be much like a V-8 engine operating on four cylinders. It will be underpowered and ineffective to accomplish the Designer's purpose. The commission of Christ to the church is simply too grand to be able to be accomplished by a handful of spiritual giants.

There is no better illustration for us than in Acts 6 when the apostles and early church leaders were faced with the limitations of their own humanity. They were the leaders of the church, and they were trying to do it all. As a result the church suffered in every area. The needs of the people were not being met effectively, and the preaching of the Gospel itself was suffering.

When the leaders realized the need to release other capable people into the work, the murmuring stopped, and the preaching of the Gospel rose to a whole new level of effectiveness. God never intended for a small group of people to do it all. He gave many gifts and many ministries in the church, and everyone is there for the purpose of divine function.

A Nation of Priests

If we are not careful, we will go back to a system where the official delegate of the people will perform all of the ministry functions of the church. Such a priest would perform rituals in the presence of onlookers whose principle function is to witness the ritual by their presence and support the efforts of the one performing by their giving.

This is one of the concepts that Martin Luther rebelled against. He believed that every believer was called to be a priest. The New Testament confirms that believers are to be a nation of priests unto God (1 Pet. 2:5-9; Rev. 1:5-6; Exod. 19:5-6). Unfortunately, in many cases this concept has been restored to the church from a doctrinal perspective but is still awaiting restoration from an experiential or practical perspective.

Entering into the Doctrine

If the church is going to grow and prosper in our day, there must be a major shift in the philosophy and practice of the church. This shift must first take place in the hearts of leaders. Leaders can enjoy being in the spotlight. They can enjoy being placed on a spiritual pedestal. They can enjoy getting most of the credit for victories. They can enjoy the fruits of their own people's ignorance. Sometimes their own insecurities in relation to their own call can keep them from truly releasing others.

Whatever the case, progressive leaders in today's church must make member activation a principle concern and a central focus. We need to define our goal. Do we want a nice church body that has few problems that takes good care of its pastor? Or do we want a well-trained, well-equipped army of people who are able to affect their communities and reach out to the world?

If all we want is to fulfill Christ's charge to the church, then we will do everything we can to assist every single member in finding his or her place. This means ministering to those working for the church and those working outside the church. This means producing a Christian community that is ministering within the four walls of the church but at the same time has a vision to take it to the streets. This means seeing a full release of every gift, every ministry, and every grace that was found in Christ as He functioned on the earth two thousand years ago.

Often people do not respond properly because they have not been taught properly. Paul was concerned about the issue of ignorance when it came to the knowledge and function of ministry (1 Cor. 12:1). The first step in the process of change is giving people truth from which to draw. The Holy Spirit will work in the lives of people with the word of truth that has been sown into their hearts.

Hindrances to the Function of the Body of Christ

There are at least three classical, non-formal teachings in the church that have crippled the church's ability to function as a body. One of them is that being a preacher of the Gospel is the highest calling there is. A second one is an overemphasis on "full time" ministry that gives the impression that getting your salary from the church is somehow superior to having a "secular" job. And the third one is that ministry is what takes place behind a microphone in the corporate gathering of the church.

All three of these non-biblical concepts have kept too many players out of the real game. Too often the church has been like a football game. There are twenty-two players on the field desperately in need of rest and forty thousand fans in the stadium desperately in need of exercise. Let's look at these three misconceptions.

Preaching is not the Highest Calling

I have heard preachers make this or similar statements from the pulpit on a variety of occasions. In a moment of great anointing a preacher makes the declaration that "Bless God! Being called to preach the Gospel is the greatest of all professions." Of course, the preacher is speaking out of his own sense of calling, and in a sense this is most likely true for him.

Unfortunately, this statement can have a very negative effect on those in the congregation listening to it. They can have two negative responses. First, they can feel inferior to whatever calling they possess, knowing that they can never be number one or in the "highest" calling. This can, in effect, demoralize them or cause them to devalue their own callings and giftings.

Second, they can feel that if their life is going to amount to anything, they must go to Bible school and try to become preachers. For this reason, we have many people aspiring to be preachers who have not been called by God to be one. These people mean well, they make major sacrifices, but they rarely become successful and fulfilled at what they do.

If the Body of Christ is going to be activated, we need to know that all ministries are needed and vital to the overall success of the church. Even the ministries that seem to be less important are essential to the well-being of the body. We need to realize that God will not judge us on the basis of the ministry that we had; He will judge us on how faithful we were to do what God called us to do.

The highest calling or the greatest ministry is the one for which God has called someone. To the preacher, preaching is the highest call, and that should be his or her attitude. However, to someone who is called by God to serve in some other way, it would be foolish to pursue preaching. In fact, it could actually be walking in disobedience to pursue preaching.

When people understand this, they understand that no ministry is more important than another in God's eyes; they will take pride in what God has called them to do and not belittle or minimize it. God has called each one to an important task. He has made each individual perfectly suited to the ministry to which He has called them. Everything about them is consistent with that purpose, and their great goal in life is to discover and enter into that purpose.

This is what Paul refers to as pressing the mark of the high calling in Christ Jesus. Paul was trying to apprehend the thing for which he was apprehended. When God put His hand on our lives, He did it with purpose in mind. Our goal is to discover that purpose and enter into it.

Full-Time Ministry is for Everyone

The second great misconception among Christians is that somehow working for the church is spiritual and working outside of the church is secular. Often when you hear people talking about their situation, they get rather boastful about the fact that they are in full-time ministry. What they mean is that they draw their salary from the church. Unfortunately, it has nothing to do with how hard they work, just the fact that the church pays their salary. In point of fact, there may be many people who are working much harder than they are, but are not drawing a salary from the church, and they may be more effective.

This misconception comes from a wrong definition of ministry. Too often we think of ministry as a title rather than a function. We hear people refer to "the ministry." Usually they are referring to a position in the church. They are "full-time ministers" if they have both the position and the salary that goes with it. This is a usage of the term ministry that is totally foreign to the Bible.

Unfortunately, when people in the congregation hear concepts like this, there is a tendency for them to feel almost ashamed of what they are doing because they are in the "secular" world.

The biblical concept of ministry is serving. It is taking the gifts, talents, and abilities that God has given to you and using them to serve God and others. Anytime you take something that God has given to you and use it to honor God and touch someone in need, you are ministering, and that activity is spiritual. It makes no difference if you are getting paid to do it or not. In fact, if you are getting paid to do it, the service you render may be less of a ministry than if you are not being paid and you still do it.

Leaders must be careful not to exalt what they do to the level that members of the body have a low regard for what they do and settle for being attendees of and financial donors to their programs or "ministry."

Actually everyone is a minister because everyone is to be a servant. In addition, everyone is to be a full-time minister. That is, everyone should be a full-time servant with their eyes wide open at all times to see the needs that God has placed before them. They should have sensitive and caring hearts to take the resources that God has given to them to touch the lives of others and so minister as Christ would have in that given situation.

Ministry Occurs Outside the Church Service

Often those who participate in the services of the church, whether it be through song leading, praying, ushering or preaching, view their involvement as their ministry. Too often we feel that our ministry should find expression in the corporate gathering of the church or we don't really have a ministry. For this reason people who feel they have the gift of exhortation or prophecy feel stifled if they cannot "perform" in the public meeting of the church. People who feel uncomfortable in front of people settle for being spectators.

The truth is that the public gathering of the saints is to ministry what the locker room is to a football game. It is the place where we get encouraged and inspired. It is a place where we go over our game plan so that when we leave the locker room and play the game, we will have the best possible chance of winning the game.

Our church services are the same. For most of the people the church service is not meant to be the place where ministry functions. It is to be the place of equipping, encouragement, inspiration, and challenge in relation to the real game that takes place as soon as they leave the worship service. Ministry begins when the saints walk out of the door and into the real world.

There will never be enough opportunities in the context of a worship service for every saint to exercise some gift or fully function in some way. Only a small group of people will be able to participate. But there is plenty of room if we see ministry as something that takes place during the week between the locker room meetings. The gifts of the Spirit and the ministries that have been put into God's people are for the street.

When you follow the life of Jesus and see where He did most of His teaching and preaching, it was not in the context of the synagogue meeting. It was as He walked along the trails of life. Jesus wants to continue to function the same way He functioned when He was here on the earth. He still wants to touch the tax gatherers, the women at the well, the man lying in the street seeking healing, the children by the side of the road, and the multitudes that are in desperate need. We encounter them every day. We rarely encounter them in our church services.

Leaders Must Decrease

There is something that plays to the ego of leaders when people believe that what they do is more holy, is higher and nobler, and is special in God's eyes. But if the Body of Christ is to arise in these days, leaders must be willing to decrease. John the Baptist said it in his day. He realized that he only existed to prepare the way for Jesus. When Jesus came, his usefulness was gone. He had done his job. Now it was time for him to decrease and for Jesus to shine.

In a similar fashion, the purpose of leaders is to equip the Body of Christ to function. There is something nice about being treated like God's "man of the hour, full of faith and power." But what God wants to do today is not going to be done by a few big-time ministers who come on the scene in the last days. The work of the Kingdom is going to be done when leaders lay their lives down for the saints, equip them, and release them into their areas of function. It will get done by this many-membered entity called the Body of Christ functioning fully as God has intended.

Discussion Questions:

1. Name two functions a church should have to develop their members.
2. What hinders the purposes of God concerning the ministries of His people and how can that be rectified?
3. What is the highest calling or greatest ministry of God?
4. Explain why working in the secular arena for the Christian should be viewed as spiritual.
5. Define ministry from a biblical perspective.

Chapter 17

HOUSE-TO-HOUSE MINISTRY

There are not many specific methods outlined in the New Testament concerning the program of the church. One exception to this is the apparent universal existence of house-to-house ministry in the New Testament church.

It appears that this house-to-house ministry went well beyond individual fellowship among believers. It seems to have included a certain amount of structure to minister to the needs in the churches and to reach out in evangelism.

There is no question that the fastest growing churches in the world today have some form of small-group ministry. Is this just another fad? Or have they tapped into a divine principle or a pattern that should be considered by every church seeking to follow the biblical model?

The Great Commission

When Jesus met with His disciples after His resurrection from the dead, He spent a good deal of His time issuing orders as the commander-in-chief of the army of God called the church (Acts 1:1-3).

As you study the four Gospels and the book of Acts in relation to this time period of forty days, you will find that these commands of Jesus were a little overwhelming, especially when put in the context of the disciples' having recently exhibited a lot of fear and personal doubt.

When you put all of the verses together, it is clear that Jesus commanded them to preach the Gospel to every creature beginning at Jerusalem and ending up at the ends of the earth, to make disciples out of those who responded, to baptize those who responded, to teach those who responded to observe everything that

Jesus has ever said, and to pastor His people into maturity and productivity. In their spare time they could heal the sick, cast out devils, raise a few dead people and, if they still had time left over, they could pick up a few serpents along the way (Matt. 28:19-20; Mark 16:15-20; Luke 24:27; John 21:15; Acts 1:8).

What a challenge! No wonder Jesus further instructed them to wait in Jerusalem until they were empowered from on high. They would need supernatural help if they were going to accomplish this supernatural task. With the help of the Holy Spirit, these once-fearful disciples changed the world in their generation.

The commission that Jesus gave to the disciples is a commission that is still on the shoulders of the church today. Everything that we do as a church has to be done in the light of God's commission in Genesis 1 and Jesus' commission to His disciples given after His resurrection.

The church is God's instrument on the earth today for the fulfillment of His divine purposes. There is no other plan; there is no other organization or group of people to which we can turn for its success.

A Strategy for Success

The early church was successful because of two things. First of all, they had been obedient to Jesus in waiting in Jerusalem for the empowering of the Holy Spirit in their lives. Their task could never be accomplished in their own strength. The book of Acts is really a book of the acts of the Holy Spirit in and through the church.

The early church was also successful because they appear to have had a strategy for the fulfillment of the commission. They used a two-pronged attack in fulfilling Christ's charge. This two-pronged attack is seen in Acts 5:42 where the early church leaders focused on the public teaching and preaching in the corporate gathering of the church and evangelistic endeavors, and they carried the same ministry into the homes of the believers.

They appear to have focused on the large gathering in the courts of the temple (Acts 2:46-47). They appear to have focused on smaller gatherings in the homes of believers to reinforce what was taking place on the larger scale.

This two-pronged attack made it possible for the multitudes who had received Christ in the outpouring of Acts 2 to continue steadfastly in the apostles' doctrine, in the breaking of bread, in fellowship, and in prayers (Acts 2:42).

The Present-Day Challenge

It is clear that the church is approaching a day of great outpouring and harvest. Jesus made it clear that before His return there would be a harvest the likes of which the world has never seen. Perhaps this goes against your personal theology. Perhaps as you look around and see what appears to be a rise in the level of wickedness, you wonder what the last days will be like.

It is clear in the Bible that while the love of many will wax cold and many will fall away from the faith, the end times will also be marked by the greatest harvest and ingathering of souls that the world has ever seen (Matthew 13:27-30, 39). In addition to a numerical expansion in the Kingdom of God, the end times will be marked by a church that has come to full stature (Eph. 4:13-16), is without spot or wrinkle (Eph. 5:25-27), and is a sharp threshing instrument moving mightily against Satan and the kingdom of darkness (Rom. 16:20).

In other words, the end times will be marked by great visitation and revival where multitudes will be swept into the Kingdom and added to the church. Christ's parables of the Kingdom, Peter's miracle draught of fish, and Joel's vision of the latter rain outpouring all seem to indicate that the "glory of the latter house" will far surpass anything that has been seen heretofore.

What does all of this mean for today's church? What does it mean for pastors in these days? It surely means many things, but one thing is obvious – the net of the church will have to be prepared structurally to handle what God is about to do.

The Need for a Strategy

Multitudes of people have always brought with them multitudes of problems. In Acts 6 when the number of the disciples multiplied, suddenly problems, murmuring, and greater needs arose.

What is the church to do? What is the pastor to do? How can the church effectively reach out and also minister to the needs of the people? Can one person standing behind the "sacred desk" one hour per week effectively get the job done? How does one person touch a community? How does one person minister to the lives of one thousand, two thousand, or ten thousand people? How can a local church handle the very thing for which it has prayed for centuries – growth?

Many churches in the world today have begun to grow rapidly. As they have, they have crossed a line where they have had to make a choice in their ministry. When the local church gets large, five changes can easily take place.

1. **The church can become *program oriented* rather than *people oriented.*** All of the energy of the pastoral staff must be given to keeping programs going that will hopefully touch people's lives. Soon people can get the feeling that the programs are more important than people and that they are only a small part of a massive, insensitive, and impersonal piece of equipment.

2. **The church can become guilty of *pulpit pastoring* rather than *personal pastoring.*** The pastor preaches a shotgun message on Sunday morning hoping to hit the needs of most of the people, but he is never able to minister to the personal needs of any one person. The individual has no personal

relationship to his pastor, and the pastor cannot even call his own sheep by name.

3. **The church can become an *assembly hall* rather than an *assembly line*.** The church is to be a place where people's lives are put together and where that which is missing is put into place. In many large churches, however, it is easy to feel that church attendance and tithing are the only important barometers of spiritual life and that the only value an individual has is to fill a certain spot once a week. As long as he is "not forsaking the assembling" together, he is considered to be doing fine.

4. **The church can become an *orphanage* rather than a *family*.** It is difficult to raise children effectively in a group. One or two parents for fifty children will never be able to develop an intimate relationship and fellowship with those children. Most likely the children themselves will never feel close to either parent or to the other members of the family.

5. **The church can become a *ministry center* rather than an *equipping center*.** When a local church becomes large, it is difficult to help each person into his or her unique ministry. We can only offer certain services to people that will hopefully keep them going for another week rather than effectively equipping the saints themselves to do the ministry.

God is placing a great challenge before the church in these days. It is the challenge of growth. It is fairly easy to assist a group of twenty-five people to become mature men and women of God. But how can one handle a multitude? God wants large churches. He created the church for growth. All of the principles of God's Word must be workable for small churches and large churches alike. God is raising up an army of trained servants in these days to march effectively against the gates of hell. There must be a way to fulfill His glorious commission.

Toward a Solution – Exodus 18:13-26

The problem facing the church today is not unlike the problem faced by Moses when he led the people of God out of Egypt and toward the land of promise. [We dealt with this briefly in chapter 2.] Here was one man trying to be the chief counselor and decision maker of all three million people. It sounds absolutely ridiculous when you think about it, and yet sometimes you can be so close to a problem that you cannot see the obvious solution. It took a visit from his father-in-law to pinpoint the problem.

The problem in Israel was serious for a couple of reasons. First of all, Jethro was careful to point out that Moses was going to "wear away" (Exod. 18:23). When a pastor is ministering to a small number of people, he can do it all, and usually does. But as the number of people increases, the pastor must begin to release responsibility to others or the burden will become too heavy for him to bear.

When Jethro came to visit his daughter and grandchildren, he had no time to spend with Moses, because Moses was never home. When you pastor three million people, there is always someone in trouble or going through a difficult problem. Moses loved the people more than his own life. Therefore, he put his own personal needs and the needs of his family after the needs of the people. This left Moses with no time for himself, his family, or his personal relationship to God. When you love people and you have a desire to help them, this is usually the result.

Every morning when Moses got up, there was a line outside his tent. There were people who needed answers, people whose lives were in turmoil, people who had to make critical decisions about their life and future. How could Moses say no to these people? He didn't! Every day from sunup to sundown (even after sundown) Moses talked, shared, and counseled with the people.

Day after day, week after week, month after month, it was the same. The waiting line never went away, but Moses himself was wearing away.

Jethro did not need a special revelation to know that Moses would never last at this pace. Out of concern for Moses, his own daughter and his grandchildren, Jethro had to rebuke Moses for the sake of his life. No one man was ever meant to carry the burden of so many people. "The thing that you are doing is not good" (Exod. 18:7).

In addition to Moses' personal health and family issues, there was another reason why the situation was serious. Jethro saw that what was taking place was not good for the people. People just cannot stand in line day after day without getting frustrated and giving up. If people know that you are too busy for them, they will wait until their problems are so big that only God Himself will be able to solve them. In addition, if the people have to wait so long in line, they will be tempted to not come for help at all and give up before they see a leader.

The Jethro Principle

Jethro saw that as long as Moses was by himself and continued his present approach, the job would not get done, and the people's needs would never be met. If this condition were to continue, it would ultimately jeopardize the entire plan of God to bring a believing people into the Promised Land.

Jethro proceeded to give Moses some "fatherly" advice, which later proved to be the same advice that God gave Moses (Num. 11 and Deut. 1). He suggested three main changes in Moses' approach. First of all, he suggested that Moses needed to get back in right relationship to the Lord and learn once again how to put the government on God's broad shoulders. Often when we get busy it is so easy to let that time with the Lord slide. Unfortunately, it is that time with the Lord where we find strength, our answers, and the grace to deal with everything else.

Second, he suggested Moses take up the mantle of teaching on a corporate basis. Rather than individually trying to teach each person the divine principles they needed to navigate a particular situation, he suggested that Moses begin to publicly teach all of the people in three main areas, and in doing so he would equip the people to make their own decisions and to solve many of their own problems, because they would have truth upon which to draw.

He told Moses to teach the people the Word, the way to walk, and the work to do. That is, he should teach them how to walk, focusing on practical principles of living as believers. And he should teach them about their personal responsibility before the Lord to be workers in His vineyard. Every member of the family of God has a work to do.

Third, he suggested that Moses bring others into the work. He encouraged Moses to select qualified individuals who had their own lives in order and delegate some of his responsibility to them. He gave him the principle of team ministry.

Jethro further suggested that Moses place these individuals over groups of people according to their individual capacities whether it be for ten, fifty, one hundred or one thousand. These support leaders would take care of the day-to-day concerns while only the most difficult issues would come to Moses. Moses saw the wisdom in this plan and implemented the suggestion, saving both himself and the congregation of the people.

In Jesus' Ministry

Jesus Himself demonstrated this same principle of ministry when He fed the five thousand (Mark 6:34-44; Luke 9:14-15). It would be difficult for one person to feed five thousand hungry people. In preparation for the miracle feeding, Jesus instructed the disciples to have the multitudes sit on the ground in companies of fifty and one hundred. Then He broke the bread, gave it to His disciples who in turn distributed it to the people. It is interesting that John's Gospel emphasizes the fact that they gave the food to those who were sitting down as Jesus had instructed (John 6:10-11).

Jesus had a plan to feed (pastor, shepherd) His people. One person could not reasonably do it all. If all are going to eat to their fill and no one is going to be overlooked, there must be a strategy. Things must be done decently and in order. Ultimately, only those who are cooperating with the strategy will be guaranteed what they need.

In the Early Church

In the early life of the church, multitudes were not the problem – making sure that the pastoral work generated by the multitudes got done was the problem. Because the heart of the leadership was that of servants, it became very easy for them to want to be personally involved in every need in the church. When the number of the disciples multiplied, this became an ever-increasing impossibility.

As a result, the needs of some were neglected (Acts 6:1-6). An even worse thing occurred, however. Because the apostles were trying to meet all of the needs of the people personally, they ended up neglecting their primary call to prayer and the Word. Everyone was in effect being hurt because they so loved. The public ministry of the Word of God was suffering.

They learned very quickly that "many hands make light work." They chose other able individuals to share the task of ministering to the personal needs of the growing church. They refocused on their primary function and, as a result, the Word of God increased and more responded to the Gospel (Acts. 6:7).

Today's Challenge

Today the church is facing the same challenge of growth. It is exciting to see the promises of harvest coming to pass. However, as the people come, they will come with great needs. The church must be prepared to advance to minister effectively to these needs or we will limit what God wants to do through each and every local church. It is my persuasion that God will only give us the quantity that we can handle.

The solution that Moses found, that Jesus demonstrated, and that was discovered by the early church is a solution that still works today. That solution could be summarized as follows:

1. Concentrate in public (in the temple) on the preaching and teaching of the Word, focusing on principles of practical living, putting the tools into people's hands to be personal problem solvers.

2. Divide the congregation into segments as Jesus did when He fed the five thousand.

3. Place over these segments, individuals who are qualified to carry such responsibility.

4. Work to train and equip these individuals to function as leaders in their defined area of responsibility.

The Two-Pronged Attack

The New Testament church used a two-pronged attack in ministering to the needs of the people and fulfilling Christ's commission to make mature ones of all nations. They had the public gatherings, which was absolutely vital for the worship life, inspiration, and marching orders of the church. They also had smaller gatherings. They continued in the temple and from house-to-house (Acts 20:20). The corporate gathering is important for the unity of the church and outreach potential. The smaller gatherings are important for many other reasons.

There are many aspects of church life that can be fostered by the smaller groups in any local church. Small groups are not meant to be in competition with the larger gathering. On the contrary, the small group should be a tremendous complement to the corporate assembly life. If the small group is designed in such a way that it competes with the main gathering of the church, it will become divisive, repetitious, and perhaps even boring. But if the small group is providing something that is not being touched by any other phase of body life, it will be a source of life and strength.

Multiple Facets of Small Groups

Small-group ministry will take on different forms in different settings depending on the vision of the leadership, the strengths of the local leadership team, and the primary focus for such gatherings. Strictly speaking, no plan is wrong and no plan is to be considered universal in its application. The principle of the small group is universal, but the application may vary from one place to another.

Regardless of the primary purpose of small groups in the life of the local church, they will most likely satisfy a combination of needs. Some of the primary purposes that are met by the small gathering include the following:

1. **Pastoral Care and Discipleship.** God has definitely given His church the burden for pastoral care and discipleship. Our desire should go beyond just birthing people into the Kingdom; it should involve providing effective covering and accountability that precipitates growth and brings people to a place of personal fruitfulness and ministry. It is impossible to pastor a crowd in any individual way. The small-group approach is a biblical way of feeding a multitude of people.

2. **Building Relationships and Fellowship.** It is clear that God wants the individual members of the church to be more closely linked to one another so that they can be in position to better minister to the needs of one another as the Bible clearly directs. This was a top priority of the church in the

book of Acts, and the small group helps to keep individuals from being alone in the midst of a large number of people. This is more important for the more passive, reserved, and quiet personality, and yet all will benefit greatly by their personal involvement.

3. **Assimilating New People into the Church.** Whether people are newly saved or simply new to the church, there needs to be a means whereby they can quickly feel a part if they are going to be permanently established and genuinely committed to the vision of the local church. It takes several years to feel a part of a crowd, but in a few brief contacts in an intimate setting, people can feel loved, cared for, and needed.

4. **Evangelism.** God wants every believer to be reaching out to others in their spheres of influence. The small group is a perfect place to introduce new people to other believers in the Body of Christ. Through the small group, it is possible for them to gain the support and the relationships that they need for them to be established.

5. **Releasing People into Their Gifts and Ministries.** It is clear from the Bible that every believer has a ministry and can be used by God to reach out beyond the church walls. They also can function in gifts of the Spirit and can be used to edify the body of believers (1 Cor. 12-14). Where do the passages like 1 Corinthians 14:26 find their fulfillment in the life of a local church where everyone has something to contribute as they come together? In a large and growing church it is impossible for everyone to participate in some way. However, in the small-group setting, everyone can be involved in some way in any given meeting.

6. **Identifying and Multiplying Leaders.** Many people are called by God to be leaders in the local church. However the

traditional model of church ministry drastically limits the opportunity for leadership to function in the local assembly. Not only does the small-group approach open the door to opportunity to many in the congregation to lead in a significant way, but it also affords those especially gifted to be identified and released to greater areas of responsibility. A much higher percentage of the congregation could grow in their capacity for leadership if there were more opportunities open to them as their current level of ability.

7. **Accountability and Personal Growth.** The small group is a great place to go over the Word that is being emphasized in the corporate life of the church to assist in accountability and seeing that word established in the lives of individual believers. It is a place where the more mature believers can serve as a pattern and an encouragement to those who are not living up to their potential in the grace of God.

Models that have Proven Effective

Because of the obvious strengths of the small-group ministry in the local church, many pastors have come home from church-growth seminars with great plans to grow their church through small groups, only to face disappointment and, in some cases, ruin. Part of the problem is that small-group ministry or any other thing that is added to the program of the church cannot just be tacked on to an already full ministry program.

In addition, it will take a long time for the people in the church to get comfortable with a ministry that forces them to get out of their traditional comfort zone and enter into a small setting where they will become vulnerable to others. As a result, some pastors have given up in the process.

Some pastors have gone into such programs not being totally convinced, not counting the ultimate cost, or not laying the proper foundation for change. In order to understand how to minimize some of the negative effects, I have done a rather thorough study of those churches that seem to be doing well with small-group ministry, have been doing it for a good length of time, and seem to be having the desired success.

The reason for the study is to discover what these successful local churches have in common. I have discovered at least nine common denominators of the most successful small-group churches.

1. **The small-group ministry is seen as the main program of the church.** Small groups are not an add-on to an otherwise full schedule of activities in the church. If you add small groups, you will have to eliminate other phases of church life that you presently have in motion. Otherwise there will be a constant competition for leadership, and some of the people will use their other fulfilling involvements as an excuse not to get involved in the small-group ministry.

2. **The small-group ministry must be led, fanned, and envisioned by the senior leadership of the church.** It is a fact that 80 percent of the success of small-group ministry is dependent on the senior pastor of the local church. This is not an area that will succeed in a corner, and it cannot be delegated to a few fanatics who want to move out on their own in this area. In order for small groups to succeed, there must be much pulpit time given to casting a clear vision. There must be ongoing exhortations and testimonies, which will require time in the corporate gathering. This also means that the senior pastor will have to get personally involved in the training of key leaders. But most of all, it means that every leader in the church from the top down will have to be committed to personal involvement in the groups.

3. **The small groups must meet fairly often.** If the small group is going to have any chance to fulfill the purposes

for which it was established, it will have to meet fairly often, preferably once a week. Again this means that the senior pastor will have to look at the overall program of the church to see that the small group is not in competition with a full schedule of weekly services. When adding small groups to the program of the church, it should most likely replace one of the other happenings in the program of the church.

4. **The small groups must be growth orientated.** One of the greatest difficulties that you will have is multiplying groups. Part of the problem is that people become comfortable in their group and they want things to stay just they way they like them. It's ironic, but groups that do not birth new groups end up becoming ingrown and usually dissolve after about two to three years. All groups should be open to new people at all times or have a natural life cycle because of the unique purpose of that specific group. Birthing new groups should be seen as a primary purpose from the very beginning. It is even helpful to put goals out that reflect this (e.g. six months to a year).

5. **The small groups must become the vehicle through which most care ministry occurs.** Again, when you structure the church around small groups, those small groups become ministry centers. You can handle just about everything regarding ministry to the believer through this channel including: personal discipleship, visitor follow-up, pastoral care, hospital visitation, wedding and baby showers, and even evangelistic endeavors.

6. **The small group must be small in size.** If the small groups are going to succeed at the purpose for which they are designed, the smaller they are the better. The

average size of small groups should be around ten to twelve adults. Once you get to a maximum of fifteen or sixteen adults, that group should birth a new group. If a group gets too large, most homes cannot accommodate it, you might end up with too many children, and it ceases to be conducive for adding new members. It can actually become more like a small local church, which is obviously not the goal.

7. **The small groups must become the center for the release of the body ministry in the church.** The small group is the care unit of the church where the members of the group take care of the needs of one another. This is where all of the "one another's" of body life can take place. This is where the members love one another in tangible ways. They comfort one another, they pray for one another, they edify one another, and they pour out their lives for one another.

8. **The small groups must exist for building relationships and a caring, nurturing community both for believers and the newly converted.** Sometimes where small groups get into trouble is when they are used as the primary means for equipping the saints and training leaders. These are functions of the five leadership ministries of apostle, prophet, evangelist, pastor, and teacher (Eph. 3:11). Not every small group will have this level of ministry within it and can end up in error if it tries to function in this way. In addition, the small group is not to become a place of group therapy or counseling. Those kinds of issues are best handled privately with proper pastoral oversight. The small groups should be focusing on serving the needs of the people coming into the groups.

9. **The small group must be a priority function of all the leadership of the church and every single staff person in the church.** The small groups will not be a success if they are not fully supported by the leadership of the church and other staff members. It will soon be interpreted that if you are more mature or that you have "arrived," you no longer need the small group. Not only that, but people are more inclined to follow your example rather than your words. All leaders should be actively involved in the small-group ministry, and they should seriously consider leading such a group.

These are some of the common denominators of successful small-group ministries around the world today. Every successful program may not be true to all nine of them, but they will share in a strong majority of them.

There are a few simple observations or issues that affect small group's success:

- Leaders must be prepared for every meeting so that something significant takes place.

- There needs to be strong emphasis on training of leaders, and every leader must have an intern leader who is being trained to start his or her own group.

- The focus of the corporate gathering is for worship, edification, and the equipping of the saints.

- Sermons should be geared toward equipping people to reach out in evangelism and service. Every believer should be equipped to lead someone to the Lord, to exhort and disciple them. Every believer must be equipped to minister to the felt needs of others.

- Corporate gatherings should be celebrations in honor to God and thanksgiving for the harvest.

Cautions in the Development of a Small-Group Ministry

Not everyone who walks down the path of small-group ministry finds long-term success. There are often very good reasons for this. Some potential pitfalls can be avoided if we do those things that will maximize our potential success. Here are ten suggestions that may help you to succeed.

1. **Do your homework.** Find the model that is best suited to your situation. This will involve being personally aware of what you are trying to achieve in the groups themselves. Find other churches that are successfully using that model. Visit those churches and study their material carefully. Try to talk to the person who has been most directly involved with the small-group ministry and let them share their journey with you including the good, the bad, and the ugly.

2. **Be convinced yourself.** Do not attempt to get others excited about this new venture until you are fully persuaded in your own mind that this is the way you want to go. First of all, you do not want to get a bunch of people excited about something that may or may not become a reality. They will only get frustrated, and you will have created another problem. Second, and perhaps more important, this must be approached as a conviction, because there will be many opportunities for discouragement along the way. Third, this cannot be something that you try for a year or two. It is a long-term commitment that may never cease. The specific form that the small groups take may change from time to time, but the idea of small groups will be with you forever.

3. **Lay a proper foundation.** Do not go into this as a new function of body life without saturating your local church

with the biblical basis for what you are trying to accomplish. If people are going to get on board, they must be convinced that this is a superior format to their traditional ideas about "church." You might even begin a pilot program with a select few to work out the "bugs" and arouse interest in others. This may be a good way to train some of your first leaders.

4. **Go slow.** Take your time establishing this new program in the local church. There is no reason to rush. Give your people time to accommodate their thinking every step of the way. The idea is not to divide your flock. The idea is to bring everyone along with you as you go.

5. **Be patient.** Results will not come immediately. It will take some time to reap a harvest from this program. It will take a lot of working the soil, a lot of sowing of seed, a lot of watering and fertilizing, and a lot of pruning. But as you are faithful, results will come. The normal experience is to begin with a certain level of enthusiasm only to see that enthusiasm wear off. The temptation will be to "shut it down." However, if you will persist through some early challenges and not give up at the first sign of trouble, the small-group ministry will eventually pay off – big time!

6. **Choose leaders wisely.** Choosing leaders is a major key to success. When you release people into the hands of others, you must be confident that they will not hurt the flock. In Acts 6 they had specific qualifications for those who would minister to the needs of the people. We must have specific qualifications as well. Leaders must be people who fear God, love the local church, understand their relationship to authority, and have demonstrated a true heart of loyalty and faithfulness. This should be their spiritual condition before they are selected as leaders (1 Tim. 3 and Titus 1).

7. **Train leaders well.** Nothing will ensure failure more quickly than to give someone a responsibility without a clear job description and the appropriate training for the task. Leaders should be prepared in advance before the program begins, and there should be opportunities for further training as time goes on. The senior leadership of the church should be directly involved in such training so that a strong bond is formed with those who will be functioning in their behalf.

8. **Stay close to leaders.** Keeping a close relational tie to those who are leading the groups is essential if unity is going to be maintained. It is so easy for leaders to slip into their own worlds and lose touch with the corporate vision. Relationship is the key to success. Jesus personally spent time with his leaders so that small issues could be dealt with quickly and the needs of those leaders could be met as well. The small-group leaders will need a pastoring touch in their lives just as much as anyone else.

9. **Monitor the results.** The only way that you can know if you are succeeding is to have some form of evaluation as the small-groups progress. Are the groups really doing or accomplishing what you set out to do with them? There needs to be a context where reports can be received, problems can be identified, failures can be evaluated, and success can be honored. Anything that is left to itself will eventually degenerate into something other than its intended purpose.

10. **Make course adjustments as needed.** When issues arise that indicate a problem, don't be afraid to make minor adjustments along the way. No matter who you are, you will not hit the right mixture the very first try. Eventually you should get to the right mix for you, your people, your culture, and your specific community. It is important not to breed any "sacred cows" when it comes to how this program

functions. Remember, in the Bible we have a general method but not the specific application of the method. The specific application may differ from one local church to another. It may differ in varying seasons in the life of a specific local church.

A Net for the Harvest

The Bible is clear that in the last days there will be an ingathering of souls much like the miracle catch of fish that Peter experienced when he responded to Jesus' command to let down the net. The local church is to be a net that is let down into the sea of humanity, fishing for the souls of men. If the net is going to be successful, it must be properly prepared, it must be washed, it must be mended, and it must be cast into the sea.

Small-group ministry is a structure that will serve to catch the harvest that God wants to bring into His house. We have an opportunity today to get that structure (net) ready so that when God does move, the harvest will be preserved.

Discussion Questions:

1. What biblical example reflects a house-to-house ministry?
2. How did Jethro help Moses organize a plan for the work he had to accomplish?
3. Describe the two-pronged solution for church growth in today's church.
4. Give several facets and their benefits of small groups within a church.
5. As a result of this study what would you like implemented in your own church that would help growth?

Chapter 18

WORKING WITH MINISTRY TEAMS

When speaking of ministry teams there are commonly two distinct types: ministry task teams and ministry leadership teams.

Ministry Task Teams

Within the idea of ministry task teams, most churches employ two types of gatherings for productive purposes: work groups and committees.

Work groups are collections of people who come together for a particular duration to accomplish a specific task. The task is not necessarily vision-driven, and the group's focus might not be the future. A work group generally does not have the special combination of spiritual gifts and natural talents required to accomplish the plethora of outcomes that move the church toward the fulfillment of God's vision.

A committee is a collection of individuals who meet for discussion and perhaps to make recommendations regarding policy, programs, or plans. Committees typically have little, if any, authority to act. Often they provide the organization with ideas, preferences, or suggestions that a leadership body then considers and passes judgment upon.

A ministry task team, in general then, is a group of people who come together to accomplish a task that has been predetermined by a leader or leadership team. Examples may include: Worship teams that prepare & present music for church services; maintenance teams that clean and maintain the buildings; and nursery teams who take care of small children and babies.

Ministry Leadership Teams

A leadership team is a small group of leaders with complementary gifts and skills who are committed to one another's growth and success and hold themselves mutually accountable. They, in turn, lead a larger group of people toward a common vision, specific performance goals, and a plan of action. Examples include: Elders as a leadership team lead a church; a diverse leadership team may lead a youth ministry. Hopefully, a leadership team of diverse strength would lead each ministry area in a church.

Two Key Characteristics of Ministry Task Teams

1. **Task teams help their leaders develop the ministry plan.** The task team provides input to the leadership team during the ministry planning process. The task team will ultimately be responsible to carry out the plan. The leadership team is not always close enough to the actual implementation to plan the task alone (Ex: 10 Spies; Nehemiah 3; Deacons - Acts 6). The leadership team can develop a separate elitism (often called the "ivory tower" syndrome) without regular interaction with task teams.

2. **Task teams implement the plan for their ministry areas.** Task teams must be empowered with authority to fulfill their task. It is critical to combine responsibility with authority. Task teams operate tactically and do not usually define the task itself, but focus on the details of how their task is to be accomplished. Task teams are narrow in scope, but as they focus on how to accomplish their task, they must also know how their team fits in the overall organization. Task teams do not typically initiate ministry plans or strategies.

Point to Ponder: The leadership team is primarily responsible to initiate the ministry plan (which comes from the vision) while task teams work with leadership teams to refine and implement the plan.

Eight Key Characteristics of a Ministry Leadership Team

1. **Small Group.** A large group cannot lead. Anyone who has been involved in effective leadership knows that once a team gets beyond six people, it becomes unwieldy and degenerates into compromises that reflect the lowest common denominator. At this stage, the focus of the group is not upon a commonly held vision but upon producing some tangible outcome with which everyone is comfortable. That is not leadership, it is accommodation. Effective leadership teams typically have three to five people. Less than three leaves you without the horsepower to get the job done. More than five produces inefficiencies and excessive compromise.

2. **The Leadership Team members are Biblically qualified.** The team members must each be biblically qualified leaders. A leadership team is a collection of leaders – not warm bodies willing to help out, not people with titles, but individuals who possess the calling, character, and competencies that qualify them as leaders. Since the very purpose of the team is to provide leadership, it must contain individuals who have that capability. Further, the notion of leaders implies that there are also followers. A leadership team is of no significance unless it is helping followers to understand, adopt, and accomplish a common vision.

    a. Leadership team members must meet the character and spiritual qualifications listed in I Timothy 3:1-7 and Titus 1:5-9. When a team member does not meet biblical standards it can cause many problems: Division among the leaders or followers; disproportion of the ministry workload; the qualified leaders always have to do more than the unqualified; or lack of confidence from those following the leaders.

b. ***Point to Ponder:*** **Luke 12:48** From everyone who has been given much, much will be demanded; and from the one who has been entrusted with much, much more will be asked.

3. **The Leadership Team has a Team Leader.** Teams need a leader who acts as their catalyst or coach. A team of ministry leaders, not one single leader, led all the churches in the New Testament. Every church had a leader (like a team captain) whom the other leaders recognized as their leader. The team leader is a catalyst or initiator among the other leaders. This team leader must be a servant who esteems and encourages others. The team leader will be the most influential in the decision making process and will usually have the final word on decisions. The key is for the leader to respect and include team members in making decisions so that they function together.

4. **The Leadership Team is represented by a diverse mix.** One of the most important attributes of effective leadership teams is that the leaders have a combination of gifts and skills that complement one another. A good leadership team consists of diversely gifted leaders with differing leadership styles and personality temperaments. One of the worst imaginable scenarios is to have three or four people with identical gifts and talents working in a team: You will experience tension and conflict of world-class proportions! The team should be as balanced as possible by having the gifts found in Ephesians 4:11-12 and Romans 12:6-8 represented within the team.

5. **The Leadership Team trusts each other.** True teamwork requires trust, and trust is built by spending considerable time working together with integrity. The leadership team should spend time together apart from the ministry work and

include their families. This will build deeper and more trusting relationships. In a true team, the leaders are committed to one another's growth and success in ministry. Granted, these individuals may not become best friends, but they must respect one another and care about their colleagues' personal maturation. Unless team members experience such ongoing growth, the team will suffer. Because a team is an expression of community, mutual concern is an indispensable ingredient in the team dynamic. A team in which the members are not committed to one another is a team that may produce some desirable results, but it is not likely to achieve its full potential as a team.

6. **The Leadership Team has strong accountability.** One of the distinctives of leadership teams is their determination to evaluate their own efforts and enable one another to live up to specific standards – both team standards and individual standards. One reason leaders fall into disgrace is that they do not have people who know them and whom they trust to bring them into accountability. No team or system works without true accountability. Accountability for a leadership team should include high standards for character, performance, and commitment. Great teams are comprised of leaders who have developed sufficient trust, rapport, and vulnerability to keep one another honest, focused, productive, humble, and inspired.

7. **The Leadership Team submits to one another (Common Vision).** It is the corporate vision that brings the team together and facilitates its passion to move forward as one. The vision unites and excites those who wish to be part of the process. The vision serves as the filter through which efforts are examined and success is defined by progress made toward fulfilling the vision. The vision is the core concept that the team communicates to the population it is leading. Not only must the leadership team be united in its

acceptance of and devotion to the vision, but unless the team can inspire others to own the vision, the team will fail in its efforts. Each team member (particularly the team leader) must respect the gifts and strengths of the individual members and defer to them in their strength areas. Team members must place the common good of the team ahead of their own needs / agenda. Most major decisions should be unanimous or made by common agreement. This empowers each leader to have an equal voice among the team.

8. **A Leadership Team has goals and a plan.** A vision that has no goals and plans associated with it is merely a fantasy. A team without goals and plans is merely a social club. Leaders must move toward the vision by identifying realistic and measurable goals before they can facilitate the development of specific courses of action that will produce the required outcomes.

When these elements are combined, the result is a powerful assembly of individuals whose ability to serve others is multiplied beyond what any one could accomplish alone.

Leadership Teams are comprised of Three Elements.

1. **The leadership team leader.** The team has a leader that God raises up as a player/coach and as a catalyst for the team. The team leader is primarily responsible to facilitate the leadership team, to help the team members maximize their role and bring the entire vision to pass. When consensus is not reached in the team, the final decision rests with the trusted leader (or the team's progress will stall).

2. **The leadership team vision.** The team has a common vision that forms the purpose and direction of the entire ministry. The vision will almost always originate from the team leader, but each member plays a significant role in

shaping, refining, and expanding the vision. The vision cannot be completed without the whole team.

3. **The leadership team members.** The team consists of members that God brings together to accomplish a common vision. Each team member will have a unique gift-mix, leadership style and personality type that will suit them well to serve in a specific role on the team.

Five Primary Functions of a Team Leader

There are five functions of a team leader. *First*, he maintains the focus of the team on the vision and goals. *Second*, he facilitates positive relationships among the team members. *Third*, he helps individuals on the team grow personally. *Fourth*, he prepares the agenda for each team meeting. The team leader should receive input from the team members and acquire needed resources. *And fifth*, he models growth and productivity personally. As the team leader grows, the team members will follow. If the team leader stagnates or stops growing, the members will follow him there, too.

John Maxwell has listed what he thinks are the ten characteristics of an effective team leader.

- Effective leaders influence others.
- Effective leaders know how to prioritize.
- Effective leaders have integrity.
- Effective leaders create positive change.
- Effective leaders are problem solvers.
- Effective leaders possess a positive attitude.
- Effective leaders develop people.
- Effective leaders have vision.
- Effective leaders are self-disciplined.
- Effective leaders develop their team members.

Point to Ponder: *"Leadership is influence, nothing more, nothing else"*

Six Behaviors of an Effective Team Leader

1. **Builds up each team member.** Effective leaders focus not only on the team as a whole, but on building up each individual team member as well.

2. **Puts the interest of the team first.** Effective leaders remember their primary role is about the interest of the team, not about their own advancement.

3. **Balances guidance and control.** Effective leaders understand the balance between providing guidance and controlling the final outcome. The leader must guide or facilitate the team dialogue toward the desired goal. At the same time the leader must not squelch team creativity by over controlling the team.

4. **Believes in their team members.** The leader knows that anything less than complete trust will result in a weakened team and favoritism. Should mistrust arise; the leader must resolve the issues effectively to re-establish trust. Speed in resolving the issues are not as important as thoroughness. However, momentum will be lost until the issues are resolved. The leader is not the ministry dictator but is the guardian of the vision, the one who makes sure it doesn't dilute.

5. **Motivates the team toward excellence.** Without someone to stand guard against slippage of standards, chances are good that teams will settle into an average or mediocre mode of performance. Leaders must know how to draw the best out of their team members.

6. **Challenges the team to take risks.** The leader knows that a team who always plays it safe doesn't accomplish much. The leader knows that uncalculated risks that lead to failure discourage future risk taking.

Six Results Produced by an Effective Team Leader.

1. **The team is focused on the vision.** Opportunities present themselves all the time for positive results, which feels good, but has nothing to do with moving the ministry toward the vision. Great leaders recast the vision frequently (monthly) for team members.

2. **The team works in harmony with one another.** The strongest team is a diverse group of individuals. The potential for creativity is high, but so is the potential for conflict. Conflict presents an opportunity to clear the air, resolve differences and become closer than before the conflict occurred. Effective leaders facilitate positive and productive relationships among team members.

3. **The team members are steadily growing personally.** The leader models personal growth and prioritizes personal mentoring of the team members. Ideally, each team member is continually in the process of becoming a better leader and disciple.

4. **The team focuses on long-term goals, not current activities.** Current activities can be all-consuming, and when they become the focus, the group moves into management mode. The effective leader keeps reminding the team to look at what they are doing in light of the overall objective, i.e. the vision.

5. **The team produces creative solutions to current problems.** Effective leaders stimulate input and creativity

from their team. The team is highly encouraged to produce creative suggestions. When creativity stalls, it is often because the leader has failed to inspire, or has been pushing too hard.

6. **The team is well funded.** Effective leaders understand it is their role to ensure proper resources are available to accomplish the mission. If someone other than the leader takes responsibility for funding the organization, that person will eventually become the primary influencer.

Shaping a Team Vision

Vision Begins Working within the Leader

> **Proverbs 29:18** Where there is no revelation, the people cast off restraint; But happy is he who keeps the law.
>
> **Habakkuk 2:2-4** Then the Lord answered me and said: "Write the vision and make it plain on tablets, that he may run who reads it. [3] For the vision is yet for an appointed time; but at the end it will speak, and it will not lie. Though it tarries, wait for it; because it will surely come, it will not tarry. [4] "Behold the proud, His soul is not upright in him; but the just shall live by his faith."

Vision leads the leader. Vision is a concept that is not yet real. It is a clear mental picture of a preferable future imparted by God. It is thinking about what could be before it exists. It is seeing more, seeing before, and seeing farther than those you lead. Think about your city or village. What do you want to see as the future there?

A leader's function is to see and move their team toward the future. The role of vision is to help the leader clarify and communicate this future. Vision could come as vague as a dream or as precise as a goal or mission statement. But it must come from the leader. And it must be the beginning of a leader's strategy.

Vision comes from within the leader personality. What is your passion? What do you dream about? Leaders must listen closely to what God has put into their heart to capture a vision – listening to the voice of the Holy Spirit, to past experiences, and to what you want to see changed around you. This could take time to develop. If the vision you are pursuing doesn't come from within – from the very depths of who you are and what you believe – you might be able to accomplish it, but you won't be able to strategically lead it.

Vision is like a leader's magnet. Positive pole: One of the most valuable benefits of vision is that it acts like a magnet – attracting, challenging, and uniting people. It also attracts finances and other resources. Negative pole: Another valuable benefit of vision is that it pushes some people away: It pushes away those who do not fit with the vision. It pushes people away from their comfort zone into greater service.

Five Phases of Team Vision

1. **God gives the leader vision.** A vision from God inspires the leader for the future ministry direction. The scope of the vision surpasses the leader's own individual capacity. It will take more people besides the leader to accomplish the vision.

2. **The vision draws the team.** The visionary leader communicates the vision and others are drawn to the vision (some potential leaders, some followers). As people are drawn to the vision, few will become part of the leadership team (then over time leaders will be raised up from within from among the followers.

3. **The vision is shaped by the team.** The leadership team pursues the vision together, refining and shaping it along the way.

4. **Team members (may) change.** The pursuit of the vision takes place with new team members joining the team and possibly some members departing the team.

5. **The vision and team mature over time.** The team and vision have four possible pathways over time. The team indefinitely pursues the same vision (with periodic refining). The team fulfills the vision and considers new direction. The vision changes significantly or is ended and the existing team pursues a new vision. The existing team disbands and a new team is formed to pursue the original vision (possibly with the original leader as well).

Four Ways the Vision Shapes the Team's Response

1. **Vision reveals God's purpose.** God has a unique vision for your ministry team that aligns with His purpose. God's purpose is never the accomplishment of a vision. Vision is what God calls us to, as a means to accomplish His purpose.

2. **Vision shapes the ministry.** This unique vision is key to shaping the ministry team and the ministry organizational structure. You can only lead a person to a desired place if you articulate what that place is. The vision will set the purpose for team, which in turn will help set its shape.

3. **Vision becomes irresistible.** The vision becomes irresistible to those whom God calls to be part of the team. A God-given vision will attract team members who will excitedly climb on board and go where God is going.

4. **Vision focuses team resources.** The vision directs the team's energies and resources strategically. Vision helps direct and generate needed resources. Without a clear vision, resource allocation tends to be reactionary rather than proactively determined.

Group Application: Describe the vision God has given you or the ministry you are a part of. Describe how the vision has drawn people and a ministry team. Are there any hindrances at this time? At what phase or stage is the development currently?

Five Ways Vision Impacts a Team

1. **Vision inspires people.** Vision inspires people by providing a hopeful picture of some future reality. Vision for the leader is like air for humans; without it you die. With no clear destination defined, most people fall into a mode of maintaining whatever they are doing, without seeking to improve or pursue greater causes.

2. **Vision attracts people.** Vision attracts people to a cause by giving them something worth investing their lives in. Every human being has a deep need to feel like he is giving his life to something worthwhile. Vision breaks people from the mundane of everyday life and gives a reason to exist.

3. **Vision builds cooperation.** Vision builds cooperation and unity by providing something to rally around. Cooperation and unity is not something you can just decide to have. It is a by-product of pursuing a common vision.

4. **Vision sustains longevity.** Vision sustains longevity by giving the team a reason to persevere through difficult times. If people have a purpose, they are more likely to stick it out, especially during the inevitable tough moments and seasons.

5. **Vision facilitates evaluation.** Vision facilitates evaluation on an ongoing basis by defining goals that can be continually measured. Unless a target is identified, how can you know whether you hit it? With a clearly defined vision, a team can evaluate whether they are accomplishing what they set out to do.

Four Keys to Shaping the Team's Vision

1. **Know God.** You must know God intimately. The better you know God, the better you will know His vision for the team. The vision must reflect the character, nature and purposes of God, or it isn't His! Hearing from God requires intimacy with Him. Prayer, fasting and other spiritual disciplines are critical.

2. **Know your team.** You must know the team's mix of gifts, talents, temperaments, and character (strengths and flaws). The better you know your team members, the better you will know what part they can play in shaping the vision. Without this knowledge, more outspoken temperament types may well dominate the discussion, leaving out the wisdom, creativity, and insights of quieter team members.

3. **Know your team's role.** You must know the team's role in the overall ministry. The larger the ministry, the more teams you will have. Each team is a sub-set of all other teams. Therefore, every team's vision must be inter-dependent with all the others. It is important when shaping a vision to determine what part of the overall vision is your team's responsibility.

4. **Know the group your team will lead.** Your team must know the larger group they lead. No matter how wonderful the vision, you are only the leader if you have followers! Therefore, the larger overall group's ownership of the vision

is critical to success. The primary danger in a team shaping a vision is what some have termed "Group Think." Group Think can occur when a conclusion is reached that doesn't hold up when exposed to the group that was not a part of the dialogue.

Discussion Questions:

1. Define both a ministry task and a ministry leadership team.
2. What is the main purpose of a ministry leadership team?
3. What are the three ingredients that comprise a leadership team?
4. Name the five functions of a team leader.
5. Describe several ways a vision impacts a team.

Chapter 19

ORGANIZATION FOR PASTORS

The mid-sixth century B.C. was a time of gloom for the people of God. Most were still in captivity in Persia, though God's servant Zerubbabel had returned in 538 after the decree of Cyrus followed by Ezra's trip in 458 B.C. The report from this second trip reached Nehemiah in the castle of the Persian King at Susa (Neh. 1:3-4).

We know nothing of this servant before the opening of the book that bears his name, but immediately we learn that God's Word has introduced us to a leader with both a servant heart and supervisory hands. The Book of Nehemiah teaches us that spiritual leadership does not scorn proper administrative principles, particularly the principle of organizing one's work. After clear emphasis on prayer (1:4-11), a clarification of priorities (2:1-5), and quite specific preparation for his task (vv. 6-10), Nehemiah unfolded his plan for the development of the walls in the city (vv. 11-18). In chapter 3 we see his organizational commitment to two very crucial principles: decentralization of responsibility and delegation of work and authority. As a leader Nehemiah had identified with the people, initiated a workable solution for their problems, and led them in invoking the faithfulness of God on the project. This 2,500-year-old-model stands before us today.

"Organizing," as we use that word within the context of this book, means to arrange, acquire, and allocate adequate resources in order to achieve clear objectives. Perhaps it would be useful to briefly review several key principles of organizing.

1. **Organizing serves no end in itself:** We do not create organizational machinery just so we can say we are organized. Machinery does not constitute ministry and can become a barrier rather than a blessing. In any organization the possibilities for failure are greater than those for success,

even though the emphasis of modern-day literature focuses almost exclusively on the latter. So wise leaders allow for failure, forgive it, and even plan for it by always organizing "Plan B" as a backup for organizational strategies.

2. **Organizing should always grow out of need:** The selection of the original "deacons" in Acts 6 provides a beautiful example. Until the need arose for food distribution to the Hellenistic widows, no organization in the church carried out that function. Original frameworks in churches and Christian organizations tend to outlive the needs which gave them birth.

3. **Organization depends on decentralization:** Decentralization moves decision-making to the lowest possible level. Obviously this also leads to maximal participation in the ministry, one of the biblical goals toward which leaders must be striving all the time.

4. **Organizing should be flexible:** Organizational variables abound in every program of ministry – immaturity of the people it serves; differences in culture even within the same country; changes in time and people; and changes in needs which call for different kinds of ministries than we initiated ten or twenty years ago.

5. **Organizing works best with wide participation:** Since the body of Christ consist of a universal priesthood of believers, involvement in the ministry is crucial for every member of the congregation. This gives them ownership, which leads to productivity instead of a spectator mentality we so often find in local congregations.

6. **Organizing requires records and reports:** Planning depends on available data, and the more comprehensive and

accurate the data, the better the planning process can proceed.

Introduction to Organization

Notable Quotes:

"Unless he manages himself effectively, no amount of ability, skill, experience or knowledge will make an executive effective."

"If we do not successfully manage ourselves, we will not be successful in managing others."

Time management and organization are matters of EXCELLENCE. To excel means *"to go beyond or above; to outdo, to surpass."* The Greek concept means: *To exceed a fixed number of sequences; to be increased, as in talents – invest, work with, improve them; to be abundantly furnished with or to be pre-eminent.*

The Bible challenges us to excel (abound) or go beyond the normal limits:

- In our expression of righteousness

    Matthew 5:20 For I say to you, that unless your righteousness exceeds the righteousness of the scribes and Pharisees, you will by no means enter the kingdom of heaven.

- In our demonstration of love one to another

    Philippians 1:9 And this I pray, that your love may abound still more and more in knowledge and all discernment,

- In a lifestyle that is pleasing to the Lord

    1 Thessalonians 4:1 Finally then, brethren, we urge and exhort in the Lord Jesus that you should abound more and more, just as you received from us how you ought to walk and to please God;

- In edifying the church

    1 Corinthians 14:12 Even so you, since you are zealous for spiritual gifts, let it be for the edification of the church that you seek to excel.

- In the work of the Lord

    1 Corinthians 15:58 Therefore, my beloved brethren, be steadfast, immovable, always abounding in the work of the Lord, knowing that your labor is not in vain in the Lord.

    1 Thessalonians 4:10 and indeed you do so toward all the brethren who are in all Macedonia. But we urge you, brethren, that you increase more and more;

Time management and organization are matters of STEWARDSHIP. Stewardship is the practice of systematic and proportionate giving of time, abilities, and material possession based on the conviction that these are a trust from God to be used in His service for the benefit of His kingdom. It is the recognition of God's ownership of one's person, one's powers and one's possessions and the faithful use of these for the advancement of Christ's kingdom in this world. Man is responsible for becoming all that God has made it possible for him to become. We increase our ability, stability and responsibility as we increase our accountability to God.

To organize is to bring together or form as a whole or combination as for a common objective; to organize systematically. What is God's relationship to organization? Well we know that God is a God of order and arrangement who delights in bringing order out of chaos. He did this in creation (Heb. 11:3). The word "framed" means to arrange, adjust or put in order. He wants this to be characteristic of the church.

God is very systematic in His approach to problems and projects. Creation testifies to this (Genesis 1-2). His approach to world evangelism bears this out (Acts 1:8). God wanted Adam, who was made in the image of God to share this attribute. Maintenance and organization extend the boundaries. God has given every one of us, who are made in the image of God, a specific work to do. When we fail to plan, we plan to fail. God wants every one of us to increase our capacity to get the job done. As we are faithful, God wants to expand our capacity and give us more work and responsibility. The reward of being faithful is that you are given more work. Jesus said, "For whoever has, to him more will be given, and he will have abundance; but whoever does not have, even what he has will be taken away from him (Matt. 13:12). The difference between a productive, efficient person and a frustrated, unfruitful one is in many cases organization and self-management.

Tips on Personal Organization

First, you must recognize your need. Jesus said, "Blessed are the poor in spirit, for theirs is the kingdom of heaven" (Matt. 5:3). Some symptoms of a management problem could include: unfinished projects, unfulfilled goals, frustration, lacking a sense of direction (reacting to problems), no sense of personal accomplishment, a feeling of being overwhelmed, a low sense of value, life out of control and experiencing guilt (feeling your letting people down).

Second, find someone who is doing well and follow them. The apostle Paul wrote "Imitate me, just as I also imitate Christ" (1 Cor. 11:1). What we lack we are to look to others in the Body of Christ to supply. Find out what they <u>are doing</u> that you are not. Find out what they <u>are not doing</u> that you are.

Other tips that will help are to:

- **Control your telephone.** You don't want to be interrupted by a phone or anything else in the middle of writing a report, preparing a sermon, or doing something else that takes deep mental concentration. Trying to get jobs done between phone calls is both annoying and counterproductive.

- **Learn to say no!** For some reason most of us in Christian work find that answer difficult. Even when we do turn down some new task or speaking engagement we feel compelled to give a number of reasons or excuses. But we stand under no obligation to serve people who are not a part of the specific organization or ministry God has placed us in. Even within that primary arena of service there may be exceptions to what we should do. So it becomes important to say no without giving reasons. Many of us try to do too much. We forget that God isn't impressed by what we do as much as by what we are. The more we focus on what God wants us to be, the more time management will fall into place. The efficient leader says, "I do things right" and of course, we all favor that choice. The effective worker, however says, "I do the right things" and that could hardly include everything we are asked to do. Saying no may very well be a spiritual discipline cultivated after we understand the objectives and priorities of the ministry to which God has called us.

- **Rigorously maintain an appointment book.** People who fail to meet appointments leave the following impressions: They are careless (They could care less). They are unconcerned and indifferent. They are selfish (Your time is more important than my time). They are irresponsible. Don't schedule appointments too close together. Try to leave ½ hr. in between to do cleanup and pray. Do things on time. Try to plan out the week in advance. This will save you time in transition. It will also give you weekly goals to accomplish. Keep paper and pencil handy at all times. Make lists of the things that you are going to do. Keep them in prominent places. Review them daily. At the end of every day list the next things you were going to do. Do the unexpected at the first available opportunity. Try not to let it hang so you can get on your normal schedule. And maintain a schedule for usual and customary activity.

• **Have and maintain a place for everything.** This includes a filing system for sermons, notes, magazine articles, etc. The key word here is "retrieval." Anybody can put things in a folder, put the folder in a file drawer and close the closet door. The question is, can you find it again when you need it? Organize your environment. Order begets order.

• **Know your own personal limitations.** Don't make promises that you cannot keep.

• **Order a large wastebasket.** Somebody has called this function "wastebasketry." Some leaders suggest we should deal with every piece of paper only once. That may be a bit idealistic. But let's focus for the moment on the "toss" action. Junk mail, brochures, flyers, contest in which somebody just can't wait to give you a million dollars, and such items fill up that big wastebasket in a hurry.

• **Set realistic goals and plan accordingly** (Personal, family, ministry and perhaps business life, etc.) We will deal with this in the next chapter.

- **Make a place for leisure time.** Everyone needs some time to recreate. This is where the ability to plan and dream gets re-energized.

- **Delegate some activities to others while retaining control.** You should not be doing anything that someone else can do.

Discussion Questions:

1. Why should a leader have a plan 'B' when organizing a strategy for a goal?
2. Define organizing as used in the context of this chapter.
3. What are three challenges the Bible gives us to go beyond our limits?
4. How can we increase our ability, stability and responsibility?
5. Give two major tips on personal organization.

Chapter 20

SETTING AND ACHIEVING GOALS

The primary characteristic of administrative leadership is purpose. When one looks at films of Roger Bannister running the four-minute mile there seems to be nothing particularly spectacular. It's just another race among milers of similar abilities who stay extremely close throughout the run. But when that final inner command told Bannister to start his kick, he moved out ahead of the pack, reached the finish line, and fell exhausted. It seemed as though he had measured his energy to the last foot to achieve his goal. One is reminded of the final achievement statement of the Apostle Paul in his very last letter to a friend. Writing from the prison in Rome he said, "I have fought the good fight, I have finished the race, I have kept the faith. Now there is in store for me the crown of righteousness, which the Lord, the righteous Judge, will award to me on that day – and not only to me, but also to all who have longed for His appearing" (2 Tim. 4:7-8).

Goals are like signs. They correctly point out that the real evidence of effectiveness in administrative leadership rests in achieved goals. There are three assumptions about all organizations:

1. **All organizations have goals.** In many churches crisis management appears to be the order of the day – every day. The leadership seems to focus exclusively on problems, rushing from one aspect of the work to another to "put out fires." Nevertheless, all organizations have goals. They may not have them spelled out. People in the organization may not know about them. Leaders may vary in their understanding of those goals. But the very existence of the church indicates that somewhere, sometime, somebody thought about goals. How does a church go about clarifying goals and objectives? Any given congregation must understand the nature and purpose of the church. The

questions asked should reach beyond those generalizable purposes with which every evangelical congregation ought to be concerned (worship, evangelism, missions, etc.). They should identify precise kinds of things God expects of your congregation in your location at this time in history.

2. **All organizations have some structure to facilitate goal achievement.** Setting and achieving goals must take into consideration the importance of sequencing, priorities, and deadlines. Sequencing refers to the stages in the process of goal-setting. Priorities refer not necessarily to time, but importance. Putting first things first, may mean doing a number of lesser things earlier since they pave the way for the more important steps down the road. When we discuss deadlines we talk about when certain goals will be achieved in the progress toward achieving our ultimate purpose.

3. **All organizations have some administration to accommodate the structure.** Administration is simply a tool which, when properly used, can produce significant benefits for any congregation or organization. It can help that organization to be effective as well as efficient. Within its proper role, administration facilitates the structure that leads to goal achievement. Consider the following questions for your ministry:

    a. Can you state your objectives?

    b. Have you chosen what God really wants for your ministry or what seems attractive in similar ministries of your acquaintance?

    c. Does your entire staff understand and agree with your goals and priorities?

d. Do you bring others into the decision-making process?

   e. Will you know when to abandon certain unachievable goals?

   f. Do you help people toward accountability for the institution's goals?

Goal-Orientation and Problem Solving

Many churches practice solving problems (crisis management) rather than achieving objectives. Such a tendency can be measured and corrected. There is a way that you can evaluate if your ministry tends to be problem oriented. Four questions can give you some definitive clues; you need not guess nor offer subjective opinions.

1. **How often do we initiate change?** The Apostle Paul was a master innovator. Virtually every aspect of his ministry was characterized by some new way of handling a challenge in order to achieve his goals. Remember the dramatic paragraph in 1 Corinthians 9 in which Paul describes how it was sometimes necessary to relate to the weak and sometimes even to be like a slave? He ends with the words, "I have become all things to all men so that by all possible means I might save some. I do all this for the sake of the Gospel, that I may share in its blessings" (1 Cor. 9:22-23). Always difficult, in some Christian organizations, change can be downright agonizing!

2. **What has stimulated recent changes in our ministry?** Some organizations change because others force change on them. But forced change doesn't count as objective-orientation. As a matter of fact, if you have to admit that

recent changes in your ministry have come about because of pressure (either internal or external), you may be describing problem-orientation. Ministry-by-objectives has not only demonstrated strategic changes in recent years but can show that those changes came from creative thinking within the organization.

3. **Do we have room for the "free thinker"?** Not a theological radical but one whose leadership ideas differ from the way we have always done things. He may just be the person who stimulates that new idea we so desperately need. The objective-oriented organization designs an open system in which all members can have significant voice.

4. **How do we spend the time in our business meetings?** This question can be answered on a quantitative basis. Without warning, sneak a stopwatch into the next elder, deacon, or board meeting. While the group talks about problems let the watch run. During discussions about objectives and plans for future ministry, cut it off. Then measure the difference. The problem-oriented meeting spends an inordinate percentage of meeting time just solving problems. To put it another way, formal business meetings such as organization will reflect its administrative style.

How can a Problem-Oriented Organization Become Goal-Oriented?

What kinds of things can you do in an elder's meeting? Since we looked at four questions earlier, let's offer four suggestions here – four ways to develop an objective-oriented ministry.

1. **Decentralize the decision-making process.** To decentralize means to push down from the top and, therefore, to involve more people, preferably those who are closest to the actual

functions influenced by the decision. Notice how decentralized decision-making dominated the early church. In the first chapter of Acts, they select an apostle to replace Judas. God makes the choice but everyone has a voice. In the sixth chapter they decentralized the selection of the seven "deacons." In chapter 13 the church ("they") deliberates in the sending out of missionaries. An objective-oriented ministry steers away from autocratic dominance because it knows that God speaks through people, not just pastors.

2. **Ask God for a change in the people.** Changing people is more important than changing things because if you change things and God doesn't change people, those people will change the things back to the way they once were. Problem-oriented people cannot become objective-oriented people unless they change. And problem-oriented people can never produce an objective-oriented ministry.

3. **Eliminate timidity throughout the organization.** This correlates with the third question. If we really have room for the free thinker, the one who is out of step with the popular wisdom of the present leaders, then we need to let him and others know that we want his voice to be heard. Such two-way communication encourages subordinates to speak to leaders, assuming the willingness of leaders to listen.

4. **Program both administration and meetings for goal achievement.** The key here is the agenda. If we pre-package the agenda with numerous front-loaded problem issues we have arranged a problem-oriented meeting. Then, too or three hours after struggling with all the horrible problems the church faces, we make our way to discussion of future planning and goal achievement. By then everyone is tired, anxious to go home, and that portion of the agenda gets brushed over very lightly. We have affirmed that we really want to give priority attention to problems and if we still

have some spare time for objectives, that's fine. I'm suggesting the reverse of that. Front-load the agenda with specific goal/planning items and take the problems in the appropriate time. The available business meeting time could also be divided so that at a certain hour the group stops talking about one and gives its attention to the other.

How Can We Apply MBO Principles to Ministry?

MBO [*Managing-by-objectives*] is the philosophy and process of managing based on identifying purpose, objectives, and desired results; establishing a realistic program for obtaining these results; and evaluating performance and achieving them.

Can we identify specific steps that a church or other Christian organization can take to conform to this ministry-by-objectives approach? Indeed we can, and they all relate to an understanding and mutual agreement of goals and objectives on the part of every one in the organization, especially the leadership team. Pastors, for example, can take ten specific steps toward employing a ministry-by-objectives pattern in the church.

1. **Define the church's purpose and mission.** Who are you? Why are you there? What does God expect of you?

2. **Realistically assess the church's strengths and weaknesses.** What about location? Denominational affiliation? Lay leadership? Pulpit ministry? How does this advance or detract from goal achievement?

3. **Write specific and measurable objectives for the church's key ministry areas which spring from its purpose.** Involve as many people as you can in the writing, soliciting opinions from leaders and followers alike.

4. **Work to obtain a general agreement on your objectives.** We've not yet reached long-range planning, so objectives might just cover one year of ministry (though five would be better). In the last step, we asked people as individuals to contribute their views of where the church ought to go. Now we're talking to the body as a group attempting to refine our objectives to arrive at a plan which really represents the body's "call."

5. **Strive to attain job control as quickly as possible.** In a major leadership post, that may take a year or more.

6. **Develop strategies on how to use available resources to meet your objectives.** Resources include such things as money, buildings, time, equipment, and yes, even people.

7. **Determine to practice accountability.** Goals must be claimed by people. Every member needs to see where he fits and how he relates to the total picture.

8. **Design long- and short-range plans to meet objectives.** We'll have more to say about this later, so here we'll just review the axiom that a goal needs a plan to make it work.

9. **Be willing to change or modify objectives, plans, or strategies as the situational variables may require.** If one of your objectives calls for hiring a minister of Christian education within three years and for some reason that occurs in the first year, you will probably need a modification of all plans related to Christian education. On the negative side, if certain objectives were keyed to the receipt of financial contributions which did not appear, restructuring might be required.

10. **Measure progress all along the way.** A good leadership team evaluates itself and builds in a system for monitoring

progress through formal reviews, mutual accountability, and examination of achievement levels.

Four Stages in the Process of Goal-Setting

Any organization serious about setting and achieving goals will give itself to a careful sorting out of four steps or levels in that process.

1. Purpose / Mission Statements

A mission statement is not usually measurable but it describes the general direction of the organization using phrases like "fulfilling the Great Commission in our community," or "bringing glory to God." A mission statement should be tightly packaged in one or two paragraphs, accurately describing the ministry over which it lies like a flag on a castle. Mission statements are notably broad based.

2. Objectives

While the mission statement has a somewhat singular focus, objectives must be multiple focused. Specificity begins to build as we now spell out precisely what it will take to achieve the purpose of the organization. The value of setting objectives for any organization lies in the process of moving from general to specific concepts. Goals become the avenue by which we reach the point of meeting needs.

3. Goals

Get ready for even more specific thinking. Just as a single mission statement has multiple objectives, each objective has multiple goals. It seems futile just to say that goals differ from objectives by being more specific, so let's look at an example.

Under the general category of leadership development, a church developed an objective which read, "To recruit and train new leaders for boards and committees." How might this be broken down more specifically into multiple goals? Here are a couple of examples:

1. Through elevating the privilege of serving the Lord in leadership.

2. Through service activities as assistants and committee members.

Not very sophisticated you say? To be sure it was this church's first attempt at a five-year plan with specifically developed levels of objectives. But do you agree that the goals serve the objective and that the objective stays in line with what most evangelical churches would want to achieve? Planners work hard to keep from staying general too long (so that goals still sound like mission statements) and to keep from getting specific too soon (so that objectives look like realization procedures). So let's add this fourth component and get the full picture.

4. Realization Procedures (Implementation Steps)

Essential to everything we have said about setting and achieving goals is the issue of accountability. In an organization, goals cannot be set and achieved by one person or even by a small leadership task force. Yes, the vision needs to originate somewhere and the initiative for carrying out the planning process may indeed come from the pastor or a small group of staff leaders. But ultimately we must develop accountability throughout the organization.

In the Pastoral Epistles, Paul calls Timothy and Titus to be accountable to their people and to hold their people accountable. Accountability demands mutual commitment which does not attach itself automatically to offices in the church. Sometimes accountability lags because people don't understand what we're trying to do. Nothing you have read so far is operational unless people make it work. If your church or Christian organization does not have clear, concise, measurable goals, you will have a great deal of difficulty placing or accepting accountability. Accountability assumes an ability to measure. If there are no goals, there is nothing against which to measure progress ... The function of leadership is to lead. Leadership needs to lay out broad purposes and directions. But effective leadership will bring in as many people as possible to refine purposes into goals and work out ways not only to meet those goals, but to measure progress (to be held accountable) along the way.

    Implementation of the material in this chapter on setting and achieving goals could revolutionize your church or ministry. How eloquently Paul put it when he wrote, "Brothers, I do not consider myself yet to have taken hold of it. But one thing I do: Forgetting what is behind and straining toward what is ahead, I press on toward the goal to win the prize for which God has called me heavenward in Christ Jesus. All of us who are mature should take such a view of things" (Phil. 3:13-15).

Discussion Questions:
1. How does the objective-oriented ministry steer away from autocratic dominance?
2. In your own estimation, why is it important to measure progress along the way of achieving your goals?

Chapter 21

SHORT-AND LONG-RANGE PLANNING

Why should my church plan? Well perhaps another question we could ask is, "Is God a strategic thinker?" To answer the above questions, let's look at some relevant scripture verses.

Jeremiah 29:11-13 For I know the thoughts that I think toward you, says the Lord, thoughts of peace and not of evil, to give you a future and a hope. [12] Then you will call upon Me and go and pray to Me, and I will listen to you. [13] And you will <u>seek Me</u> and find Me, when you search for Me <u>with all your heart</u>.

Proverbs 3:5-8 <u>Trust in the Lord with all your heart</u>, and lean not on your own understanding; [6] In all your ways acknowledge Him, and <u>He shall direct your paths</u>. [7] Do not be wise in your own eyes; fear the Lord and depart from evil. [8] <u>It will be health to your flesh, and strength to your bones.</u>

Proverbs 15:22 Without counsel, plans go awry, but <u>in the multitude of counselors they are established</u>.

Philippians 2:1-4 Therefore if there is any consolation in Christ, if any comfort of love, if any fellowship of the Spirit, if any affection and mercy, [2] fulfill my joy by <u>being like-minded</u>, having the same love, <u>being of one accord, of one mind</u>. [3] Let nothing be done through selfish ambition or conceit, but in lowliness of mind let each esteem others better than himself. [4] <u>Let each of you look out not only for his own interests, but also for the interests of others.</u>

Ephesians. 4:11-13 And He Himself gave some to be apostles, some prophets, some evangelists, and some pastors and teachers, [12] <u>for the equipping of the saints for the work of ministry</u>, for the edifying of the body of Christ, [13] till we all come to the unity of the faith and of the knowledge of the Son of God, to a perfect man, to the measure of the stature of the fullness of Christ;

Matthew 25:14-30 *Summation:* Out of good stewardship; multiply what has been entrusted into your care.

Acts 6:1-7 *Summation:* So that you may maintain proper focus on your mission – empower others to serve and lead.

Romans 8:14 For as many as are <u>led by the Spirit of God, these are sons of God.</u>

Corinthians 1:12-2:4 *Summation:* Paul's change of plans showed integrity in his decision-making; God's grace in the process; appealing to others to understand; consistency in every ordinary planning process.

What is Strategic Planning?

Strategic planning is a <u>process</u> that helps leadership to be active and positive rather than passive about their position in history. It is <u>action oriented</u> where there is a concentrating on key decisions that will affect the future; <u>participatory</u> and highly tolerant of controversy; and <u>sensitive</u> to the many elements which affect the success of a given strategy; such as: Biblical / theological mandates; the leading of the Holy Spirit; traditions, values and aspirations; social, cultural, and environmental trends; abilities and priorities of leadership; institutional strengths and weaknesses and special opportunities, resources, etc.

Why then the resistance? Why do we fear the process of developing Holy Spirit directed strategies for our churches? We lack discipline, experience, faith in the process and the resources and know-how. We also lack accountability, tend to resist change and tend to write off planning as worldly.

What are the Common Pitfalls of Planning?

1. We make it too complex.

2. We don't reach conclusions and make an action plan;

3. Or we make an action plan without coming to conclusions.

4. The action plan isn't simple and compelling.

5. We don't revisit and revise the plan.

6. We let the process take too long.

7. We don't listen enough to God in prayer and instead trust our own instincts.

8. Strategic planning is a process that God through His Holy Spirit must direct. Let's be people of prayer and trust Him for His design for our church.

In this chapter we will talk about short-range planning as being anything up to a year and long-range planning any period beyond that. Most churches need to start with a one-year plan, work up to multiple years, and eventually work on at least a five-year plan subject to revisions on an annual basis. Many of our failures, particularly failures in achieving goals, are due to either poor planning or a total lack of planning.

Where Do We Commonly Go Wrong?

1. **Often our objectives never get cleared up**; they remain unrelated to a quality mission statement and, therefore, unable to give birth to legitimate goals.

2. **Sometimes planning fails because we don't involve people.** Even if the pastor and board carry out the planning function, actual realization of the goals must involve a much wider group of people. Planning can be a very useful way of involving many people in considerable depth. The act of asking individuals or groups to consider alternate or optimum ways of reaching their goals, or the act of asking them to make proposals to the organization can be the trigger for a series of events. It cannot only give people the feeling of having participated in the organization, but can also stimulate a host of new ideas.

3. **Effective planning depends on identification of legitimate resources.** When we think only about finances (and many churches limit their planning to this dimension), we cripple the planning process – all resources essential for goal achievement must be spelled out.

4. **Just as planning can fail because of poor objectives, it can fail because of poor goals.** Goals must be specific, measurable, and realistic. Even then not all planning succeeds, but at least we give it a chance.

5. **Planning sometimes fails because the planning group either did not understand the mission, objectives, goals, and implementation steps of the organization**, or, if charges with creating these, did not understand the process of goal-setting. Such a group will often build into the plan projects or ideas which do not relate to the objectives of the ministry.

6. **Since planning is based on evaluation, the process requires a clear-cut assessment of the previous year (or years).** Fuzzy evaluation leads to fuzzy planning, causing future fuzziness in evaluation, and on it goes – planning and evaluation form an inseparable cycle.

Foundations for Effective Planning

We need to discuss how to actually design a plan. Some people feel that planning denies faith and represents unbiblical activity. The models of Joseph in famine relief; Moses in desert survival; David in military strategies; Solomon in massive building projects; and Paul in missionary itinerating should lay to rest any suspicion that long-range planning is unbiblical. Before we get into process, however, let's talk about principles one more time.

Principles of the Planning Process

1. **Planning is an investment, not an expenditure of time.** The housewife who writes out a list of tasks to be accomplished on a morning outing in town does not spend time by prioritizing those tasks in relation to geography, opening and closing times of certain businesses, and the urgency with which they must be achieved. A fifteen-minute investment in such an analysis might pay off three- or fourfold on the trip itself.

2. **Planning requires careful attention to immediate choices because immediate choices greatly expand or narrow future options.**

3. **Planning is cyclically based on evaluation.**

4. **Planning demands acting objectively toward goal realization.** Remember our axiom? A goal needs a plan to

make it work. Likewise, a plan needs clear-cut objectives and goals to give it any reality or meaning. Only when those objectives and goals are owned and acted on does planning become a process rather than a blueprint.

5. **Planning helps us note the relationship between determining what we want to do and realizing that end.** To put it another way, a direct and strategic ratio exists between the planning of an event and its occurrence.

6. **In planning, specificity increases as the event draws near.** Even short-range (up to one year) planning (sometimes called project planning) we can see this principle at work.

7. **Planning requires maximum participation.**

8. **Planning demands that the effort applied be commensurate with the results desired.** The more careful the planning, the more likely the results (goal achievement). The more careless the planning, the less likely that those dreams and visions will translate into goals and actually come to pass.

Evaluation and Analysis in Planning

Analysis is two fold: looking in the mirror and looking out the window. The more data we collect, assuming they are accurate, the better the planning process. Sometimes the evaluation stage is painful as we dig up things we would just as soon forget.

Planning becomes more difficult in a new church or one in which poor records have been kept. The shaky data base reduces the analysis and evaluation to guesswork. Even then, however, we must gather all the information we can, using the best possible tools.

Assumptions in the Planning Process

After gathering all the data we can, internally and externally, we make some "assumptions' regarding what will happen in future years. Don't miss the important distinction between analysis and assumption. The analysis deals with the past and assumption with the future. Such *"forecasting," builds a scenario of future trends on an extrapolation of the past.* Assumptions are constructed on the basis of analysis and interpretation of what appear to be valid trends.

The planning which follows the forecasting must initially focus on analysis of mission, clearly defining the role which the church or institution plays in its current setting. As we look out the window (external analysis), we want to be able to say something intelligent about the economic environment of our ministry, the demographic environment (demography has to do with population shifts numerically, geographically, and in other ways), certainly the moral/religious environment, and possibly the political and educational arenas.

The assumption then becomes a pivot point in the planning process. On the other hand, we look back and review our evaluation to make sure that our assumptions have been correctly drawn from an accurate analysis. Then looking toward the future, we build our objectives, goals, and realization procedures on the basis of our assumptions.

Common Questions about Effective Planning

Should Christians Plan Long-Range?

God's leaders throughout history have done long-range planning with His apparent blessing. Sometimes (particularly eschatology) it gets in the way, but only because we think "wrongly." One can believe in the imminent return of Jesus Christ and yet recognize any kind of date-setting as unbiblical nonsense. Paul clearly taught this view, yet urged in all his letters that the churches develop "long-range Christians" whose spiritual lives would build toward maturity.

To the Galatians Paul wrote, "Let us not become weary in doing good, for at the proper time we will reap a harvest if we do not give up" (Gal. 6:9). The apostle spoke quite frequently of planting, watering, and reaping. There has never been a farmer who reaped a harvest without some kind of planning. The soil must be prepared at just the right time of the year, the seeds planted after the danger of frost has passed, and the young plants given water and warmth. The skillful mind and hands of the farmer must plan every phase from planting to harvest.

The analogy certainly applies to all phases of Christian ministry. Without proper planning for all phases of ministry, we cannot expect the kind of harvest God promises from the seed of His Word. Teachers who are adequately trained to plant, water, and reap can change a lackluster traditional Sunday School program into a dynamic Bible-teaching and evangelism center.

Isn't Planning a Denial of Faith?

On the contrary, the question betrays little understanding of biblical teaching on leadership. It strikes me as being similar to the question of why we should spend any time studying for preaching or teaching when the Holy Spirit is perfectly capable of giving us precisely what we should say as we stand up to speak. Without doubt; but the Scriptures emphasize that the Holy Spirit activates us in the study process as well as in the speaking process. The tone of the Pastoral Epistles urges Timothy and Titus to be students of God's Word so that by careful instruction they could bring to naught the words of false teachers.

Likewise, the role of faith and hope can be as active in the planning process as in the realization process. Hope looks not for the future which it can engender, make, or put at its disposal but rather for the future which God puts at its disposal. Hope expects the future which God promises.

Who Should Be Part of the Planning Team?

Good question. Not everybody in the church or Christian organization holds adequate qualifications to serve on the planning team. People who do not believe planning is biblical will hardly make good members. Negative, pessimistic people who constantly explain why things can't be achieved would only slow down the process. Legalistic types, who feel bound by all traditions of the past feel uncomfortable and threatened struggling with the potential of the future.

Biblically, we can see a marvelous contrast in mind-set between the Pharisees and the early missionaries, particularly Paul. The former were landlocked in the past and determined to preserve it in the present. The latter were grateful for the past, dissatisfied with the present, and eager for what God had in the future.

Why Do Plans Sometimes Fail?

Why is it that sometimes after we have planned, those plans do not develop? Consider these problems expounded in a book by Jeffry Timmons under the heading "Why Plans Fail."

1. No real goals – a goal statement that does not describe an end state is not a goal.
2. No measurable objectives.
3. Failure to anticipate obstacles – actually a plan should be flexible enough to handle obstacles, whether anticipated or not.
4. Lack of progress review – these provide corrections in direction, pace, and reality.
5. Lack of commitment – the unwillingness to see a plan through to its completion.
6. Failure to revise objectives – this links up with number 3 and calls again for flexibility in the plan.

7. Failure to learn from experience – we need to listen to feedback and with every obstacle ask, "What did we learn this time?"

Concluding Thoughts on Planning

We've noted earlier the experience of planning in the lives of Biblical characters. Let's close the chapter by citing some helpful planning proverbs and a planning prayer.

God Plans for Us

Jeremiah 29:11-12 "I know the plans I have for you," says the Lord, "plans to prosper you and not harm you, plans to give you hope and a future." (NIV)

God Expects Us to Plan

Proverbs 16:3 Commit to the Lord whatever you do, and your plans will succeed.

God Describes Planning as a Group Process

Proverbs 15:22 Plans fail for lack of counsel, but with many advisers they succeed.

It is God Who Will Make Our Plans Succeed

Proverbs 16:3 Commit to the Lord whatever you do, and your plans will succeed.

And for all those who read this chapter and share the tasks and burdens of planning, here is the prayer of David: "May He give you the desire of your heart and make all your plans succeed" (Psalm 20:4).

Discussion Questions:

1. Name three scriptures that describes the directives concerning planning.
2. What four things are we to know about strategic planning?
3. What are two pitfalls of planning and how could they be avoided?
4. Give a scriptural example of long-term planning?
5. In what ways does God tell us that planning is good?

Chapter 22

ASSESSING NEEDS, GIFTS, AND CALL

Long before we think about training and placement, even prior to the process of recruitment, we must grapple with *assessment – an analysis of the present situation with special focus on needs, gifts, and call.* In the spiritual framework of the body of Christ, God calls the biblical servant to minister to others, and he must effectively carry out that ministry in the attitude of Christ-like perspective and the reality of spiritual power. In order to do so he needs help in understanding the *needs* which require the ministry, the *gifts* which respond to the ministry, and the *call* which places him in ministry. Certain qualifications and characteristics mark effective leaders. An effective leader must:

1. Be wholly dedicated to God's glory (Eph. 1).

2. Understand the principles and practice of God's grace (Acts 20:24).

3. Have a burden and concern for the entire body (1 Cor. 12; Eph. 4:11-16).

4. Stand firmly for reconciliation (2 Cor. 5:11-21).

5. Model godly living in his own family and the body (Phil. 3:17; 1 Thes. 2:9-10).

6. Lead in accordance with biblical principles (Luke 22:24-27).

7. Serve others willingly (1 Peter 4:10-11).

8. Endeavor to make disciples (Matt. 28:18-20).

9. Reproduce himself in new leadership (Acts 11:19-30).

Obviously all of these are more applicable to professional staff but this is not a chapter about professional staff except as they bear responsibility for the development of leadership. One of the surveys implemented by the Win Arn Church Growth Center uncovered "Ten Questions Most Often Asked by Church Leaders." They spotlight the importance of our subject in this chapter.

1. How can I see more members involved in sharing their Christian faith with others?

2. How can we help our present members to be more open to newcomers and make them feel a part of the fellowship?

3. How can we involve more members in the ministry of our church?

4. How can our new members find a place of belonging in their new church home?

5. How can we train a task force in developing a successful ministry program?

6. How can our evangelism program be more effective in reaching unchurched persons in our community?

7. How can we build a strategy in placing members in positions that enhance their spiritual gifts?

8. How can I help our members discover that evangelism does not mean tight collars, stomach butterflies, and sweaty palms?

9. How can we close our "back door" so the people who join our church don't become inactive in the first year?

10. How can we keep our church staff and leaders at the "cutting edge" of effective growth and ministry insights, and all pulling together toward the same common goals?

At best we can respond to this vast area of need assessment by breaking it down into a broad-narrow focus for ministry which begins with the world and ends at a specific point of service.

Needs of the World

A decision of leadership in the local church must treat the wider subject of volunteerism, a major issue of public concern in America today. When Ronald Reagan was President, he argued for four years that the nation should pay less attention to government and more attention to volunteerism. Early in his first administration he told a story about a high tide and storm-generated surf in Newport Beach, California.

> All through the day and cold winter night, volunteers worked filling and piling sandbags in an effort to save those homes. Local TV stations, aware of the drama of the situation, covered the struggle. It was about 2:00 A.M. when one newscaster grabbed a young fellow in his teens, attired only in wet trunks. He had been working day and night – one of several hundred of his age-group. No, he did not live in one of the homes they were trying to save. He was cold and tired. The newscaster wanted to know why he and his friends were doing this. The answer was poignant, and so true it should be printed on a billboard. "Well," he said, "I guess it's the first time we ever felt like we were needed."

Just a few years later a Gallup Poll showed that Americans are volunteering more than ever. Fifty-two percent of the population is involved in some voluntary action and 31 percent in organized, structured volunteerism on a regular basis. Interestingly, the largest percentage of volunteers, serve in religious activities (19 percent).

We live in a needy world and the response of the church must be more than sandbagging floods and handing out food baskets. The fulfilling of the Great Commission in the broadest sense requires the enlistment of many volunteers on a level unprecedented since the first and second centuries of the life of the church. In the entire world there are just 60,000 missionaries from North America. But one Protestant denomination (Southern Baptist Convention) counts 100,000 of its members living overseas, each a potential lay witness, even in countries where missionaries are denied entry.

Needs of the Nation

At the end of the twentieth century, America reeled like a drunken sailor staggering by multiple blows to the head. Consider just a few of the horrifying statistics.

> There are about 2.22 million unmarried-couple households in the United States.

> Fourteen million children are living in poverty in the United States.

> More that one half of the children in America now live with one parent.

> The school dropout rate is 25 percent overall and 50 percent for blacks and Hispanics.

> Thirteen million Americans have drinking problems, and so for every person who suffers from alcoholism, another four people are directly affected.

> An estimated 23,500 people are killed annually in alcohol-related traffic accidents and 700,000 more are injured.

In New York City the 1985 revenues from marriages were $779,420; for annulments and divorces, $3, 690,750.

Nearly half a million births occur to young girls each year as well as 400,000 abortions and 134,000 miscarriages.

The body of Christ may be an unheeded voice crying in the midst of anarchy and chaos, but that voice must at least be heard. This chapter argues that it cannot be properly heard without a revival of leadership involvement.

Needs of the Community

Vision must inseparably relate to needs. An assessment of community needs in a large urban congregation would be very different from a small church. But needs assessment must be made. Goals and objectives derive from a proper understanding of needs. Part of that vision on the part of pastoral staff must be a commitment to the development of leadership and volunteerism. I like the way Menking deals with the issue of pastoral vision.

> To be held responsible for the realization of this vision seems unfair. It is easier for you to say, "The laity did not see," than to confess, "I did not enable them to see." There is no doubt you may resist this. You do not have control over other people's responses. Lay people are free to reject the vision. In your heart you know this does not relieve you of the responsibility to have, to share, and to work for a vision of ministry. This is the burden and the challenge of your labors as an institutional leader.
>
> Vision takes time to realize, and therefore requires patience and persistence. For that reason these two questions always have to be asked:
>
> How long will it take to translate this vision into a ministry?

Will I be here long enough to be the midwife for this vision?

Needs of the Church

Too many pastors trap themselves into crisis management, rushing about week by week just trying to hold the place together a little while longer. Ministry opportunities deteriorate to frantic dilemmas as we practice *ex post facto* recruitment (desperately searching for someone after the vacancy is apparent). In large measure such activity reflects failure in long-range planning, goal setting, and delegation.

Before we can announce needs we must be aware of needs – not only present but future. Self-evaluation questions help us in this kind of process.

1. What percentage of the church's total budget is allocated to education, missions, evangelism, worship, etc.?

2. How do we keep and use records?

3. Is there a properly designed organizational chart?

4. Do all ministry positions have job descriptions?

5. Is there provision for effective leadership training?

6. Do we have a strategic plan for reaching out and assimilating new members?

7. What is the process of decision-making in our church?

8. How are people appointed or elected to positions?

9. When was the last time we did a gift or talent search?

10. When was the last time we did a community or prospect survey?

11. How much do we understand about the various age-groups in our congregation, their needs, and what are we doing to meet these needs?

12. What opportunities do we anticipate in new ministries over the next three years?

One of the needs may be more professional staff. Failure to develop leadership may suggest that the pastor (assuming he is the only full-time staff member) gets so overloaded with general pastoral duties he has not time and perhaps no training to carry out this strategic ministry. It might be time for that church to bring a minister of Christian education on staff.

Needs of the Specific Ministry

We have a tendency to spread volunteers so thin across the ministry that they are unable to achieve satisfactory effectiveness in any role. A Sunday School teacher, for example, needs to grasp precisely the needs and characteristics of the age-group he teaches. An elder or deacon needs in-depth analysis of biblical responsibility and ministerial accountability for those important roles.

To be sure, a great deal of this takes place in the training process and we will come to that later. Here it may be helpful for us to grasp some of the reasons why we have been ineffective in recruiting volunteers in the local church and, therefore, why those volunteers do not serve satisfactorily in ministry. There are at least five areas of breakdowns that can occur in recruiting volunteers.

- Most volunteer ministry jobs in the church are not clearly defined; job descriptions are almost never written.

- Tradition often squelches new and creative ideas and approaches.

- Time and talent sheets have helped officially reject people's gifts every year.

- Clergy and leaders alike are often very poor at delegating.

- The jobs to be filled often receive more attention than the people filling them.

I'm particularly concerned about the last one. Churches have lists of 'slots to fill' and often recruit more on the basis of 'taking turns' rather than sharing gifts." Members of the pastoral staff, confident of their own gifts and call, must design a deliberate strategy to assist every believer in the congregation to discern, develop, and deploy his or her spiritual gifts in ministry.

Effective Leadership Centers in Spiritual Gifts

When we refocus the task of ministry away from the exercise of spiritual gifts in the power of the Holy Spirit by means of God's grace, we have forgotten our organismic base and function only as an organization. Too many a time, the pastor, as shepherd of the flock, ignores the fact that we, the people of God, are enabled by the Spirit in order to carry out the tasks God has given the church. For a pastor or people to believe that such undertakings, whatever they might be, can be accomplished for any length of time without Spirit empowerment is to misunderstand what it means to be the body of Christ.

Spiritual Gifts can be Discerned

Pastors who want leadership to center in spiritual gifts must approach their preaching and teaching with the assumption that people can ascertain their own spiritual gifts. Christian ministry does not have to become a neurotic compulsion to duty, but rather joy. Serving Christ can proceed on the basis of the delight criterion.

How wrong to assume that because we enjoy some particular service that ministry cannot be God's will for us. Or to deduce that because something is distasteful, it must be God's plan for us. Wouldn't God more likely assign us gifts the employments of which bring pleasure, not misery? Like Jesus, in doing the Father's will we should find delight, not drudgery.

That gives rise to the first important question – what do you enjoy doing? The second helps us as well – what service has God been blessing? Do you see fruit from your teaching? Do people trust Christ as a result of your evangelism? Help people in your congregation understand God's blessing on their ministry as an affirmation of spiritual gifts.

Still a third question might be worded this way: How have others encouraged you? God gives us parents, pastors, teachers, and friends to help us in making key decisions – and this is certainly a key decision. Churches should probably be taking more initiative to assist members in identifying spiritual gifts.

But the most important question asks, what has the Holy Spirit told you? The inner witness of the Spirit cannot be limited to confirming our salvation. He wants us to know our gifts and how to use them. Spiritual gifts can be discerned.

Spiritual Gifts can be Developed

A spiritual gift is not a full-blown power to perform. Once a believer recognizes his spiritual gift(s), development becomes the next step. Spiritual gifts serve the body of Christ, its up-building and its ministry. They are geared to the way we serve people. We teach people; we help people; we lead people. In the church we must recognize the mutuality of the body. A spiritual gift does not belong to its recipient; it is Christ's, and each of us becomes His steward (Rom. 12:3-8).

A strange mind-set has infected the church in recent years related to the use of spiritual gifts. Instead of accepting gifts as a means to serve other Christians, many people in the local church have assumed a showcase mentality, placing their spiritual gifts on display for other people to see, but they are not touched by them. There is much more talk about spiritual gifts in some churches than there is of using them for serving the body of Christ.

The object of spiritual gifts, to build up the body of Christ, was evident in the early church as it was built up in both numbers (quantity) and in spiritual maturity (quality). Today, the Holy Spirit is just as anxious to produce these same results in the local church through the ministries of Spirit-filled and gifted people.

Spiritual Gifts can be Deployed

Only when professional staff members in the church are confident and effective in their leadership roles can leadership development be realized. The deploying of spiritual gifts depends not only on their discernment and development, but also on the entire leadership climate in which a layman finds himself.

Many people feel they lack a call, training, and authority. They help others, but this is not viewed as ministry. Some people believe the pastor is paid to do this. Where ministry is still perceived as what a pastor does, it is a challenge to share the ministry dimension of helping others. But here we face a problem. When spiritually gifted laymen are recruited, trained, and enlisted, the deployment of their spiritual gifts often threatens the pastoral staff. What happens then offers a sad indictment on the contemporary church – pastors unwilling to share the ministry.

While there is always the cost of time to enable and deploy others, the positive side of deploying people is that more will be done for others and laity will have a significant and meaningful way to exercise their faith commitment. When that happens, you will be functioning as a biblical leader.

Effective Leadership Requires Clarity of Call

The whole issue of "call" has been a battleground since the publication of *Decision-Making and the Will of God*. In that significant book Gary Friesen argues for less attention to specific calls and more attention to general service according to biblical principles and common sense. I have no taste here to argue either case or even to enter the discussion. Let us assume that in some way, at some time, God calls believers to ministry in general, to ministry in a specific organization, and to ministry at a specific task. Let's take those one by one.

Call to Ministry in General

I like the Living Bible treatment of 1 Peter 4:10-11.

God has given each of you some special abilities; be sure to use them to help each other, passing onto others God's many kinds of blessings. Are you called to preach? Then preach as though God Himself were speaking through you. Are you called to help others? Do it with all the strength and energy that God supplies, so that God will be glorified through Jesus Christ – to Him be glory and power forever and ever. Amen.

From teaching in Sunday school to tent making in Bangladesh, God calls His people to service. The variety of spiritual gifts indicates a variety of ministries available and those ministries do not all need to be designed and programmed by the local church. We need to help people understand the importance of self-initiated ministries which God directs them to undertake.

Encouraging men and women of all ages to understand themselves as people whom God can use as part of His kingdom is the first step. Where does one go for such insight and counsel? Certainly, we begin with God's Word. Understanding the biblical concept of being one body and that the work of Christ is done by the body of Christ, rather than individuals, is an important concept.

This means that there needs to be a group of men and women who have committed themselves to encourage one another and encourage themselves as a local church to understand their individual and corporate vocational tasks.

Call to Minister in a Specific Organization

Understanding God's call need not be viewed as some mystical revelation-in-the-night experience. It's probably more like an inner confirmation from the Lord that He wants one of His people in a certain kind of ministry. The words "specific organization" in this context could refer to service with one mission board rather than another; giving one's life to the military chaplaincy rather than to a local church pastorate; evangelizing teenagers with Youth for Christ rather than Young Life; or choosing to work in a Tuesday night club program rather than in children's church on Sunday morning. These are not accidental or unimportant decisions. Lay people need to understand God has gifted them and called them first to ministry, and then to a certain kind of ministry.

God may leave an open door, allowing us to choose within the "circle" rather than narrowing us to the "dot." But what a tragedy to enter the insurance business if God has called you to serve in Central Africa, or to run off to Central Africa if God wants you in the insurance business. Such decisions are made by spiritually mature, growing, committed believers – not baby Christians.

Call to Ministry at a Specific Task

We all have many important things to do but none of them can be more important than the ministries to which Jesus Christ has appointed us. Paul wrote, "Faithful is He who calls you, who also will do it" (1 Thes. 5:24). God never calls us to a task without also promising to supply all that we need to accomplish that task. That's the innate beauty of God's appointment to ministry ... and that's why we can say with the Apostle Paul: "I can do all things through Christ who gives me strength" (Phil. 4:13).

So there you have it. Development of leadership in a local church begins with an assessment of needs, gifts, and call. We base that assessment on a proper and biblical understanding of leadership, both pastoral and lay. Remember, to do this we need to use proper assessment tools. A thorough assessment represents information from several sources including the potential leader. Interest and experience inventories are very helpful; personal interviews provide valuable insights; spiritual gift inventories add a crucial dimension; and discussions in leadership development teams put all the pieces together.

Foundation to all of this, however is a solid program of pulpit and classroom teaching which emphasizes repeatedly the significance of lay involvement in the ministry of the local church.

> For by the grace given me I say to every one of you: Do not think of yourself more highly than you ought, but rather think of yourself with sober judgment, in accordance with the measure of faith God has given you. Just as each of us has one body with many members, and these members do not all have the same function, so in Christ we who are many form one body, and each member belongs to all the others. We have different gifts, according to the grace given us. If a man's gift is prophesying, let him use it in proportion to his faith. If it is serving, let him serve; if it is teaching, let him teach; if it is encouraging, let him encourage; if it is contributing to the needs of others, let him give generously; if it is leadership, let him govern diligently; if it is showing mercy, let him do it cheerfully (Rom. 12:3-8).

Discussion Questions:

1. Name several qualifications and characteristics that mark effective leaders.

2. After reading the list of "Ten Questions Most Often Asked by Church Leaders", what question best needs to be asked in your church?
3. What are some of the self-evaluation questions that could be asked in order to get a needs assessment of a church?
4. What can members of the pastoral staff do in order to assist every believer to discern, develop and deploy spiritual gifts in ministry?
5. Can ministry be biblical outside the church?

Chapter 23

RECRUITING EFFECTIVE VOLUNTEERS

One of the most frustrating problems that pastors face today is the motivating and sustaining of active participation of their lay leaders. Yet the recruitment and development of lay volunteers remains the key that unlocks the door to church growth. The more members that become involved in church ministry roles, the easier it is to find the right people best qualified and gifted for a particular ministry. Unfortunately, history shows that without an intentional priority and effective plan, most churches never reach these realistic possibilities.

Some leaders have consistently approached every leadership need with negative assumptions – nobody is interested, nobody will volunteer, nobody will stick it out. There are three things we are not to practice in effective recruiting.

1. **General public announcements.** Apart from being futile, such a shotgun approach offers genuine risks since the pellets might hit anybody and produce volunteers unsuitable for the ministry.

2. **Last-minute announcements.** Understanding the need does not mean recognizing on Wednesday night that a Primary Department class appears to be teacher-less for the coming Sunday. As we noted earlier, long-range planning and a personal development strategy should identify needs in the present program and opportunities for new ministry in expanding programs long before the crisis hits.

3. **Pressurized appeals.** Arm-twisting usually belittles the job merely to secure an affirmative answer and get the position filled.

On the positive side, this chapter will teach you how to determine high standards, design an atmosphere of service, and develop effective servants.

Determine High Standards

For many pastors, they have not been taught in their seminary training the administrative process nor how to work with people in anything other than preaching, classroom, or individual counseling sessions. Developing people in small groups may even seem foreign to him. Sooner or later however, a pastoral leader must learn that when a church considers leadership training, it must first determine standards (1 Tim. 4:11-12). Four areas ought to concern every Christian leader looking for potential volunteer workers either in the local church or in parachurch ministries.

Spiritual Maturity

The first area is both the most obvious and the most necessary. We're not talking here about the potential for spiritual maturity someday; that would describe everybody in the congregation. Rather, we need to focus on present evidence of spiritual maturity and the quality of spiritual life. A brief reading of the qualifications for elders and deacons in 1 Timothy 3 can bring to the surface the importance of this standard.

It is entirely possible for people to be highly gifted, but still to be weak or unstable in character. You must realize how much growth and character would be necessary for the person to be able to offer effective leadership for God's people. For many people it would require an enormous amount of change: for some it is probably not possible. However, when you have a person who is basically sound in his or her character, and they have the openness and willingness to be used by God, often God will add gifts to that person and He can accomplish great things through them. Let the standards you develop be clearly supported by the Word of God.

Leadership Skills

While spiritual maturity focuses on life qualities, leadership skills focus on service qualities. Training will develop leadership skills, but there should be some visible evidence of the skill even before training begins. The wise leader pays attention to putting the right people in the right slots. Trained teachers build effective ministry; the more effective any ministry is, the easier it is to recruit new leadership.

But how do you spot people with leadership skills? Let me suggest at least three qualities such people will demonstrate.

1. **The ability to win the respect of others.**

2. **The ability to gain people's trust.** To whom would most members of your congregation turn for help if they had serious problems? Whom would they like to have as a prayer partner? Who would be selected to lead meetings effectively?

3. **The ability to take the initiative with organized and directed goals.**

Some years ago the American Association of School Administrators released a criteria sheet to enable local school boards to select competent educational leaders in their communities to serve on the board. Here are some of the items they suggested:

1. Is the candidate reputable as a person and as a public worker and recognized as such by the intelligent leaders of the community?

2. Does she/he have personal courage, exercised with appropriate tact, in facing opposition?

3. Is the candidate likely to avoid fanfare and self-publicity in this post?

4. Does this candidate have the ability to deal democratically and effectively with employees?

5. Is this candidate one who has propensity for keeping his feet on the ground, willing to recognize legitimate precedent, yet also willing to consider appropriate change?

Such a list of standards would have to be adapted for use in the church and many more could be added but it might give you some idea in setting up your own criteria for the selection of lay leaders.

Learning Potential

In addition to life qualities and service qualities, we must set standards which deal with intellectual qualities. Some people regularly hold important roles in church ministry, but really do not have the potential for leadership.

Recruitment is not an end in itself; it merely leads to the next step which is training. And we can cause great grief for the training aspect of the program if we allow a breakdown in the recruitment phase. Potential leaders tend to be organized people who understand goals and priorities. They make wise use of their leisure time, are able to focus with intensity when necessary, and can handle occasional discouragements. In other words, they are mature people who are able to work without playing and to play without feeling they ought to be working.

Cooperative Attitude

Remember that every new volunteer must fit in with the team you already have. Just bringing any person to fill an empty slot could create havoc in an already functioning unit. People with cooperative attitudes know how to relate well to others. An open admissions policy preempts the kind of quality control which enables us to select the right people under the leadership of the Holy Spirit and in line with what God's Word requires.

Design an Atmosphere of Service

Often churches have been guilty of viewing lay ministry only from the "employer viewpoint." We recruit volunteers as a means of accomplishing the work of the church or of a particular program. On the contrary, however, the volunteer activity must also accomplish the personal goals of the volunteer. There are two purposes for volunteer church work – one is to develop the church program and the other is to develop the individual. People who aren't growing as they serve stagnate early and become candidates for complaining rather than contributing.

There are seven "attitude competencies" which must be a part of the personal and professional profile of the recruiter(s).

1. Vision for a potential volunteer serving the church.

2. Belief that people are more important than positions or programs.

3. Willingness to work with volunteers to see them reach full potential.

4. Love for the volunteers.

5. Belief in the importance of the church's ministry.

6. Desire to help volunteers develop.

7. Belief in the abilities of the volunteers.

Elevate Ministry Involvement

Assuming we have recognized spiritual gifts, emphasized the significance of call, and taken into consideration experience and personal interests, we now stand at the crucial first public step – elevating the opportunity for ministry. Churches are doing a number of good things in this area – teacher appreciation banquets, distribution of ministry certificates, appropriate recognition for teachers and leaders who take advantage of conventions, seminars, and training programs – but elevating ministry involvement is a constant task for the pastor and all other leadership staff.

Explain Ministry Involvement

The concept of job description is crucial. Many don't like the term because they feel it connotes a secular position rather than ministry. But we use the word "work" commonly and the Bible even applies it to our service for the Lord (Col. 3:23). Training volunteers like staff provides the key to all good volunteer programs.

It begins with someone having thought through the question and having written a position description. The position description should describe what the job entails and what qualifications are needed to do it. Having a position description is the first indicator that the organization expects a high level of commitment from its volunteers and that it intends to choose them carefully with respect.

Worker orientation offers a corollary to an effective position description. Orientation is part of the training, but we want to view it here as preliminary to the formal training process. Finding effective people is only the first step; launching them into ministry is just as important. As we stress spiritual opportunities and explain ministry responsibilities, we want to thoroughly detail what we expect. Many later failures can be traced back to inadequate orientation.

Evaluate Ministry Involvement

We're not ready to examine supervision and evaluation, but remember the importance of announcing to all volunteers right up front that their ministry will be evaluated. Actually, evaluation starts right at the beginning as we ascertain whether a potential worker meets the standards which have been set. Then we measure his or her progress in the orientation and training program. Finally, we evaluate the actual ministry. Sometimes we might want to try a probationary period, such as, a substitute teaching role for three or six months. On other occasions an internship could be used for early evaluation purposes. The secret lies in communicating the idea that evaluation is neither negative nor punitive – it offers a service to the volunteer to help him improve in ministry.

Expect Ministry Involvement

Many leaders do not expect people to respond affirmatively to request for ministry involvement. Sometimes leaders bring this problem on themselves by asking others to be involved in inadequate and improper ways. <u>In developing good relations with volunteers you must remember five "nots" in working with them.</u>

1. *Volunteers are not members of the staff.*

2. *Volunteers are not full-time workers.*

3. *Volunteers cannot be taken for granted.*

4. *Volunteers are not paid.*

5. *Volunteers are not bound to a job in the church for long periods of time.*

<u>To these five "nots" we must add three "needs."</u>

1. *Volunteers need to hear thanks.*

2. *Volunteers need recognition.*

3. *Volunteers need to be treated courteously.*

Does our failure to obtain involvement bring about a lack of expectancy or does our lack of expectancy create negative response? It could be a little bit of both. In order to build an achievement-oriented atmosphere we begin by understanding people and placing a high value on them. We must credit everyone with more potential than limited intelligence and unlimited time.

Develop Effective Servants

If a leader has never held a managerial role in business or industry, he or she may not be familiar with the concept of quality control. He or she may tend to spiritualize (almost mysticize) the process of recruiting workers while at the same time practicing the most pedantic processes for filling the many and frequently open ministries in the church. In order to develop effective servants one must realign his or her understanding of standards and retune the whole atmosphere of ministry which he or she has created.

In addition, he or she needs to take definite steps to improve the recruitment process which starts with a better focus on potential volunteer candidates.

Match Persons and Positions

Assuming we have identified gifts, interest, call, and needs, we are at the point of putting together ministry opportunities with ministering people. At times that may require protecting people from themselves, those ever-eager souls who will take on yet another ministry for whatever good or questionable motivation. Part of a leadership role is to protect those workers who have demonstrated their usefulness and have been asked to assume too many responsibilities. It may take just one more job to send an already overloaded superintendent / treasurer / secretary / janitor to that nice church down the street.

Follow Proven Procedures

Recruitment continues all year, aiming to keep a ready reservoir of servants in order to protect the stability of the church's ministries. Recruitment must be coordinated.

Proven procedures take in virtually everything we have said so far – determining the standards; elevating the ministry; explaining ministry involvement; evaluation; attitudes of expectancy; matching people and positions; writing careful job descriptions; preparing and using a prospect list.

Let's add a few more practical guidelines before we discuss how to approach the potential volunteer.

1. Start early – enlistment should take place at least three months before the person actually begins serving in order to allow time for orientation and training.

2. Make all contacts face-to-face if possible. Sometimes a phone call may be necessary, but direct conversation is much better.

3. Have your information in hand. Know the experience, gifts, and interests of the potential volunteer so you can genuinely affirm the committee's selection in light of the best information available.

4. Anticipate excuses.

5. Assure him of your help and prayer.

Specify Persons, Tasks, and Time

Ask specific people for a specific ministry for a specific length of time.

1. Specific people. No general announcements or universal invitations. We are approaching people who have been prayerfully selected by the appropriate committee or recruitment team.

2. Specific ministry. We don't ask these people to serve "in general" but attempt to match our understanding of their spiritual gifts, interest, and experience with the various needs in the church. The specific opportunity we wish to discuss is the one that seems to best fit all these important variables.

3. Specific time. Serving Christ in the church is not a life sentence in one unchanging post. I recommend that you set a one-year boundary and recruit volunteers for that specific time frame.

Of course this does not mean that we expect a complete turnover on an annual basis. It does mean, however, that we don't want people accepting a position in August and then resigning it in November just because they tire of the preparation and study. The time factor must be emphasized; people will not understand one-year ministry appointments unless you clearly communicate that concept.

When a vacancy appears sometime during the ministry year, the appointment should be made just until the end of the year, at which time all workers are evaluated and reappointed or assigned elsewhere.

Detail the Responsibilities and Duties

The greatest sin in volunteerism is in not adequately defining the task to be completed. Even simple requests will perform better if the task is written down. Why? A written objective is usually much clearer and easier to understand than a verbal request. Before approaching a volunteer, the following elements of the job should be determined: the exact job, the timetable, the final results desired, and the working relationships.

There is some overlap here with our earlier discussions about explaining ministry involvement. Perhaps the very nature of this crucial dimension of recruitment requires double handling. The person contacting potential volunteers needs to be able to talk intelligently about each specific ministry, the tasks that the volunteer will be asked to perform and specifically when the ministry will begin. Obviously this process must be bathed in prayer and we never want to rush an answer on the part of the recruit.

One more dimension requires our attention. College recruiters refer to it as "student retention," holding onto the people you already have. That means that we need to learn to plug up the leaks in the present leadership program which cause both present and potential volunteers to become discouraged. Why do lay leaders leave the ministry?

1. Because willing people become overworked and burned out.

2. Because volunteers don't receive much-needed help.

3. Because lay people have personal and spiritual needs of their own which aren't being met in the framework of their ministries.

4. Because we do not adequately show appreciation.

5. Because they have not been provided proper equipment and materials.

6. Because they have not been trained adequately for the ministries they have been asked to carry out.

7. Because friction has developed between or among workers in a given ministry area.

8. Because they have lost interest, enthusiasm, and commitment for the ministry.

9. Because supervision is inadequate or perhaps even abrasive.

10. Because evaluation has not been carried out or results have not been identified as a positive thrust for ministry improvement.

Recruiting is everybody's job – people currently involved in ministry need to be finding new volunteers for ministry. Keep the process dignified and spiritual. Trust God to provide workers you need. In detailing the process of recruitment, we may use terms like "job," "position," and "work," but we must always emphasize the spiritual and biblical dimensions of ministry.

Remember, people rarely perform above the level at which they were recruited. If we play down the importance of ministry just to get them to say yes, we must expect a minimal performance. We must appeal to opportunity and benefit. Mutual ministry serves both the church and the volunteer whose family, parenting skills, relationships with other people, and general spiritual life should be enhanced by his or her involvement in ministry.

Discussion Questions:

1. Four areas ought to concern Christian leaders looking for potential volunteer workers. What are they?
2. What are the two reasons we recruit volunteers?
3. Describe in your own words how we are to treat the volunteer.

4. List three important proven procedures that will help recruiting volunteers go smoothly.
5. When reading the list of why volunteers leave the church, do you see similar reasons in your own church situation? If so, what can you do to rectify the problem?

Chapter 24

BUILDING THE LEADERSHIP AND RESOLVING CONFLICT

There are four requirements for building a leadership team:

1. **Building a strong leadership requires a clear strategy.** The team leader (and any other decision makers) must pray and determine the direction, strategy and course of ministry. Strategy is based on the vision. Once the ministry strategy is clear, you can determine what other leadership roles are needed for your leadership team.

2. **Building a strong leadership team requires intentionality.** You should create a profile list of the attributes, skills and functions needed for each leadership position. The profile will be unique for each position. The profile should be different than the profile of the team leader. The leader and other team members should be prayerfully looking for the team to be filled with the right people. Lift specific requests up in prayer to the Lord. Make needs known to others who could connect you with the right person. Look among the people in your ministry for someone who could be promoted to a higher leadership level.

3. **Building a strong leadership team requires loyalty.** King David asked three basic questions of his potential team members in I Chronicles 12:14-18: (1). Have you come in peace? Do you have a rebellious spirit? Are you here to unite or divide? (2). Have you come to help me? Do you understand that you are under the authority of the team leader? Is your purpose to accomplish our goals or your own? (3). Do you plan to betray me? Do you have any

hidden plans or motivations? Do you have the courage to stand with me when things get difficult?

4. **Building a strong leadership team requires patience.** The team leader and team members must be patient to allow God to bring His choice, not yours. It is very difficult to take away a position or assignment once it has been given. Morale and momentum are lost when this happens. Allow the entire team to confirm the selection of new members (as well as other governing bodies). Do not make selection decisions alone. Build synergy and trust with group input. This is essentially critical at the leadership level.

In selecting the leadership team members, you should follow certain criteria. The team members should be people of:

- **Character.** This would include: honesty, integrity, self-discipline, teachability, dependence, perseverance, and a good work ethic.

- **Influence.** He or she has the ability to know where they are going and persuade others to come.

- **Positive Attitude.** They are able to see situations and people positively. This is a key asset in life – it makes them a no-limit person.

- **Excellent People Skills.** They have a genuine concern for others. They also have an ability to understand others – he or she is a person who chooses to make people-interaction a priority.

- **Evidence of Gifts.** He or she has evident gifts that simply need to be developed.

- **Proven Track Record.** He or she is a person who has learned from their mistakes. One who does not continually repeat the same mistakes over again.

- **Confidence.** People are drawn to confidence. Strong leaders recognize and value confidence in others. This requires wholeness of self-worth.

- **Self-Discipline.** Emotional self-discipline means having control over your own emotional reactions. A leader cannot let his or her emotions be affected by others. External self-discipline involves time management and other habits.

- **Communication Skills.** A leader cannot reach his or her potential without strong communication skills. Clear communication allows them to cast vision and get response!

- **Seeks Excellence**. He or she has a willingness to continually grow, make changes, and take risks. Someone who seeks solutions of satisfaction.

Resolving Conflict within the Team

There are three principles of team dynamics.

1. **First is that a team experiences formation** (We have already taken some time to talk about this).

2. **The second principle of team dynamics is that a team will experience conflict.** You are working with leaders. As a result, each tends to be decisive, visionary and authoritative in their approach to the accomplishment of any given task. The goal of the team is to reach unity, but team members come from very diverse backgrounds.

3. **The third principle is that well-managed conflict helps all team members grow.** The team leader's primary role at this stage is to help the team come together. The current team priority ceases to be the overall mission and becomes team building. Effectiveness comes from interdependence. God's ideal for team leadership is <u>not dependence</u> ... where one is unwilling or unable to provide anything for himself or the team. God's ideal for team leadership is <u>not co-dependence</u> ... where certain members enable other team members to fail to do their share. God's ideal for team leadership is <u>not independence</u> ... where each team member continues to operate independent of other team members. God's ideal for team leadership is <u>interdependence</u>. This is where each team member brings strengths and weaknesses to the mix. Effort is made to learn one another's contribution to the team. When a team achieves interdependence each team member's contribution is celebrated. When a team achieves interdependence each team member's challenges are shared. When a team achieves interdependence the team accomplishes more than any one member can alone.

Ten Common Problems that Cause Conflict

1. **Floundering.** Teams often start enthusiastically, but wane before the goal is reached. When progress is stopped, it becomes a breeding ground for conflict.

2. **Overbearing Participants.** Sometimes one influential member exerts his authority to the extent that other team members are intimidated to join the creative process.

3. **Dominating Participants.** Teams sometimes have a member who is very talkative and dominates all conversations.

4. **Reluctant Participants.** Teams often have members who are reluctant to speak up during team meetings. Due to fear or ulterior motives, they form another meeting later with one or two other members, thus creating conflict.

5. **Acceptance of Opinions as Facts.** Some express personal opinions with such confidence that they are taken as facts. When those "facts" are proven untrue, conflict arises.

6. **Rush to Accomplishment.** A member who is impatient to get immediate results can sometimes push the team to start a project before the planning phase is completed.

7. **Personality Conflicts.** Even among committed members, different personalities and styles of communication can produce conflict.

8. **Ignoring ideas.** Everyone offers an idea, now and then, that just won't work. When the team just ignores the idea or, worse, ridicules it, conflict can come.

9. **Digression.** As the team builds personal relationships it may tend to lose focus on the task at hand. Some will like this digression; others will be frustrated by it.

10. **Feuding Members.** Sometimes unresolved conflicts existed between team members before they joined the team. They may bring that conflict into the team and draw others into it.

Point to Ponder: "Never confront power with power. Confront power with truth. The first instinct is to respond defensively – resist that temptation."

Six Aspects of Team Conflict

1. **People view conflict differently.** Some view conflict as a sin to be avoided. Others view conflict as an opportunity to

assert their authority and establish their position. Both views have some strong bases in truth. Galatians 5:7 strongly suggests that conflict is a result of sin. Ephesians 6:12 suggests that spirit-empowered authority is needed to resolve conflict. The power view of conflict is the creative tension between law and grace / justice and mercy. When a leader understands this, conflict becomes an opportunity to establish the truth while demonstrating grace. The result is a tighter, more unified team.

2. **Unhealthy views of conflict.** A defensive or authoritative response to conflict tends to polarize the team into sides someone has to win and someone has to lose and escalate the conflict. When handled incorrectly, the issue becomes irrelevant. Both sides are convinced the other side is rebellious. Both sides feel they are appointed by God to remove the troublemakers and "save" the ministry.

3. **A positive view of conflict.** Each side can break the reactive cycle by choosing not to respond to perceived threats. Jesus said to, "Bless those who curse you, and pray for those who spitefully use you. To him who strikes you on the one cheek, offer the other also. And from him who takes away your cloak, do not withhold your tunic either (Luke 6:28-29). Paul instructed us to, "Be angry, and do not sin": do not let the sun go down on your wrath (Eph. 4:26). Refusing to react defensively is the key to breaking the cycle of mistrust. This is the essence of the Apostle Paul's teaching, "Consider others more than yourself" (Phil. 2:3). Responding to power with truth places Christ at the center of the conflict. In order for truth to prevail, all team members must recognize that no one side has the whole picture. They can only arrive at the truth together. Conflict is resolved when we turn to Christ and recognize we need each other.

4. **Attempting to resolve conflict too soon.** A common mistake a leader can make is to resolve the conflict too quickly. Sometimes we think we see the solution immediately and rush to judgment too quickly. When the leader first begins to ask team members for the source of the conflict, he will often get symptoms that must be evaluated to accurately assess the problem. Sometimes team members will offer solutions to the problem before the problem is even fully understood. Those solutions are flawed because the understanding of the problem was flawed. Sometimes we dislike the pain of conflict; we "agree to disagree" for the sake of unity. But unity is not the absence of conflict; it is the presence of agreement. While some people have learned to embrace conflict as a necessary part of team building, no one really likes it. Saying, "Let's just get along" may produce temporary relief from the tensions. But unless the root cause of the conflict is exposed it will reappear with more intensity. Effective leaders learn to look deeper and to live with pain until the root of the problem is discerned.

5. **Keep focused on the vision during the conflict.** While conflict is being resolved, the leader must keep the team's focus on the vision. The team must stay focused on the big picture, the vision. Otherwise the conflict might be resolved, but the vision doesn't get accomplished. The leader must remind the team that we need each other to accomplish the vision.

6. **Positive benefits of conflict.** The leader must point the team's attention to God's purpose in allowing the conflict. Conflict, properly handled, serves to draw the team together. Conflict forces us to find common ground. Conflict produces more creative energy. Conflict causes individual team members to learn more about themselves and potentially become more like Christ. Conflict exposes our

own need for change and can cause us to grow. Conflict causes us to face issues not faced before.

Six Actions to Resolve Team Conflict

1. **Evaluate yourself.** Ask: what is it about me that is helping to cause this conflict?

2. **Refuse to assign blame.** The blame game is Satan's tool to destroy unity.

3. **Prohibit any gossip.** Gossip is talking with someone who is neither part of the problem nor part of the solution.

4. **Listen carefully to the opposite view.** Seek to understand others rather than only trying to be understood by others.

5. **Challenge all team members to seek the Lord.** Ask: Why do you think the Lord is allowing this in your life?

6. **Assemble the team to find a solution.** Typically, a solution discovered by one team member will be flawed. Normally, if you don't include all the people involved in the conflict in the closure session, they will not experience closure.

Discussion Questions:

1. What are the four requirements of building team leadership?
2. What criteria should you follow when selecting your team members?
3. What are the three dynamics of a team?
4. What are some common problems that cause conflict?
5. Name the six actions to resolve team conflict.

Chapter 25

TRANSITIONING TO LEADING WITH TEAMS

Eight Principles for Transitioning to Team Leadership

1. **The senior leader is the primary influencer.** Anyone of influence can initiate the change, but the senior leader must support change. If the senior leader is not the primary influencer in the transition, members faithful to the senior leader will be confused whether or not to agree with the changes. If the senior leader is not the primary influencer in the transition, and the transition succeeds, he may be the primary influencer after the transition is complete.

2. **Teach the value of teams first.** Teach the value of teams before you start teaching the vision of a team led ministry. The first mistake leaders make is to share a vision of where he wants to lead the ministry, without first leading the group to understand the value of the change. Once the group sees the value of team leadership, they will ask the senior leader to help them get there. It is much easier to lead someone where they want to go than it is to lead them where you want them to go. Effective leaders don't push their followers; they gently lead them.

   Point to Ponder: A constant in all leadership experiences is that most people resist change, even when it is in their personal best interest.

3. **Clearly define new terms for the environment.** Every discipline has terminology that goes with it. Every new word, phrase and/or concept must be clearly defined and

consistently used. Once definitions are established, use the terms in every possible forum, verbally and in print.

4. **Obtain common agreement.** Gain firm consensus among your existing leaders before launching the transition. Common agreement is that point in which everyone can say with integrity I will support this decision. If the key influencers in the ministry do not have ownership of where you are going, you will fail to gain the support of the entire ministry. Each leader will influence his own group in the direction he is leaning.

5. **Start with a prototype team.** Start with a prototype team before you switch the entire ministry or church over to the new model of team ministry. Form a small group of influential people to begin team formation. Key members of this transition team may comprise the senior leadership team once the transition is complete. The prototype leadership team should draft a clear and comprehensive transition plan moving from macro to micro. The plan begins with the highest overview possible. Once the highest levels are set, move to the next highest level in light of the plans made at the highest level. Continue that process until your transition team has evaluated every ministry in the church from a Team-Led perspective.

6. **Recruit new leaders for the team.** Identify and recruit new people who have strong leadership potential and an openness to operate in a team environment. Often those who flourish in a solo leadership model struggle in a team environment. Often those who lack the confidence or special skills for solo leadership do very well in a team environment.

7. **Match leaders strategically.** Match up leaders strategically to produce compatible and competent teams, based on aptitudes, temperaments and giftings. As your organization

begins to adopt the team model they will be looking for increased effectiveness to reassure their decision. Initial teams must be very carefully selected to maximize early success. If the prototype team fails to form successfully, it will diminish congregational confidence in the team model.

8. **Build momentum but moderate people's expectations.** In the transition there is a small percentage of your people that "buy in" initially. With every success, more members will adopt the new paradigm. A major mistake of leaders zealous to transition to a team model is overstating benefits. Avoid expressions like, "Once we establish teams we will have more effectiveness and remove all conflict!" Leaders must prepare the organization for the learning curve of having functioning, effective leadership teams.

Four Implementation Phases for Leading with Teams

1. **Preparation Phase** – committed to research (Yr. 1). A committed group of 2 or 3 innovative leaders should be working together at this stage. The value of working together and functioning as a community needs to be mentioned occasionally to the general group. The vision of teamwork is not taught at this stage.

2. **Development Phase** – committed to develop the system – (Yr. 2). A core team of 10 to 12 "early adopter" type leaders form a prototype team. The vision begins to take shape and form. The organization infrastructure is developed. This core team begins to build a support core of leaders around them. The value of teamwork is preached more.

3. **Transition Phase** – transition to teamwork model (Yr. 3). A support team of 30 to 40 members is required at this stage. The vision of teamwork at every level of the ministry is now being taught and preached to the general ministry group.

4. **Operational Phase** – "breaking point" in the process (Yr. 4). If the general group adopts the vision, you move into the "operational" phase. If the general group rejects the vision, you move into the "loss of vision" phase.

Eight Pitfalls to Transitioning to Leading with Teams

1. **Leaders resist change to retain position or power.** They may fear the new system will not work as effectively and the ministry will suffer. They may not trust the other prospective team members to handle their roles effectively. They may truly believe that it is easier to do it yourself than to train others.

2. **Replacing departing leaders without sensitivity.** Any time there is a major transition in a ministry, there will be some who will not be able or willing to go with you. Departing leaders have some influence in the body; if replacing them is not handled well you will lose members.

3. **Senior leaders incorrectly assess their own gifts/style.** The senior leader may assume that he is a macro level-directing leader, when actually that is not his strength. Once the senior leadership team is established it may be determined that the senior leader is actually more gifted as a Strategic Leader of a Team Building Leader. The senior leader may recognize this, but still find it difficult to relinquish "directing leadership" to another team member.

4. **Staff members incorrectly assess their own gifts/style.** Often members of the staff are very valuable to the ministry but do not have the giftings to view the big picture or the gifting to assist in vision formation. You must help them see they will be frustrated in a role that is outside their gifts, but how valuable they are to the ministry serving within their giftings.

5. **Rushing the transition process.** Change takes time. Most ministers take two to three years to adopt the values of team leadership. It then takes another two or three years to fully implement. The larger the organization the more methodically the transition process must be.

6. **Allowing teams to be too large.** The most effective teams usually have no more than seven members. Optimally, effective teams can have 3-5 members. The larger the team, the more difficult it is for all members to bring meaningful contributions to the creative mix. The larger the team, the harder it is for the directing leader to facilitate the personal growth of each member.

7. **Allowing leaders to serve on multiple teams.** Dual loyalty rarely works and time commitment conflicts are inevitable. Even if the leader can effectively switch from one role to another, it is very difficult for followers to keep up with which role the leader is in at a given time.

8. **Allowing teams to continue when they should disband.** Every team has an effective life cycle. Some teams achieve a depth of true camaraderie rarely attained elsewhere and do not want to let go. The priority of the team must be vision first, relationships second. Otherwise, the team will stay together and take on a life all its own, even though it ceased to be an effective leadership team long ago.

Common Mistakes Pastors Make

Introduction – Good News and Bad News

The bad news is that mistakes will happen. There is no perfect pastor. Sometimes mistakes may involve immature decisions on your part. Other times it may be that you are treading waters without experience to draw from.

The good news is that mistakes can be minimized. You can and must learn from the past. You also must identify common problems that others make as well.

Some of the common mistakes that pastors make are:

Mistake #1 – Setting in leadership too soon.

Paul waited 3-5 years before ordaining elders. Elders need to be shaped, proven, tested, etc. Any outside minister who joins the church needs time to develop as a sheep first – give him authority slowly.

Mistake #2 – Changing too much too soon.

The problem in the pastor is that while the pastor has vision – he wants to get to it too soon without setting a proper foundation. The problem in the people is that they tend to love tradition and tend to always resist change. People don't have the same grace to be able to change as quickly as leaders. Having people follow in a slower manner can help to keep a leader from going too fast.

Some possible solutions that can be of help include making sure that all changes are carefully thought out and clearly the will of God. Make sure you properly prepare the ground to plant the seeds to receive change. Write, spell-out, and make plain (communicate clearly) the vision before you implement it (Hab. 2:2). Be patient with people in the changing process. Only focus on one change at a time. And remember to keep your eye on the vision for long term not just the immediate.

Mistake #3 – Not marrying the flock.

Evidences of this problem are seen when you are not loving people more than you're your own ministry. Jesus instructed us about the shepherds' role when He said, "I am the good shepherd.

The good shepherd gives His life for the sheep. But a hireling, he who is not the shepherd, one who does not own the sheep, sees the wolf coming and leaves the sheep and flees; and the wolf catches the sheep and scatters them (John 10:11-12).

Other symptoms of this problem may include: moving from place to place in ministry. Keeping other options open at all times. Not developing close relationships. Not committing to the people no matter what the future holds and using threats to leave as a means of manipulation.

Some suggestions for dealing with this problem are to let the people know of your love for them both verbally and through your demonstration. Plan to build for the long haul and reap fruit in your old age and put roots down and develop love for your city.

Mistake #4 – Using gimmicks to build the church.

While everyone wants to see growth, the problem with using gimmicks is that you will have to continue to use more spectacular gimmicks to keep the people. In dealing with this, do not make numbers your only goal. You will also need to take care of the growth you already have. Stick to the basics – they still work. Visualize an oak tree instead of a mushroom. Serve a balanced diet and disciple people through long term relationships.

Mistake #5 – Demanding submission to authority.

You must gain authority by teaching. A lot of talk about submission shows a leader to be insecure. Practice things that bring authority. Provide an example for people to follow. Paul instructed Timothy, "Let no one despise your youth, but be an example to the believers in word, in conduct, in love, in spirit, in faith, in purity (1 Timothy 4:12). Other ways to gain authority in the eyes of your people:

- Submit to authority in your own life.

- Hold up a clear vision before the people.

    Luke 6:39 And He spoke a parable to them: "Can the blind lead the blind? Will they not both fall into the ditch?

- Demonstrate love for people in practical ways.

- Make careful and wise decisions.

    1 Kings 3:28 And all Israel heard of the judgment which the king had rendered; and they feared the king, for they saw that the wisdom of God was in him to administer justice.

- Feed the people with green grass.

- Spend time in the presence of God as an individual.

Mistake #6 – Financial Mismanagement.

Some possible problems include: the debt or overhead of the church is above what the congregation can afford or borrowing money from a member in the church; no effective budgeting or reporting to the congregation; not keeping accurate books; not counting the offerings in a wise way, or being accountable for financial decisions. The solution to these matters is to live within means and opposite of all the above.

Mistake #7 – Talking too much.

By this I mean that you confide to one person about another person. Obviously you must keep confidential areas confidential

Mistake #8 – Not admitting mistakes when they occur.

Why? Pastor's mistakes are obvious. Pastors who hide their mistakes will repeat them. Some way to minimize mistakes:

- Do not make decisions alone
- Draw from the experiences of others
- Learn from your own mistakes
- Be sure you hear a matter before you judge it
- Go slow when making changes – avoid impulsiveness
- Stay humble and teachable
- Wait on God for decisions.
- Keep your vision and goal in sight.

How do you undo mistakes that you have made in the past? First, admit them. Second, learn from them and third, go on from there.

Proverbs 24:16 For a righteous man may fall seven times and rise again, but the wicked shall fall by calamity.

"Error ... is to follow something which does not lead to that at which we wish to arrive." St. Augustine

Discussion Questions:

1. Describe in detail two principles for transitioning team leadership.
2. Explain one pitfall to transitioning to leading with teams.
3. What common mistake can a pastor make and what should he do to avoid it?
4. How can a pastor gain authority in his congregation?
5. After thoughtful consideration and self-evaluation, what area do you think you will need to improve in order to prevent or minimize mistakes in your ministry?

Chapter 26

BIG PASTORS OF SMALL CHURCHES

What is success? – What is the goal for which you are reaching?

In the secular world:

- Success tends to be measured by possessions
- Success may be measured by financial independence
- Success can be measured by the size of accomplishments
- Success can be measured by the people you control

In much of the church:

- Success can be measured by possessions
- Success can be measured by numbers

In God's mind:

- Success in ministry is achieving God's goal for your life.
    - The example of Paul – Fought a good fight, finished the race.
    - The example of Jesus – "It is finished." – Did what God wanted Him to do.
- Success in our ministry is not in our hands alone.
    - God chooses
    - God determines the kind of ministry

> **1 Corinthians 12:10** to another the working of miracles, to another prophecy, to another discerning of spirits, to another different kinds of tongues, to another the interpretation of tongues.

- o God determines the sphere of ministry

- o God determines the duration of ministry

- o God determines the success of the ministry

  > **1 Corinthians 3:6-9** I planted, Apollos watered, but God gave the increase. [7] So then neither he who plants is anything, nor he who waters, but God who gives the increase. [8] Now he who plants and he who waters are one, and each one will receive his own reward according to his own labor. [9] For we are God's fellow workers; you are God's field, you are God's building.

- o God prepares the heart of the sinner

- o God opens and closes doors

- o God orders world events – consistent with His purpose

Your Definition of Success Will Make a Difference in Your Ability to Achieve Success

- Wrong concepts will open you to serious temptations
- Temptation to covet our neighbor's house
- Temptation to pursue greener pastures
- Temptation to despise the true will of God

> **2 Timothy 4:10** for Demas has forsaken me, having loved this present world, and has departed for Thessalonica--Crescens for Galatia, Titus for Dalmatia

- Temptation to become critical of others who seem successful
- Temptation to relax in our effort
- Temptation to serve self rather than others
- Temptation to compare yourself with others
- Proper concepts will release you to more effective ministry.
- To be what God has called you to be.
- To finish the race and win
- To be a true servant to others

> **John 13:3** Jesus, knowing that the Father had given all things into His hands, and that He had come from God and was going to God,

- To be faithful where God has placed you
- To be content – accept God's plan for your life

Qualities that Make a Pastor "Big" in God's Mind

- Personal integrity

    Honesty and truth; financial stewardship and responsibility; moral purity and self control; true to convictions and standards; diligence and hardworking

- Faithfulness to God's call

    Willing to die to self; good and faithful servant

- Loving the people of God

Put needs of people ahead of your own

- Openhearted to all

    You can't be introspective. Watch for who God puts in front of us

Keys to Victory

- Keep your servant spirit and your spirit of sacrifice
- Never compare yourself with others – be yourself
- Look to God for His approval

    Hebrews 11:6 But without faith it is impossible to please Him, for he who comes to God must believe that He is, and that He is a rewarder of those who diligently seek Him.

- Guard your heart motivation

    2 Corinthians 5:14 For the love of Christ compels us, because we judge thus: that if One died for all, then all died;

- Release your expectation to God

Discussion Questions:

1. Define God's meaning of success.
2. What are the wrong concepts of success needed to be avoided?
3. Name the proper concepts of success that will release a more effective ministry.
4. What qualities does God desire in His pastors?
5. What are the keys to 'winning the race' for pastors?

Appendix 1

Expanding on the Qualifications for Spiritual Leadership Delineated in the Constitution of Master Builder Ministries

"Qualifications for Spiritual Leadership"
1 Timothy 3:1-13; Titus 1:5-9; 1 Peter 5:1-3

1 Timothy 3:2-7	Titus 1:6-9	1 Peter 5:1-3
Above reproach	Above reproach	Not under compulsion, but voluntary
The husband of one wife	The husband of one wife	Not for sordid gain, but with eagerness
Temperate	Having children who believe	Not yet as lording it over ... but proving to be examples
Prudent	Not self-willed	
Respectful	Not quick-tempered	
Hospitable	Not addicted to wine	
Able to teach	Not pugnacious	
Not addicted to wine	Not fond of sordid gain	
Not pugnacious	Hospitable	
Gentle	Lover of what is good	
Uncontentious	Sensible	
Free from the love of money	Just	
Manages his household well	Devout	

Not a new convert	Self-controlled	
A good reputation with those outside the Church	Holds fast the faithful Word both to exhort and to refute	

The character and effectiveness of any church is directly related to the quality of its leadership. That's why the Bible stresses the importance of qualified church leadership and delineates specific standards for evaluating those who would serve in that sacred position. Failure to adhere to those standards has caused many of the problems that churches throughout the world currently face.

It is significant that in his description of the qualifications for elders, Paul focused on their character rather than their function. A man is qualified because of what he is, not because of what he does. If he sins and thereby soils his character, he is subject to discipline in front of the entire congregation (1 Tim. 5:20). The church must carefully guard that sacred office.

The spiritual qualifications for leadership are nonnegotiable. They are part of what determines whether a man is indeed called by God to the ministry. Bible schools and seminaries can help equip a man for ministry, church boards and pulpit committees can extend opportunities for him to serve, but only God can call a man and make him fit for the ministry. The call to the ministry is not a matter of analyzing one's talents and then selecting the best career option. It's a Spirit-generated compulsion to be a man of God and serve Him in the church. Those whom God calls will meet the qualifications.

Why are the standards so high? Because whatever the leaders are, the people become. Hosea said, "Like people, like priest" (4:9). Jesus said, "Everyone, after he has been fully trained, will be like his teacher" (Luke 6:40). Biblical history demonstrates that people will seldom rise above the spiritual level of their leadership.

First Timothy 3 carefully outlines the spiritual qualifications for men in leadership. Paul is speaking specifically of elders' qualifications in the verses we will examine (vv. 1-7), but note that the only significant difference between an elder's qualifications and those of a deacon is that an elder must be skilled as a teacher (cf. vv. 1-7 and 8-13).

Paul begins by asserting that the man who desires the office desires a good work (v. 1). But no one should ever be placed into church leadership based on desire alone. It is the responsibility of the church to affirm a man's qualifications for ministry by measuring him against God's standard for leadership as delineated in verses 2-7.

"Blameless" – He Is a Man of Unquestionable Character

Paul began, "a bishop [or elder] . . . must be blameless" (v. 2). The Greek word translated "must", emphasizes an absolute necessity: blamelessness is mandatory for overseers. It is a fundamental, universal requirement. In fact, the other qualifications listed by Paul in verses 2-7 define and illustrate what he meant by "blameless."

The Greek text indicates this is referring to a present state of blamelessness. It doesn't refer to sins that the man committed before he matured as a Christian – unless such sins remain as a blight on his life. (No one is blameless in that sense.) The idea is that he has sustained a reputation for blamelessness.

"Blameless" (v. 2) means "not able to be held." A blameless man cannot be taken hold of as if he were a criminal in need of detention for his actions. There's nothing to accuse him of. He is irreproachable. When an elder is irreproachable, critics cannot discredit his Christian profession of faith or prove him unfit to lead others (Neh. 6:13). He has a clean moral and spiritual reputation. Since all God's people are called to live holy and blameless lives (Phil. 2:15; 1 Thess. 5:23), since the world casts a critical eye at the Christian community (1 Peter 3:15, 16), and since Christian leaders lead primarily by their example (1 Peter 5:3), an irreproachable life is indispensable to the Christian leader. Job, for example, was an elder among his people (Job 29:7, 21, 25; 31:21), and he, the

Scripture says, was morally above reproach: "There was a man in the land of Uz, whose name was Job, and that man was blameless, upright, fearing God, and turning away from evil" (Job 1:1).

A church leader's life must not be marred by sin – be it an attitude, habit, or incident. That's not to say he must be perfect, but there must not be any obvious defect in his character. He must be a model of godliness so he can legitimately call his congregation to follow his example (Phil. 3:17). The people need to be confident that he won't lead them into sin.

Spiritual leaders must be blameless because they set the example for the congregation to follow. That is a high standard, but it isn't a double standard. Since you are responsible to follow the example of your godly leaders (Heb. 13:7, 17), God requires blamelessness of you as well. The difference is that certain sins can disqualify church leaders for life, whereas that's not necessarily true for less prominent roles in the church. Nevertheless, God requires blamelessness of all believers (cf. Eph. 1:4; 5:27; Phil. 1:10; 2:15; Col. 1:22; 2 Pet. 3:14; Jude 24). Paul now begins to delineate concrete, observable qualities that define what it means to be irreproachable.

"The Husband of One Wife" – He Is Sexually Pure

"The husband of one wife" is not the best rendering according to our studies of the Greek text. We believe the words translated "wife" (*gunaikos*) and "husband" (*aner*) are better translated "woman" and "man." The Greek construction places emphasis on the word *one*, thereby communicating the idea of a one-woman man.

It is appropriate that sexual fidelity is first on Paul's list of moral qualifications because that seems to be the area that most often disqualifies a man from ministry. It is therefore a matter of grave concern.

There have been many proposed interpretations of this qualification. The view that an elder can't have more than one wife at a time has been the traditional understanding of the English phrase "the husband of one wife," but although the religious climate of Paul's day did have some who engaged in the practice, we believe that there was a fuller meaning of the phrase.

Some people say that "the husband of one wife" means a man can't be an elder if he has remarried for any reason. But Paul couldn't have been referring to remarriage because he made clear that God permits remarriage after the death of one's spouse (1 Tim. 5:9-15; Rom. 7:2-3; 1 Cor. 7:39).

Others say that Paul was prohibiting divorced men from serving as elders. But if Paul were referring to divorce, he could have clarified the issue by saying. "An elder must be a man who has never been divorced." But even that statement would pose problems because the Bible teaches that remarriage after divorce is within God's will under three circumstances.

First, divorce is justified when one partner commits continuous sexual sin. Jesus said to the religious leaders, "It hath been said [by rabbinical tradition], Whosoever shall [divorce] his wife, let him give her a writing of divorcement" (Matt. 5:31). Many Jewish men were divorcing their wives for insignificant reasons, and the only requirement was to complete the necessary paperwork.

But Jesus said, "Whoever shall [divorce] his wife, except for the cause of fornication, causeth her to commit adultery [when she remarries]; and whosoever shall marry her that is divorced committeth adultery" (Matt. 5:32). That implies fornication is legitimate grounds for divorce.

We believe that the "fornication" mentioned in that context refers to extreme situations of unrelenting and unrepentant sexual sin. God graciously permits the innocent party to be free from the bondage to such an evil partner. With that comes the freedom to remarry a believer.

Under Old Testament law, if a marriage partner committed adultery, he or she could be stoned to death. That would release the other partner from that marriage and free him or her to remarry. Although God no longer demands the death of an unfaithful spouse, the sin of adultery is no less serious. Should God's grace in sparing the life of the adulterer penalize the innocent party by demanding lifelong singleness? We don't think so. The grace that spares the adulterer's life also frees the innocent party to remarry.

Second, divorce is justified when an unbelieving partner leaves. In 1 Corinthians 7:15 Paul says, "If the unbelieving depart, let him depart. A brother or a sister is not under bondage in such cases; but God hath called us to peace." If an unbelieving partner wants out of the marriage, the believer is free to let him or her go. God doesn't require you to live in a state of war with such a partner.

Third, remarriage is permissible if the divorce and remarriage took place before either party was a Christian (1 Cor. 6:9-11). A caution should be added in this area. If an individual is brought up for a leadership position, then we must deal with potential drawbacks. A "proving time" would be necessary to determine the character qualities of the new marriage. All leaders must be willing to have their lives examined according to the specific areas mentioned as qualifications.

*** **For a full statement of Marriage, Divorce and Remarriage see Master Builder Ministries' position paper on the same.**

Some people say 1 Timothy 3:2 prohibits single men from serving as elders. But that position is refuted by the fact that Paul, who was an elder (1 Tim. 4:14; 2 Tim. 1:6), was himself single (1 Cor. 7:7-9).

The phrase "one-woman man" doesn't refer to marital status at all. Paul is giving moral qualifications for spiritual leadership, not outlining what an elder's social status or external condition is to be. "One-woman man" speaks of the man's character, the state of his heart. If he is married, he is to be devoted solely to his wife. Whether or not he is married, he is not to be a ladies' man.

Unfortunately, it is possible to be married to one woman yet not be a one-woman man. Jesus said, "Whosoever looketh on a woman to lust after her hath committed adultery with her already in his heart" (Matt. 5:28). First Timothy 3:2 is saying that a married – or unmarried-man who lusts after women is unfit for ministry. An elder must love, desire, and think only of the wife that God has given him.

Sexual purity is a major issue in the ministry. That's why Paul placed it at the top of his list.

"Temperate" – He Is Not Given to Excess

The Greek word translated "temperate (*nephalios*) means without wine or not mixed with wine. It speaks of sobriety – the opposite of intoxication. Wine was a common drink in biblical times. Because Palestine was so hot and dry, it was often necessary to consume a large volume of wine to replenish body fluids lost in the heat. To help avoid drunkenness, wine was normally mixed with large amounts of water. Even so, the lack of refrigeration and the fermentative properties of wine made intoxication a problem.

Even though wine could cheer a person's heart (Judg. 9:13) and was beneficial for medicinal purposes such as stomach ailments (1 Tim. 5:23) and relieving pain for those near death (Prov. 31:6), its abuse was common. That's why Proverbs 20:1 says, "Wine is a mocker, strong drink is raging, and whosoever is deceived thereby is not wise."

Proverbs 23:29-35 says, "Who hath woe? Who hath sorrow? Who hath contentions? Who hath babbling? Who hath wounds without cause? Who hath redness of eyes? They that tarry long at the wine; they that go to seek mixed wine look not thou upon the wine when it is red, when it giveth its color in the cup, when it moveth itself aright. At the last it biteth like a serpent, and it stingeth like an adder. Thine eyes shall behold strange things, and thine heart shall utter perverse things. Yea, thou shalt be as he that lieth down in the midst of the sea, or as he that lieth upon the top of a mast. They have stricken me, shalt thou say, and I was not sick; they have beaten me, and I felt it not. When shall I awake? I will seek it again?"

Genesis 9 records an example of the mocking effect of wine. Noah planted a vineyard, made wine, and became drunk. While he was drunk "he was uncovered within his tent" (v. 21). The Hebrew text implies some kind of sexual evil. Ham, one of his sons, saw him in that state and mocked him. His two other sons entered the tent backward to cover him up because they were ashamed of his sinfulness.

Because of their position, example, and influence, certain Jewish leaders abstained from wine. Priests could not enter God's house while under its influence (Lev. 10:9). Kings were also advised not to consume wine because it might hinder their judgment (Prov. 31:4-5). The Nazirite vow, the highest vow of spiritual commitment in the Old Testament, forbade its participants from drinking wine (Num. 6:3). In the same way, spiritual leaders today must avoid intoxication so they may exercise responsible judgment and set an example of Spirit-controlled behavior.

It's likely that Paul's usage of *nehalios* went beyond the literal sense of avoiding intoxication to the figurative sense of being alert and watchful. An elder must deny any excess in life that diminishes clear thinking and sound judgment. "Temperate" denotes self-control, balanced judgment, and freedom from debilitating excesses or rash behavior. Negatively, it indicates the absence of any personal disorder that would distort a person's judgment or conduct. Positively, it describes a person who is stable, circumspect, self-restrained, and clear-headed.

It is necessary that elders, who face many serious problems, pressures, and decisions, be mentally and emotionally stable. Elders who lack a balanced mental, and emotional perspective, can easily be snared by the devil or false teachers.

"Sober-Minded" – He Is Self-Disciplined

The Greek word translated "sober-minded" (*Sophron*) speaks of discipline or self-control. It's the result of being temperate (v. 2). The temperate man avoids excess so that he can see things clearly, and the clarity of thought leads to an orderly, disciplined life. He knows how to order his priorities.

Sophron indicates a person who is serious about spiritual things. Such a man doesn't have the reputation of a clown. That doesn't mean he avoids humor – any good leader is able to use and enjoy humor. But he is to have an appreciation for what really matters in life.

Similar to the word "temperate," "prudent" (*sophron*) also stresses self-control, particularly as it relates to exercising good judgment, discretion, and common sense. To be prudent is to be sound-minded, discreet, and sensible, able to keep an objective perspective in the face of problems and disagreements. Prudence is an essential quality of mind for a person who must exercise a great deal of practical discretion in handling people and their problems. Prudence tempers pride, authoritarianism, and self-justification.

Dictionary definitions of prudent commonly include these elements: caution, practical wisdom, and carefulness, understanding the present. In Proverbs, a prudent man "covereth shame" and "looketh well to his ways" and "responds to correction" and is "hungry for training." (Proverbs 12:16, 23; 13:16; 14:8, 15, 18; 15:5; 16:21; 18:15; 19:14; 22:3; 27:12).

"Good Behavior" – He Is Well-Organized (Respectable)

The Greek word translated "good behavior" is *kosmios*. It comes from the root word *kosmos*, which in its general sense refers to the interplay between human, divine, and satanic values. A man of "good behavior" approaches all the aspects of his life in a systematic, orderly manner. *Kosmios* conveys the ideas of self-control, proper behavior, and orderliness. Although the word is used to describe properness in outward demeanor and dress in 1 Timothy 2:9, its usage here conveys the more general meaning of "orderly" ... "well-behaved," or "virtuous" ... that which causes a person to be regarded as "respectable" by others. An elder cannot expect people to follow him if he is not respectable.

This kind of person diligently fulfills his many duties and responsibilities. His disciplined mind produces disciplined actions – "good behavior."

The opposite of *kosmios* is chaos. Elders must not have a chaotic lifestyle. That's because their work involves administration, oversight, scheduling, and establishing priorities.

The ministry is no place for a man whose life is a continual confusion of unaccomplished plans and unorganized activities. Over the years I have seen many men who had difficulty ministering effectively because they couldn't get their lives into meaningful order. They couldn't concentrate on a task or systematically set and accomplish goals. Such disorder is a disqualification.

Paul is saying here that a man who is respectable has a lifestyle that adorns the teachings of the Bible in his speech, his dress, his appearance at home, his office or the way he does business. God is a God of order. A man of God, too, should be orderly and proper (1 Thess. 4:10-12; Col. 3:23-24; 1 Tim. 6:2; Col. 4:5-6; 1 Pet. 2:12; Phil. 1:27).

"Just" – He Is Righteous Or Upright

"Just" (*dikaios*) means "righteous" or "upright." To be righteous is to live in accordance with God's righteous standards, to be law-abiding. John writes that "the one who practices righteousness is righteous, just as He is righteous" (1 John 3:7).

An elder who is righteous can be counted on to be a principled man and to make fair, just, and righteous decisions for the church (Prov. 29:7). Job is a good example of a just man:

> **Job 1:1** There was a man in the land of Uz, whose name *was* Job; and that man was perfect and upright, and one that feared God, and eschewed evil.

> **Job 29:14-17** I put on righteousness, and it clothed me: my judgment *was* as a robe and a diadem. ^{15}I was eyes to the blind, and feet *was* I to the lame. ^{16}I *was* a father to the poor: and the cause *which* I knew not I searched out. ^{17}And I brake the jaws of the wicked, and plucked the spoil out of his teeth.

God's steward, then, must be like Job. He must live a morally upright life and be clothed in practical righteousness.

"Given To Hospitality" – He Is Hospitable

The Greek word translated "given to hospitality" is composed of the words *xenos* ("stranger") and *phileo* ("to love" or "show affection"). It means to love strangers.

It is necessary for an elder to be hospitable. Hospitality is a concrete expression of Christian love and family life. It is an important biblical virtue:
- Job, the exemplary Old Testament elder, was a model of hospitality: "The alien has not lodged outside, For I have opened my doors to the traveler" (Job 31:32).
- Paul exhorts the Christians at Rome to pursue hospitality (Rom. 12:13).
- Peter writes, "Be hospitable to one another without complaint" (1 Peter 4:9).
- The author of Hebrews bids his readers: "Do not neglect to show hospitality to strangers, for by this some have entertained angels without knowing it" (Heb. 13:2).

These New Testament commands to practice hospitality are all found within the larger context of Christian love. Unfortunately, most Christians, and even some Christian leaders, are unaware that hospitality is a biblical requirement for pastoral leadership in the church. Some may even argue against such a seemingly insignificant point being a requirement for church shepherds.

Such thinking, however, shows an inadequate understanding of authentic Christian community, agape love, and the elder's work. For an elder to be inhospitable is a poor example of Christian love and care for others. The shepherd elder is to give himself lovingly and sacrificially for the care of the flock. This cannot be done from a distance – with a smile and a handshake on Sunday morning or through a superficial visit. Giving oneself to the care of God's people means sharing one's life and home with others. An open home is a sign of an open heart and a loving, sacrificial, serving spirit. A lack of hospitality is a sure sign of selfish, lifeless, loveless Christianity.

Although the shepherd's ministry of hospitality may seem like a small thing, it has an enormous, lasting impact on people. If you doubt this, ask those to whom a shepherd has shown hospitality. Invariably they will say that it is one of the most important, pleasant, memorable aspects of the shepherd's ministry.

In His mysterious ways, God works through the guest-host relationship to encourage and instruct His people. So we must never underestimate the power of hospitality in ministering to people's needs. Those who love hospitality love people and are concerned about them. If the local church's elders are inhospitable, the local church will also be inhospitable and indifferent toward the needs of others.

Biblical hospitality is showing kindness to strangers, not friends. In Luke 14:12-14 Jesus says, "When you give a luncheon or a dinner, do not invite your friends or your brothers or your relatives or rich neighbors, lest they also invite you in return, and repayment comes to you. But when you give a reception, invite the poor, the crippled, the lame, the blind, and you will be blessed, since they do not have the means to repay you; for you will be repaid at the resurrection of the righteous" (NASB).

"Loving What Is Good" – He Loves People Is An Example of Christ-likeness

Closely associated with hospitality, "loving what is good" is a positive virtue that is required of those who seek to help others and live as Christ-like examples. The Greek word used here is *philagathos*, which one Greek lexicon defines as "one who willingly and *with self-denial* does good, or is kind." William Hendriksen explains the word as "ready to do what is beneficial to others." The *Theological Dictionary of the New Testament* states: "According to the interpretation of the early Church it relates to the unwearying activity of love."

King David was a lover of goodness. He spared his enemy Saul, who had to reluctantly admit: "And you have declared today that you have done good to me, that the Lord delivered me into your hand and yet you did not kill me. For if a man finds his enemy, will he let him go away safely?" (1 Sam. 24:18, 19a). David sought to show kindness to his deceased friend Jonathan, Saul's son, by taking Jonathan's crippled son, Mephibosheth, into his own house (2 Sam. 9).

Job's friends had to admit that he was a lover of goodness: "Behold, you have admonished many, And you have strengthened weak hands. Your words have helped the tottering to stand, And you have strengthened feeble knees" (Job 4:3, 4). But the greatest example of one who loved goodness is our Lord Jesus Christ, who "went about doing good" (Acts 10:38b).

An elder who loves goodness seeks to do helpful, kind things for people. He will be loving, generous, and kind toward all and will never sink to evil, retaliatory behavior (Acts 11:24; Rom. 12:21; 15:2; Gal. 6:10; 1 Thess. 5:15; 1 Peter 3:13). In contrast, Paul prophesied that in the last days more people would be "lovers of self, lovers of money ... without self-control ... haters of good." (2 Tim. 3:3). A society that is led by lovers of good rather than haters of good is truly blessed.

"Apt To Teach" – He Is Skilled In Teaching

The Greek word translated "apt to teach" (*didaktikon*) is used only two times in the New Testament (here and in 2 Tim. 2:24). It means "skilled in teaching." It's the only qualification listed here that relates to the function of an elder and sets the elder apart from the deacon.

Like Israel, the Christian community is built on Holy Scripture. So those who oversee the community must be able to guide and protect it by instruction from Scripture. According to Acts 20, the elders must shepherd the flock of God. A major part of shepherding the flock involves feeding it the Word of God. Therefore, elders must be "able to teach" in order to do their job.

The ability to teach entails three basic elements: a knowledge of Scripture, the readiness to teach, and the ability to communicate. This doesn't mean that an elder must be an eloquent orator, a dynamic lecturer, or a highly gifted teacher (of which there are very few). But an elder must know the Bible and be able to instruct others from it.

In his parallel list of elder qualifications in Titus, Paul expands on the meaning of "able to teach." He writes, "holding fast the faithful word which is in accordance with the teaching, that he [the elder] may be able both to exhort in sound doctrine and to refute those who contradict" (Titus 1:9). An elder, then, must be able to open his Bible and exhort and encourage others from it. He must also be able to discern false doctrine and refute it with Scripture. God's Word brings growth to the church and protects it from falsehood. Therefore, shepherd elders must be able to teach God's Word.

The Holy Spirit gives the gift of teaching to those called to teach the church (Rom. 12:7; 1Cor. 12:28; Eph. 4:11). It is not a natural ability but a Spirit-given endowment that enables one to teach the Word of God effectively.

"Not Given To Wine" – He Is Not A Drinker

The Greek word translated "given to wine" (*paroinos*) means "one who drinks." It doesn't refer to a drunkard – that's an obvious disqualification. The issue here is the man's reputation: Is he known as a drinker?

The Bible contains many warning against the potential dangers of wine and strong drink (Isa. 5:11, 22; Prov. 20:1; 23:30-35; Hos. 4:11). It especially warns leaders about the dangers of alcohol (Prov. 31:4, 5; Lev. 10:8-9; Isa. 28:1, 7, 8; 56:9-12).

Elders work with people, often those who are troubled. If an elder has a drinking problem, he will lead people astray and bring reproach upon the church. His overindulgence will interfere with spiritual growth and service, and it may well lead to more degrading sins.

While Paul is talking about over-drinking, the kind of drinking that causes one to lose control of his senses and be brought into bondage, a higher law rules us in this matter. We should not do "anything by which your brother stumbles" (Rom. 14:21).

"Not Violent" – He Is Not A Fighter

You can't be an elder if you settle disputes with your fists or in other violent ways. The Greek word translated "violent" (*plektes*) means "a giver of blows" or "a striker." An elder isn't quick-tempered and doesn't resort to unnecessary physical violence. That qualification is closely related to "not given to wine" because such violence is usually connected with people who drink excessively.

A pugnacious man carries a chip on his shoulder and is always ready for a good argument, perhaps even just a good theological tussle! A pugnacious person loses control of his senses and is controlled by anger. He is always ready to fight with a combative, belligerent nature. He cannot always avoid engaging in physical violence.

Elders must handle highly emotional interpersonal conflicts and deeply felt doctrinal disagreements between believers. Elders are often at the center of very tense situations, so a bad-tempered, pugnacious person is not going to solve issues and problems. He will, in fact, create worse explosions. Because a pugnacious man will treat the sheep roughly and even hurt them, he cannot be one of Christ's under-shepherds.

A spiritual leader must be able to handle things with a cool mind and a gentle spirit. Paul said, "The servant of the Lord must not strive" (2 Tim. 2:24).

"Patient" – He Easily Pardons Human Failure

We skipped "not greedy of filthy lucre," which appears in the King James Version but not in the better Greek manuscripts. That qualification is identical in meaning to "not covetous" (v. 3), which we will soon cover.

The Greek word translated "patient" (*epieikes*) means "to be considerate, genial, forbearing, gracious, or gentle." "Gentle" is one of the most attractive and needed virtues required of an elder. No English word adequately conveys the fullness of this word's beauty and richness. "Forbearing," "kind," "gentle," "magnanimous," "equitable," and "gracious" all help capture the full range of its meaning. Forbearance comes from God and is a chief source of peace and healing among His people. So in his letter to the Philippian Christians, who were experiencing internal as well as external conflict, Paul says, "Let your forbearing spirit be known to all men" (Phil. 4:5).

The gentle man stands in vivid contrast to the pugnacious man. A gentle man exhibits a willingness to yield and patiently makes allowances for the weakness and ignorance of the fallen human condition. One who is gentle refuses to retaliate in kind for wrongs done by others and does not insist upon the letter of the law or his personal rights. "Graciously amenable," says one commentator, "yielding wherever yielding is possible rather than standing up for one's rights."

Forbearance is a characteristic of God: "For Thou, Lord, art good, and ready to forgive [the same Greek word used in the LXX meaning forbearing or gentle], and abundance in loving-kindness to all who call upon Thee" (Ps. 86:5). Gentleness also characterized the life of Jesus on earth: "Now I Paul myself urge you by the meekness and gentleness of Christ" (2 Cor.10:1). God fully expects His under-shepherds to shepherd His people in the same way He does. He will not let His people be driven, beaten, condemned, or divided. Thus the shepherd must be patient, gracious, and understanding with the erring – and at times, exasperating – sheep. So many wrongs, disagreements, faults, hurts, and injustices exist in this sinful world that one would be forced to live in perpetual division, anger, and conflict were it not for forbearance. So elders must be "gentle" and "forbearing" like Christ.

In a practical sense, patience is the ability to remember good and forget evil. You don't keep a record of wrongs people committed against you (cf. 1 Cor. 13:5). That's an important virtue for a spiritual leader.

"Not Self-Willed" – He Is Not Arrogant

To be self-willed or arrogant is the opposite of being "gentle" [forbearing], which is one of the qualifications listed in 1 Timothy 3:3. A self-willed man wants his own way. He is stubborn, arrogant, and inconsiderate of others' opinions, feelings, or desires. A self-willed man is headstrong, independent, self-assertive, and ungracious, particularly toward those who have a different opinion. A self-willed man is not a team player, and the ability to work as a team is essential to eldership.

We must remember that the local congregation belongs to God, not to the overseer. The overseer is God's servant, not a master or owner, thus he has no right to be self-willed when caring for God's precious people. A self-willed man will scatter God's sheep because he is unyielding, overbearing, and blind to the feelings and opinions of others (2 Peter 2:10).

"Not A Brawler" – He Is Not Quarrelsome

The Greek word translated "not a brawler" (*amachos*) is similar in meaning to *me plektes* ("not violent," v. 3). The difference is that the latter refers to not being physically violent, whereas the former refers to not being quarrelsome. This signifies someone who is not quarrelsome and contentious, but is peaceable, a man of peace.

The contentious person domineers others, but in reality is insecure and defensive. He struggles against others, has to compete and debate others. He is not happy unless he is in charge and not willing to serve or come under anyone else. He is not willing to bend, not flexible. "It's my way or no way!" Such people, usually jealous and selfish, are motivated by pride. He is apt to contend and argue and loves controversy, strife, conflict, struggle and discord.

God hates division and fighting among His people: "These are six things which the Lord hates ... A false witness who utters lies, and one who spreads strife among brothers" (Prov. 6:16-19). Yet fighting paralyzes and kills many local churches. It may be the single, most distressing problem Christian leaders face. Therefore, a Christian elder is required to be "uncontentious," which means "not fighting" or "not quarrelsome."

By contrast, the peaceable character quality that makes a person a good elder is that he seeks peace. "With all that lies within you . . . live at peace with one another" is his motto (Romans 12:16, 18).

When you have a plurality of church leaders attempting to make decisions, you can't get very far if any of them are quarrelsome. That's why Paul said, "The servant of the Lord must not strive, but be gentle unto all men . . . patient" (2 Tim. 2:24). He must be a peacemaker.

"Not Quick-Tempered: He Is Slow To Anger"

One of God's attributes is that He is slow to anger, so His stewards must also be slow to anger. Man's anger is a hindrance to the work of God, "for the anger of a man does not achieve the righteousness of God" (James 1:20). Since an elder must deal with the people and their problems, a "hothead" will quickly find much material to fuel his anger. Proverbs warns against the perils of an angry man: "An angry man stirs up strife, And a hot-tempered man abounds in transgression" (Prov. 29:22). With his ugly, angry words, a quick-tempered man will destroy the peace and unity of God's family. The fierce looks and harsh words of the quick-tempered man will tear people apart emotionally, leaving people sick and destroyed in spirit. So a man who desires to be a church shepherd must be patient and self-controlled.

Of course, everyone experiences anger, and leaders who must deal with contentious situations often may experience a great deal of anger.

"Not Covetous" – He Is Free From The Love Of Money

The Greek word translated "not covetous" (*aphilarguros*) is a negation of the Greek words for "love" and "silver." It speaks of someone who doesn't love money. An elder must not love money or be greedy. So this qualification prohibits a base, mercenary interest that uses Christian ministry and people for personal profit. Both Paul and Peter condemn what we would call "being in it for the money" (1 Peter 5:2; Titus 1:7). False teachers, Paul points out, are overly interested in money and in personal financial gain (1 Tim. 6:5; Titus 1:11). The Pharisees were lovers of money who devoured widows' houses (Luke 16:14; Mark 12:40). The chief religious leaders of Jesus' day turned the temple into a merchandise mart for their own profit (Mark 11:15-17).

An elder should be content with God's provision. In Hebrews 13:5 the writer exhorts his readers, "Let your character be free from the love of money, being content with what you have; for He Himself has said, 'I will never desert you, nor will I ever forsake you." Paul states the matter this way: "For we have brought nothing into the world, so we cannot take anything out of it either. And if we have food and covering, with these we shall be content. But those who want to get rich fall into temptation and a snare and many foolish and harmful desires which plunge men into ruin and destruction" (1 Tim. 6:7-9). Elders, then, must model godly contentment and faith in Christ's loving provision for them.

"One That Rules Well" – He Maintains a Godly Family

First Timothy 3:3-4 says that an overseer must be "one that rules well his own house, having his children in subjection with all gravity. (For if a man knows not how to rule his own house, how shall he take care of the church of God?)." An elder's home life is an essential consideration. Before he can lead in the church he must demonstrate his spiritual leadership within the context of his family.

The Greek word translated "rules" means "to preside, having authority over, stand before, or manage." He is the manager of his home. That affirms the consistent biblical teaching on male headship in the home. Obviously there are shared responsibilities between husband and wife and many tasks that the wife manages within the home, but the husband must be the leader.

The same Greek word is used in 1 Timothy 5:17: "Let the elders that rule well be counted worthy of double honor." An elder's ability to rule the church is affirmed in his home. Therefore he must be a strong spiritual leader in the home before he is qualified to lead in the church.

He must rule his home "well." There are many men, who rule their home, but they don't rule very well – they don't get the desired results.

By implication a man's home includes his resources. A man may love the Lord and be spiritually and morally qualified to be an elder. He may even be skilled in teaching and have a believing wife and children who follow his leadership in the home, but let's say he has mismanaged his funds and is in bankruptcy. Somehow he can't seem to pull his finances into proper order. Since in the area of finances he doesn't rule his household well, he is disqualified from spiritual leadership. Stewardship of possessions is a critical test of a man's leadership. His home is a proving ground where his administrative capabilities can be clearly demonstrated.

The Greek word translated "subjection" is a military term that speaks of lining up in rank under those in authority. His children are to be lined up under his authority: respectful, controlled, and disciplined. That qualification applies only if a man has children. He's not disqualified if he doesn't have children. But if God has given him children, they must be under control and respectful to their parents.

A well-managed family means that children obey and submit to the father's leadership. The way in which that relationship is manifested is especially important: it is to be "with all dignity." The father is not to be a spirit-crushing tyrant who gains submission by harsh punishment. Elsewhere Paul writes, "Fathers, do not provoke your children to anger; but bring them up in the discipline and instruction of the Lord" (Eph. 6:4). Thus a Christian father must control his children in an honorable, respectful, and dignified way. Of course there are no perfect, problem-free children in this world. Even the best Christian fathers and mothers have child-rearing problems, but these parents resolve the problems and are involved with their children in responsible, caring ways. They guide their children through the many storms of life.

The translation, "having children who believe," found in Titus 1:5-6, is better rendered as "having faithful children," which is the choice in the *Authorized King James Version*. The Greek word for "believe" is *pistos*, which can be translated either actively as "believing" (1 Tim. 6:2) or passively as "faithful," "trustworthy," or "dutiful" (2 Tim. 2:2).

The contrast made is not between believing and unbelieving children, but between obedient, respectful children and lawless, uncontrolled children. The strong terms "dissipation or rebellion" stress the children's behavior, not their eternal state. A faithful child is obedient and submissive to the father. The concept is similar to that of the "faithful servant" who is considered to be faithful because he or she obeys the Master and does what the Master says (Matt. 24:45-51).

The parallel passage in 1 Timothy 3:4 states that the prospective elder must keep "his children under control with all dignity." Since 1 Timothy 3:4 is the clearer passage, it should be allowed to help interpret the ambiguity of Titus 1:6. "Under control with all dignity" is closely parallel with "having trustworthy children." In the Titus passage, however, the qualification is stated in a positive form – the elder must have children who are trustworthy and dutiful.

Those who interpret this qualification to mean that an elder must have believing, Christian children place an impossible burden upon a father. Even the best Christian fathers cannot guarantee that their children will believe. Salvation is a supernatural act of God. God, not good parents (although they are certainly used of God), ultimately brings salvation (John 1:12, 13).

In striking contrast to faithful children are those who are wild or insubordinate: "not accused of dissipation or rebellion."

These are very strong words. "Dissipation" means "debauchery," "profligacy," or "wild, disorderly living" (1 Peter 4:3, 4; Luke 15:13). "Rebellion" means to be "disobedient," "unruly," or "insubordinate." Wild, insubordinate children are a terrible reflection on the home, particularly on the father's ability to guide and care for others. A man who aspires to eldership but has profligate children is not a viable candidate for church leadership.

"Not a Novice" – He Is A Mature Christian

Scripture prohibits a "new convert" from serving as an elder. A new convert is a beginner in the faith, a baby Christian, a recent convert. No matter how spiritual, zealous, knowledgeable, or talented a new convert may be, he is not spiritually mature. Maturity requires time and experience for which there is no substitute, so a new convert is simply not ready for the arduous task of shepherding God's flock.

There is nothing wrong with being "a new convert." All Christians begin life in Christ as babies and grow to maturity. An elder, however, must be mature and know his own heart. A new Christian does not know his own heart or understand the craftiness of the enemy, so he is vulnerable to pride – the most subtle of all temptations and most destructive of all sins. Pride caused the devil's ruin (Ezek. 28:11-19; Gen. 3:5, 14, 15). Like the devil, the prideful elder will inevitably fall. "Pride goes before destruction," the Bible says, "And a haughty spirit before stumbling" (Prov. 16:18; 11:2; 18:1; 29:23). Biblical history shows that pride has destroyed the greatest of men (2 Chron. 26:16; 32:25).

The position of elder (especially in a large, well-established church such as the one in Ephesus) carries considerable honor and authority. For a recent convert, the temptation of pride would be too great. Pride would destroy the man, causing personal disgrace, loss, exposure, divine chastisement, and possibly wrecking his faith. It would also hurt the church. So Paul warns against appointing a new convert as an elder, "lest he become conceited and fall into the condemnation incurred by the devil."

"A Good Report of Them Who Are Outside" – He Is Well-Respected By Non-Christians

Finally, and of significant importance, an elder "must have a good reputation with those outside the church." Both the apostles Paul and Peter expressed deep concern that Christians have a good reputation before a watching, non-believing world (1 Cor. 10:32; Phil. 2:15; Col. 4:5-6; 1 Thess. 4:11-12; 1 Tim. 2:1-2; 5:14; 6:1; Titus 2:5, 8, 10; 3:1-2; 1 Peter 2:12, 15; 3:1, 16). If all believers are required to have a good testimony before non-Christians, then it is imperative that the leaders have a good reputation with unbelievers. The church's evangelistic credibility and witness is tied to the moral reputation of its leaders.

In reality, the non-Christians may know more about the character and conduct of the prospective elder than the church. Quite often the prospective elder's non-Christian fellow workers or relatives actually have more daily contact with the church leader than do the people in church. So Paul is concerned that those who may judge less sympathetically but perhaps also more realistically and knowledgeably will render a good verdict both from the perspective of their own consciences and also from their awareness of the particular man's commitment and consistency in terms of his Christian faith.

An outsider's opinion of a Christian leader's character cannot be dismissed, for it affects the evangelistic witness of the entire church, "the pillar and support of the truth." That is why Paul emphatically states "he must have a good reputation." The verb "must," the same verb used in verse 2, again stresses the absolute necessity and importance of this matter.

The reason for emphatically insisting on this qualification is that an elder with an unfavorable or sinful reputation among non-Christians will "fall into reproach and the snare of the devil" in a far more destructive way than those he leads. If a pastor elder has a reputation among non-believers as a dishonest businessman, a womanizer, or adulterer, the unbelieving community will take special note of his hypocrisy. Non-Christians will say, "He acts that way, and he's a church elder!" They will ridicule and mock him. They will scoff at the people of God. They will talk about him and will generate plenty of sinister gossip. They will raise tough, embarrassing questions. He will be discredited as a Christian leader and suffer disgrace and insults. His influence for good will be ruined, and he will endanger the church's evangelistic mission. The elder will certainly become a liability to the church, not a spiritual asset.

But that is not all. Fully aware of the devil's ways (2 Cor. 2:11), Paul adds that the defamed elder will also fall into "the snare of the devil." The devil is pictured as a cunning hunter (1 Peter 5:8). Using public criticism and the elder's own inconsistencies, the devil will entrap the unwary Christian into more serious sin – uncontrolled bitterness, angry retaliation, lying, further hypocrisy, and stubbornness of heart. What may begin as a small offense can become something far more destructive and evil. Therefore, an elder must have a good reputation with those outside the Christian community.

Practical Questions a Potential Leader Can Ask to Evaluate His Own Character Development.

1. Do I stay in close communion with the Holy Spirit?
2. Do I accept the Bible as the Word of God?
3. Do I love God's people?
4. Do I identify with God's people in a specific local church?
5. Do I willingly submit to authority?
6. Do I love the sinner and backslider?
7. Do I truly worship God with all of my heart?
8. Do I have a strong prayer life?
9. Do I have a mature attitude in pressure situations?
10. Do I let another person finish a job that I began without feeling any bitterness toward that person?
11. Do I listen to and receive criticism?
12. Do I accept it when someone else is assigned a job for which I am better qualified?

13. Do I gloat self-righteously when someone else makes a mistake?
14. Do I allow other people's opinions or do I always have to argue for my point of view?
15. Do I have inner peace during times of turmoil?
16. Do I forgive someone who deliberately ignores me?
17. Do I control my anger?
18. Do I pass up certain present pleasures to achieve long-term goals?
19. Do I finish the projects that I begin?
20. Do I put others before myself?
21. Do I face unpleasant disappointments without any bitterness?
22. Do I freely admit when I am wrong?
23. Do I keep my promises and complete my commitments?
24. Can I hold my tongue when it is best to do so?
25. Do I accept and live in peace with the things I cannot change?

Appendix 2

Marriage, Divorce and Remarriage in the Bible:
A position paper on marriage, divorce & remarriage in the church

Marriage

Some Basic Considerations about Marriage

What is marriage? God established, instituted and ordained marriage at the beginning of human history (Gen. 2-3). Marriage is a foundational institution. An attack on marriage is an attack on society itself (and on God, who built society on marriage). Marriage is also the foundation upon which the church as God's special society rests. This covenantal community is weakened as the "house" or "household" is weakened.

Marriage is not solely an institution designed to propagate the human race. While God has ordained that procreation must be carried on as one duty of marriage, and only within marriage, procreation is not the fundamental feature of marriage.

Marriage must not be equated with sexual relations. Marriage is different from, bigger than, and inclusive of sexual union (just as it is inclusive of the obligation to propagate the race). But the two are not the same.

What Marriage Is All About

Marriage is a covenant relationship made before a most holy and righteous God witnessed by family and friends and acknowledged by the church and usually civil government. Marriage and family was part of God's design right from the start (Gen. 1:26-28). God gave the man and woman a three-fold purpose: (1) to be image-bearers; (2) to take dominion over creation; and (3) to be fruitful and multiply. The eternal purpose in all of this is to extend His kingdom over all the earth.

God uses the institution of marriage to accomplish this goal in two ways. The first way is through propagation: the making and training of Godly seed (Mal. 2:15). Marriage and family is the training ground where children can be nurtured, cared for, protected, taught the things of God and loved, all for the glory of God (Gen. 1:28). This concept is supported in the choosing of Abraham (Gen. 18:18).

The second way that God accomplishes His goal for marriage is that the two (together in unity) can accomplish so much more for Him than one alone (Eccl. 4:9-12). God dealt with this issue in Genesis 2:18: "It is not good for the man to be alone. I will make him a helper who approximates [or corresponds to] him." The Covenant of Marriage is the close, intimate relationship of a husband [man] and wife [woman] to one another. The concept of the marriage relationship appears in Malachi 2:14, where a different, but very complementary, term is used: "The Lord has been witness between you and the wife of your youth to whom you have been faithless, although she is your companion and your wife by covenant."

Now, the word here translated "companion" has as its kernel idea that of union or association. A companion, therefore, is one with whom one enters into a close union (or relationship). A companion is one with whom you are intimately united in thoughts, goals, plans, and efforts and, in the case of marriage, in bodies. God's revealed goal for a husband and wife is to become one in all areas of their relationship – intellectually, emotionally, physically. The Covenant of Marriage was designed to also fill this need.

God has called some to be exceptions to His own rule and provided for their need of companionship by gifting them especially to lead the single life (Matt. 19:11, 12; 1 Cor. 7:7). According to Matthew 19:11, 12 and 1 Corinthians 7:7, there are people whom, we might say, God has singled out to Himself to lead a life of celibacy for the sake of His kingdom. This gift is never explained clearly in detail, but doubtless, in it is the "capacity" to find companionship of a different (it could never be the same) sort outside of marriage in the special kingdom works to which some are called (vs. 12). This indicates that these single persons have been gifted with the capacity to live satisfying (not lonely) lives by (in one way or another) becoming deeply involved in the work of the Lord in ways that married persons cannot (1 Cor. 7:32-34).

In the Bible, an engagement was absolutely binding. In effect, it was the first step of marriage. In the engagement the marriage covenant was made, and an engagement could be broken only by death or by divorce (Deut. 22:23; Matt. 1:16-24). Notice, the marriage, which began with engagement (and required a divorce to break it) did not begin with a sexual union (Matt. 1:25) and had to be ended by divorce. Marriage is a formal covenantal arrangement between two persons to become each other's loving companions for life. In marriage, they contract to keep each other from ever being alone so long as they shall live.

The Place of Marriage

Marriage is not only the principal building block of society in general, and of the church in particular, but it also occupies a key place in human life. God did not put a parent and child into the garden. Adam and Eve were man and wife. That shows that the primary human relationship (and family relationship) is husband and wife. That is why a man must leave father and mother and cleave to his wife. The relationship of parent and child is temporary and must be broken; the relationship of husband and wife is permanent, and must not be broken. Therefore, divorce is always the result of sin.

Divorce

A Biblical Attitude toward Divorce

Contrary to some opinions, the concept of divorce is biblical. The Bible recognizes and regulates divorce. Certain provisions are made for it. This must be affirmed clearly and without hesitation.

While God emphatically says, "I hate divorce" (Mal. 2:16), that statement must not be taken absolutely to mean that there is nothing about divorce that could be anything but detestable, because He, Himself also tells us " . . . for all the adulteries which faithless Israel had done, I sent her away and gave her a divorce bill (Jer. 3:8, Berkeley)." If God Himself became involved in divorce proceedings with Israel, it is surely wrong to condemn any and all divorce out of hand. Obviously, from this passage (and Matthew 1:18-19) it is certain that sometimes, in some ways, divorce, for some persons, under certain circumstances is altogether proper and not the object of God's hatred. Note that Joseph is called a "just man" not only for what he was about to do ("put her away" – divorce Mary) but for the attitude he had towards a lesser penalty than death which was the Hebrew penalty.

It is altogether true that God hates divorce. But He neither hates all divorces in the same way nor hates every aspect of divorce. He hates what occasions every divorce [sin] – even the one that He gave to sinful Israel. He hates the results that often flow to children and to injured parties of a divorce (yet even that did not stop Him from willing divorce in Ezra 10:44). And He hates divorces wrongly obtained on grounds that He has not sanctioned. But that leaves some things about divorce that He does not hate. He certainly does not condemn or hate divorce proceedings per se – i.e., as a process. Nor does He hate divorce when it is obtained according to the principles and regulations laid down in the Scriptures and which He followed in His dealings with unfaithful Israel. Nor does God hate the freedom that an innocent person receives because of divorce.

It is important, therefore, to develop a balanced, biblical attitude toward divorce – on the other hand, hating all those things that God hates about divorce, while recognizing that in this sinful world there are those situations in which (as God Himself demonstrated) it may be necessary to obtain a divorce.

Let us make it clear, then, that those who wrongly (sinfully) obtain a divorce must not be excused for what they have done; it is sin. But precisely because it is sin, it is forgivable. The sin of divorcing one's mate on unbiblical grounds is bad, not only because of the misery it occasions, but especially because it is an offense against a holy God. But it is not so indelibly imprinted in the life of the sinner that it cannot be washed away by Christ's blood.

The Concept of Divorce

Divorce is a human institution. The available (biblical) evidence shows that although divorce is recognized, permitted and regulated in the Bible it was not instituted by God. If Moses "allowed" divorce by regulating rather than forbidding it, we must never get the idea that God merely winked at divorce. He neither ignores it (hoping that it will go away), nor (as a practice) denounces it, but rather, takes cognizance of it and does something about it (1) to see to it that divorce is permitted only under certain circumstances, and not under others (Deut. 22:19, 29), (2) that when it is done it is done in an orderly fashion, and (3) that those who obtain a divorce are fully aware of the possible consequences (Deut. 24:1-4). It is certainly correct to say that in the Scriptures God acknowledges the existence of divorce and carefully regulates it. Our stance, then, must be the same.

Properly handled, a divorce was a formal, legal act whereby the covenant of companionship was repudiated and dissolved. In Deuteronomy 24:1-4, we see that it was a three-step procedure. The divorce did not actually take place until all three steps had been pursued. (1) There was a written bill of divorce. Writing the bill made it a legal matter. To write a bill required time. (2) The bill must be served. The one who divorced another had to personally put the bill into the other party's hand. Again, time was gained. Others could intervene. (3) The person divorced must be sent from the home. The actual rupture of the home must formally occur. The person divorced must move out of the house.

A final comment: God permitted and regulated divorce. But He did not merely regulate it. The content of regulation indicates (1) that He wished to keep people from doing more damage to one another than they might otherwise, and (2) that He intended to discourage foolish and hasty divorce actions. The process and regulations outlined in Deuteronomy 24:1-4 tended to discourage divorce transacted without adequate forethought, and divorce as a handy convenience.

Every legitimate effort, therefore, ought to be made to help persons contemplating divorce to reconsider the alternatives, and to assist divorced persons to become reconciled to one another (whenever possible) before they remarry another and it is too late to do so.

What Is Divorce?

A divorce is the repudiation and breaking of the covenant in which both parties promised to provide companionship for one another. A divorce is, in effect, a declaration that these promises are no longer expected, required or permitted. By obliterating these obligations, a divorce is intended to free the parties to make the same commitment to someone else. Of course, we have not yet established this biblically, though we have seen that this was the intention in the divorce document.

However you view it, the concept of divorce has in it the idea of severing of the covenantal relationship that previously existed.

The Two Groups in 1 Corinthians 7

Group I – Both Christians (1 Cor. 7:10, 11). Believers may not take other believers into court. Matters must be settled within the church itself. This brings up the necessity of church government becoming actively involved in discipline. When the church has no court she, by her silence, allows much breakdown and loose ends in marriage breakups. The principle when dealing with believers is Matthew 18:15

Group II – Christians contemplating divorce with unbelievers (1 Cor. 7:12-16). Believers are not prohibited from taking unbelievers into court. Principle when dealing with unbelievers – Romans 12:18

Divorce Among Believers (Preliminary Considerations)

Group I – Both Christians (1 Corinthians 7:10-11). No permission to divorce. In acknowledging the fact that divorce may occur because of sinful disobedience, Paul simply wants to warn against further complications arising out of additional sin. So that the party(s) may at all times be able to repent and be reconciled to each other. If one of the parties marries, they push their disobedience one step beyond and get themselves into an irremediable situation (Deut. 24:1-4).

What Paul is after is reconciliation; he wants these two believers to put the marriage back together in a new and more biblical way. Now, notice another important fact. Even when a separation by divorce occurs as the result of disobedience, that divorce – though sinful, though obtained on illegitimate grounds – broke the marriage. The grounds may be illegitimate; the divorce itself isn't. Believers who wrongly separate by divorce are said to be "unmarried." Until they are remarried (to each other), all rights and privileges of marriage as well as all obligations of married persons, no longer pertain. Their chief obligation is reconciliation, and therefore all that leads to it.

Divorce Among Unequally Yoked

Group II – Unequally yoked couples (1 Cor. 7:12-16). It is one thing to contemplate divorce with a believer: there are resources (the Word and the Spirit) of which both parties may avail themselves, there is a mutually basic commitment to obey Christ and there is the process of church discipline that (in the last resort) may be activated if either one or the other (or both) refuses to deal with problems. There is, therefore, hope for that marriage and every reason for insisting upon reconciliation. But here is an entirely different situation – a believer contemplating divorce with his/her unbelieving spouse. None of the resources mentioned above are available to the unbeliever except the third, and the third resource (church discipline) is not available to the believer. Thus, there cannot be the same insistence on reconciliation; the same sort of hope does not exist. And, indeed, we do not see Paul requiring it.

Rather than commanding the believer not to divorce his unsaved partner regardless of what happens, he requires something less: he (or she) must not divorce a partner who is willing to make a go of their marriage. Indeed, the believer is told to do all he/she can to hold the marriage together for the sake of the unbelieving partner (hoping he/she will come to know Christ through continued association with the believer) and for the sake of the children (who if taken out of the believer's care would be counted and treated as pagans – i.e., "unclean"). But if, after all has been done by the believer to prevent it, the unbeliever does not agree to go on with the marriage; divorce is an acceptable alternative (v. 15).

The state in which the believer finds himself following such a divorce is defined: "Under these circumstances the brother or sister is not bound." All the bonds of marriage have been removed. He or she is released entirely from every marriage obligation, and is a totally free person. Nor is there any obligation to be reconciled in marriage. "God has called you to peace."

The Exceptional Clause

Matthew, chapters 5 & 19 – Jesus made it plain that there is one ground on which believers might divorce a spouse – fornication (or sexual sin). In this case, however, no requirement to divorce the other is laid down. Fornication refers to sexual sin of any and all sorts: incest (1 Cor. 5:1), homosexuality (Jude 7) and even adultery (Jer. 3:1, 2, 6, and 8).

Adultery is unfaithfulness toward one's marriage partner. In addition to the notion of sexual unfaithfulness, adultery refers to the violation of the covenant of companionship by the introduction of another party into the picture. This third party appears on the scene in order to provide companionship (usually, if not always, of a sexual nature) instead of the wife or husband "of one's youth."

In Matthew chapters 5 & 19, Jesus' permission to divorce a spouse is based on the violating act (sexual sin) not on its effect (adultery). Why does Jesus focus on the act? Jesus covered the broad base of possibilities. He declares fornication (sexual sin) to be the ground upon which one may serve a bill of divorce because fornication covers incest, bestiality, homosexuality and lesbianism as well as adultery.

What about the situation in which the one who has been wronged wants to forgive (has done so in his heart in prayer before God), wants to go on with the marriage, but cannot yet grant forgiveness to the offender because he/she persists in sin, or (at lease) will not repent and seek forgiveness (remember, Luke 17:3, speaks of granting forgiveness to those who repent). In such cases, the reconciliation / discipline dynamic comes into play. Work through Matthew 18 principle. If unrepentive after all discipline has been exhausted the Church must excommunicate the individual.

By following the reconciliation dynamic, hopefully there will be reconciliation in most cases. Whenever the principles of biblical reconciliation are followed faithfully, discipline rarely reaches the highest levels of excommunication. Most marriages not only can be saved, with proper help they may be changed radically for good.

But in those few cases where reconciliation is refused, the believer who seeks it is not left in a state of limbo. He has a course of action to pursue, and if it leads to excommunication and desertion he is no longer obligated to remain married indefinitely. This is true only if the believer's marriage partner during the whole process of discipline has failed to demonstrate evidence of repentance and faith, if that partner has been excommunicated, and if he (or she) wishes to dissolve the marriage. Continued rejection of the help and authority of Christ and His church finally leads to excommunication.

An excommunicated party who continues to be unrepentant must be looked upon and treated as a heathen and publican (Matt. 18:17). He shows no signs of a work of grace. When he has been put outside of the church and still evidences no signs of salvation, the believing partner may deal with him as an unbeliever. This means that if he leaves the believer under those circumstances, the latter is no longer under bondage. This Group I (both Christians) situation is now treated like a Group II (unequally yoked couples).

Christ, Deuteronomy and Genesis - Key Scriptures (Gen. 1:26-28; 2:18, 21-25; Deut. 24:1-4; Matt. 5:31-32; 19:3-9; Mark 10:2-12; Luke 16:18)

We must remember that adultery always involves a violation of the marriage covenant in such a way that a third party is introduced into the picture claiming the right (or privilege) to do for one of the two parties what they have contracted to do for one another. Normally, adultery takes place while the marriage contract is still in effect. In the situation to which Jesus refers (Deut. 24) that contract has been broken for sinful reasons [other than adultery]. Therefore, while it is truly broken (and no rights, privileges or obligations of marriage are permitted or required at this point), nevertheless the divorced parties have no right in God's eyes to be in a divorced state. They are obligated to be reconciled in remarriage so that they can renew the contract and continue to pursue their vows. That is the point (1 Cor. 7:10, 11). As Paul says, they must remain unmarried (not marry a third party) not only in order to be in a position to be reconciled (as we saw earlier) but, as we now see, also in order not to commit adultery.

Adultery, then, is sexual sin with someone other than the one with whom one ought to be having sexual relations. That the marriage contract has been sinfully broken means a number of things, including: (1) That the divorced persons cannot have sexual relations with one another, even though they ought to be doing so because they ought to be married. The right or privilege to sexual intercourse has been removed because of their divorced state. (2)

That anyone who marries either of the sinfully divorced persons (who are under divine obligation to remarry one another) commits adultery as well as the divorced person he/she marries, not because he/she is still married but because he/she is obligated before God to be married. He/she has no right before God to be in an unmarried state because of divorce over some indecency or impropriety of behavior.

What has just been said, Jesus assures us, applies equally to any man or woman who sinfully divorces his/her partner (Matt. 19, Mark 10, Luke 16). One final comment on the Gospel accounts: It is vital to recognize that, unlike the Pharisees, Jesus does not restrict His discussion of divorce to Deuteronomy 24. He does not consider it the basic or definitive OT passage on the subject – it was merely a regulation that had to do with a particular kind of problem relating to marriage. Instead, He returns to the passages regarding the institution of marriage in Genesis 2. Here we see one woman for one man, united in one person (one flesh) for life. That, Jesus told them, is the way marriage is intended to be.

The Origin of Divorce for Sexual Sin

In the OT God Himself recognized (and thereby taught us) that divorce for the sexual sin of adultery is an option. He taught us this by both precept and example in His own relationship with Israel. What God has taught, let no men deny!

In a number of passages, God speaks of His relationship to His OT covenant people as a marriage. As the NT makes clear (Eph. 5:22-33), this is more than a mere analogy; rather, the biblical norm for Christian marriage is found in the relationship of Christ to His church (the prototype of which was the relationship of God to His bride. <u>Scriptures to consider:</u> (Ezek. 16:8; Jer. 2:2, 20; 3:23-25; 3:6, 8, 9; Hos. 2:13, 5, 7; Ezek 23:17-19; 23:29; Jer. 3:8, 1, 2: Isa. 50:1; Hos. 2:2; 1:9; Hos 14:1-2; 2:14, 16; Jer. 3:13-14; Hos. 2:7; Isa. 54:6-7).

It is plain from this evidence that divorce for adultery by fornication was considered a natural option for God to use in referring to His relationship to Israel. It seems also that the NT Church recognized that the words of Jesus, based on God's own example in the OT, indicate that something less than stoning – namely, repentance and forgiveness – may be required for fornication-adultery in its various forms.

Remarriage

Remarriage after Divorce

Paul allows for the remarriage of those released from marriage bonds (i.e., divorced) even in a time of severe persecution when marriage, in general, is discouraged (1 Cor. 7:27-28). The Bible allows the remarriage of some divorced persons (not those in view in Matthew 5 & 19, except for those divorced because of fornication).

So, thus far, we have established two very significant points: (1) Remarriage, in general, is not only allowed but in some cases encouraged and commanded. It is looked favorably in the NT. (2) Remarriage after divorce is not allowed, but in cases where one has been properly "released" from his spouse it is plainly declared to be no sin – even in perilous times of crisis when all marriage is discouraged. There is no reason to believe that the New Testament's favorable view of remarriage does not apply equally to all such cases.

Let's now turn to a third matter. Who may remarry after divorce and under what conditions? *First general principle*: All persons properly divorced may be remarried. What is complex is whether persons who were divorced improperly (because the divorce itself was sinful), and as a result, who are still under an obligation to be reconciled to their spouses, or whether persons properly divorced but with other obligations (to be discussed later) can so discharge these obligations that eventually they too may be free to marry. The principle that runs throughout Scriptures, in one form or another, is that God has called us to peace (1 Cor. 7:15).

God requires us to set all unsettled matters to rest; He wants no loose ends dangling.

It is proper, then, for some divorced persons to remarry just as after the death of a spouse (1 Cor. 7:39) so long as they "marry in the Lord" (i.e., Christians must marry Christians). While they are free to marry, they are not free to marry any and every person; they may marry only believers.

Persons with a Past

General principle: When a person is converted, he is to "remain with God in the state in which he was when he was called (1 Cor. 7:24; 17, 20, 26). Paul made this a rule for all the churches (v. 17). This implies that a convert, from the date of his conversion, starts a new history from square one. (This doesn't exclude the necessary fulfillment of civil or moral obligations. True repentance always leads to such fruit.)

It seems well established that once a believer was forgiven and had forsaken a sin, he was no longer considered a fornicator, a drunkard, etc. (1 Cor. 6:9-11). Why then should we continue to call a breaker of the covenant of marriage such?

It is important to note that forgiveness (even in the case of a repentant believer who sinned after conversion), involves not only cleansing but also comfort and restoration to full fellowship among the members of Christ's church (II Cor. 2:7-8).

Before declaring a repentant, wrongly divorced person free to remarry another, we must ask: (1) have you freed yourself of all past obligations? (2) Have you sought forgiveness not only from God but also from your former wife, children, relatives, others involved? (3) Have you made every effort at reconciliation (where possible)? (4) Have you made every effort to right all wrongs (so far as possible) regarding such matters as voluntary repayment of any unfairly-obtained monies, rights, etc., in a divorced settlement, assuming obligations for child-support, etc.

Moreover, since a past divorce proves that there has been a failure in marriage we must: (1) Counsel all formerly divorced persons before remarriage about any sins in their lives that may have contributed in some way to the outcome. (2) Counsel them about any wrong attitudes or ideas about marriage (or marriage partners) that he may have developed during the previous marriage and the divorce proceedings with a special emphasis on love as giving, not getting.

"Dealing With Divorce and Remarriage"

Principles:

Marriage:
- Is a divinely ordained institution
- Is the first and most fundamental institution
- Is covenantal and binding
- Is a covenant of companionship
- Is the place for true intimacy
- Is to conform to the model of Christ and His church

Divorce:
- Always stems from sin
- Is not necessarily sinful
- Always breaks a marriage
- Is never necessary among believers
- Is legitimate on the grounds of sexual sin
- Is legitimate when an unbeliever wishes to divorce a believer
- Is forgivable when sinful.

Remarriage:
- Is possible for a divorced person
- Is possible for a sinfully divorced person through forgiveness
- Is possible only when all biblical obligations have been met
- Is possible only when parties are prepared for marriage
- Is possible when both parties are Christians

Divorce, Remarriage and Church Leadership

There are many encouragements in scripture to remarry (Rom 7:3b; 1 Tim 5:14; 1 Cor. 7:8-9, 39). The phrase - "husband of one wife" (found in 1 Tim. 3:2, 12; Titus 1:6) – does not mean that a man could not remarry. If only thinking of those who might have married someone who was divorced – logically you would also have to exclude anyone who was remarried. Paul could have said only those who have been married only once. He was not concerned about how many times a man had been married, but about how many wives he had! The life of an officer must be exemplary and God wanted the example of monogamous marriage held before the church. In the 1st century, it was common for some men to have more than one wife.

The literal Greek phrase used by Paul is "a man of one woman," or a one woman man," also emphasized the man's character and faithfulness in his present condition. The phrase "one-woman man" doesn't refer to marital status at all. Paul is giving moral qualifications for spiritual leadership, not outlining what an elder's social status or external condition is to be. "One-woman man" speaks of the man's character, the state of his heart. If he is married, he is to be devoted solely to his wife. Whether or not he is married, he is not to be a ladies' man. Therefore, even a single man could be judged by his relationships with other women.

Unfortunately, it is possible to be married to one woman yet not be a one-woman man. Jesus said, whosoever looketh on a woman to lust after her hath committed adultery with her already in his heart" (Matt. 5:28). First Timothy 3:2 is saying that a married – or unmarried-man who lusts after women is unfit for ministry. An elder must love, desire, and think only of the wife that God has given him.

This interpretation also clearly indicates that an examination of someone's present faithfulness in marriage and quality of relationship is the issue, not one's former relationships. In other words, has the individual repented for all sins, including marital, and is presently not repeating them?

If Paul did not forbid remarriage among elders and deacons – What of divorced persons holding office? God does forgive all sins in Christ. Forgiveness does not clear one from every consequence of his sin. Forgiveness means that God will not hold one's sin against him. The forgiven person will not be judged eternally for that sin; Christ was judged in his place. But social consequences must still be met.

Now, there are consequences of sin that are for life, and some that are not. The only issue in question is how does the Bible speak about this particular question? The answer, it seems, is that the Bible teaches that some consequences of past sins for eligibility as an officer in Christ's church are lifelong, and others are not. For instance, if before conversion a man married more than one wife, his polygamy does not keep him from membership in Christ's church, but it does prohibit him from bearing office in that church. And this is not because God and the church have not forgiven him, but because an office bearer must "be an example in all things" (including monogamous marriage practices).

Now is the question at issue like that? Not quite. A qualification for an office bearer is that he "must be above reproach" (1 Timothy 3:2) and also "must have a good reputation with outsiders" (1 Timothy 3:7). Titus reiterates this by saying he "must be blameless" (Titus 1:6). The circumstances of his divorce and/or remarriage may be such that a person for years afterward (perhaps even for the remainder of his life) would fail to qualify because of the bad reputation that he bears as a result. On the other hand, his lifestyle subsequently may be such that God has changed his reputation. Moreover, he may not have sinned at all in obtaining a divorce, if granted on biblical grounds.

No one perfectly fulfills all of the requirements for elders and deacons, but these are the specific areas we should examine in those who will become leaders. If an individual is weaker in a specific area, the attitude of the heart and the steps taken to insure an overcoming of this area is important. The intention of the Scripture is not an examination for perfection, but an examination of character example and heart intention.

The general tendency is to pick on divorce and this quality, which makes us inconsistent with the other qualities. Rarely do you find someone arguing that if an individual has ever used wine in excess in their past, they cannot serve as a leader, but you do find this for this clause. Even after salvation we do sin, but the key is our attitude of repentance and willingness to do all necessary not to repeat the habit or sinning. One key is forgiveness from God and the rest of the church. Ed Glasscock, in his article entitled "The Husband of One Wife Requirement" makes the following statement about the tendency to make individuals who have been involved in divorce leprosy cases, keeping them out of areas of service in Christ: "Some would treat divorce and remarriage as the unpardonable sin and practically force some genuine, godly Christians into a life of spiritual exile, treating these forgiven children of God as though the blood of Christ could not thoroughly cleanse them."

In our desire to have high standards, we can actually erect barriers not intended by the Word of God. However, the standard of excellent character is critical, and thus it is important in all areas (not just divorce and remarriage) to examine carefully how we deal with each individual being considered for leadership.

If an individual has been divorced and / or remarried prior to or after salvation and is brought up for a leadership position (specifically as an elder or deacon), then we must cautiously deal with potential drawbacks. It is worthy of note that the Bible has these restrictions regarding elder and deacon offices, but not for other ministries within a local church. A "proving time" of perhaps a year or more, depending upon the individuals involved, would be necessary to determine the character qualities of the new marriage. In this way, the qualifications could be clearly upheld.

All leaders must be willing to have their lives examined according to the specific areas mentioned as qualifications (1 Tim. 3:1-13; Titus 1:5-9). It is not the one area of "husband of one wife" that should have this qualification alone. Thus, it is possible that individuals, who have had bad habits financially, go through a "proving time" to be sure that the testimony of leadership is not brought down in the community through lack of character. This would apply to any other qualification as well. For a more complete examination of these character qualities see *"Qualification for Spiritual Leadership: Expanding on the Qualifications for Spiritual Leadership Delineated in the Constitution of Master Builder Ministries, a New Testament Church – 10/22/01"*.

Since each case differs, and since we have these clear biblical criteria to determine who is eligible for office, it is wrong to add church by-laws, especially when they are less flexible than the Scriptures themselves. The church has no right to forbid what God allows. It is the job of the existing officers in each instance to determine whether or not a given individual fits those qualifications.

www.ingramcontent.com/pod-product-compliance
Lightning Source LLC
Chambersburg PA
CBHW051032160426
43193CB00010B/916